Use What Works

Nicole Hancock and Steve Moiles

HAYDEN McNEIL

Hayden-McNeil Sustainability

Hayden-McNeil's standard paper stock uses a minimum of 30% post-consumer waste. We offer higher % options by request, including a 100% recycled stock. Additionally, Hayden-McNeil Custom Digital provides authors with the opportunity to convert print products to a digital format. Hayden-McNeil is part of a larger sustainability initiative through Macmillan Higher Ed. Visit http://sustainability.macmillan.com to learn more.

Copyright © 2015 by Nicole Hancock and Steve Moiles

All rights reserved.

Permission in writing must be obtained from the publisher before any part of this work may be reproduced or transmitted in any form or by any means, electronic or mechanical, including photocopying and recording, or by any information storage or retrieval system.

Printed in the United States of America

10 9 8 7 6 5 4 3 2 1

ISBN 978-0-7380-8077-2

Hayden-McNeil Publishing
14903 Pilot Drive
Plymouth, Michigan 48170
www.hmpublishing.com

Hancock 8077-2 F15

Use What Works

Table of Contents

Welcome to Students	4
Chapter 1: The Writing Process: Not Just a Lucky One-Shot Deal	5
How the Writing Process Makes Writing Less Stressful	6
What the Writing Process Often Looks Like	9
The Recursive Writing Process	11
Chapter 2: Reasons to Write: Everyday Life and College	17
Why Bother to Write?	17
What Rhetoric Is: Something You Already Do	19
What Audiences Expect	23
Chapter 3: Reading and Writing Strategies: What an Essay Could Look Like	26
What an Essay Is, and Why It's Important	26
How the Parts of an Essay Work Together	27
Essays are About Ideas, Not Formulas	30
The Importance of Being an Active Reader	33
Chapter 4: Invention	39
Freewriting	40
Aural Invention: Talking It Out, Recording, Instant Messaging, Voicemail	43
Brainstorming	44
Questioning	45
Clustering	46
Drawing	47
Storyboarding	48
Chapter 5: Your First Draft	53
How to Start Writing	54
What a First Draft Is—And Isn't	55
How to Avoid Common Writing Traps	56
Essay Strategies to Consider (Common Development Strategies)	59

ANNOTATED SAMPLE 61

Chapter 6: Rethinking Revision 66
    How to Work from a Discovery Draft 68
    How to Create a Revision Agenda 68
    Does Your Draft Have "Good Bones"? 69

Chapter 7: Feedback: Getting and Giving It 74
    What Peer Review Is and Why People Use It 75
    Good Peer Review Does Not Happen Accidentally 76
    Different Approaches to Peer Review 77
    How Conferences and Tutoring Can Help Writers 84

Chapter 8: Global Revision 88
    From Discovery Draft to Audience Draft 87
    On The Need for Connection: Fitting the Puzzle Pieces Together 88
    How to Add Details 94
    When Audience Starts to Matter 100

Chapter 9: Redrafting for Deeper Development 104
    Strategies for Development 105
    When Complications Improve an Essay—Going Deeper 110
    How to Complicate an Essay 112

Chapter 10: Localized Revision 117
    Paragraphs 117
    Transitions 119
    Introductions 122
    Conclusions 127

Chapter 11: Editing for Correctness 133
    Looking for Error Patterns in Your Writing 134
    Fixing Problems with Sentence Boundaries 136
    Fixing Problems with Verbs 143
    Fixing Problems with Pronouns 147
    Fixing Problems with Modifiers 149
    Fixing Common Punctuation Errors 152
    Finding and Fixing Spelling Errors 156
    Proofreading: The Final Soundcheck 159

Chapter 12: Editing for Style 162
    Finding the Right Tone 163

Editing for Word Choice	168
Editing for Conciseness	170
Editing for Clarity	171
Editing for Sentence Variety	171
Getting Active Voice into Your Writing	174
Noticing Other Writers' Styles	176
Breaking the Rules on Purpose	177

Student Essay Walk-Throughs: A Collection of Multiple Drafts by Student Writers 179

Questions for Discussing Student Drafts	179
Sample Essays	181
Alaine Loehr, "What 'We Are the World' Means to Me" (invention + five drafts)	182
Terrence Westbroke, "Does Mark McGwire Belong in the Hall of Fame?" (four drafts)	191
Evelyn Minick, "How Families at Home Cope with Military Deployments" (invention + peer review + instructor conference + three drafts)	199
Travis Wilson, "The Hunt" (a draft featuring plagiarism)	210
Karlos Martin, "The Helping Hand" (four drafts)	216

THEMATIC PAIR: TWO ESSAYS ON BULLYING

Rachel Beck, "Being Bullied (three drafts + peer editing + instructor feedback)	223
Evan Brown, "An Unexpected Lesson" (invention + outlining + three drafts)	230

THEMATIC PAIR: WRITING ABOUT SOMEONE WHO MATTERS TO YOU

"A Special Woman Known As Lucy" (avoiding a "Dead Grandma Essay")	238
Suggestion Box: When You Want to Write about Someone Who Matters to You	
"My Promise to John" (successful essay about an influential person)	241

Assignments & Writing Opportunities 247

Journal Prompts	248
Assignment Bank	254
Special Writing Tasks	265
Index	272
Special Features List (Exercises, Suggestion Boxes, Looking for a Challenge)	275

Welcome to Students

Have you ever . . .

- found yourself continually erasing what you've just written?
- worried so much about how to get started that you couldn't start the paper at all?
- felt you had to have a good plan for your paper, wandered off to another topic, and had to start all over again?
- had a really interesting idea but weren't sure how to write it so you went back to a dull but safe idea instead?
- made sure every detail was correct as you went along, only to lose track of where you were going?

These problems can be frustrating, but many writers face them. They need not overwhelm you. You have the potential—this semester—to become a stronger writer.

Use What Works is a book about getting your ideas on to the screen and/or page. It's also a book about working with your writing so that it does what you want it to do.

Maybe you think writing is an activity for others—a skill for people who want to publish a book, or a hobby for people born with a "writing gene." That belief (if you hold it) may leave you feeling that writing is just a course you have to pass and a bunch of assignments you need to turn in. We want you to see college writing for what it should be: a way to communicate your important ideas.

Writing your ideas your way will require effort, but it will be worth it. You will have to think about your writing more deeply than you have before, and your writing will be more powerful as a result. We think you're up to the challenge. Between us, we've worked with thousands of students, and we've seen most of them become stronger writers through the use of the techniques you'll learn in this book. We respect the hard work it takes for people to become more effective writers.

One last thought. We've both heard students say, "Writing isn't anybody's idea of fun." We'll accept the sentiment those students expressed—that is, writing had never been enjoyable for *them*—but we do not agree that writing can never be fun. When you find an idea that matters to you, and you suddenly realize that you want to make that idea matter to your readers, well, that's an important and sometimes very enjoyable experience. We hope you'll have that experience a number of times this semester. Try the strategies in this book. Find out—and use—what works for you.

Wishing you a great semester and good profit from the investment of your time and energy,

Nicole Hancock
Steve Moiles

Chapter 1: The Writing Process: Not Just a Lucky, One-Shot Deal

At a Glance...

- You're not expected to write an essay perfectly on the first try.
- Writing is a system with many parts working together toward one goal.
- Using the writing process can help you navigate this system and gain control over what you want to say.
- The writing process usually consists of the following stages: invention, drafting, redrafting, and editing.
- The writing process is recursive, so you can jump back and forth among phases.
- Trying something different can help you discover what works *for you*.

For Discussion or Writing: Describe a time when you tried to do something complicated for the first time. What thoughts went through your head? What concerns and hopes did you have? What skills did you already possess that helped you with the complex task? How does that experience relate to your work in this class?

Note: Your instructor may ask you to share your response with the class.

If You Had to Get Everything Right the First Time...

Imagine you've just walked into a thrift shop for the first time, with only ten minutes to spare, expecting that you'll find clothing in the right sizes for each member of your family. Or imagine getting behind the wheel of a car for the first time, expecting that you should be able to manage driving down the side of a steep mountain. Or picture yourself stepping into a kitchen that is not your own, facing a pantry stocked with ingredients you haven't cooked with before, with Gordon Ramsey waiting to judge your gourmet cuisine.

What the Writing Process Means and Why It's Important

Students often enter a writing class with unrealistic expectations, similar to those described above. Such expectations can cause students to think they stand no chance of succeeding. But we have good news for those students—and for you: *Writing essays is not a one-shot deal.* In other words, the process does not involve immediate failure or success. Writing is not an activity that requires you to get everything right the first time.

This means that you can start with a topic you're interested in, find something important you want to say about that topic, and go from there. You can figure out what you want to say, and how you want to say it, as you go. You can change your mind along the way. You can add new ideas, change or even get rid of things you wrote the other day that you're no longer satisfied with, and you can re-order your topics. Making changes is a very normal thing to do when writing. It does not mean you've "messed up" or that your paper will fail. In all likelihood, your paper will become stronger the more you work on it. That's especially true if you get some feedback on it from readers whom you trust.

There is no such thing as a perfect paper, and you don't have to wait until you have finished yours before you show it to anyone. A good piece of writing is something that a person produces over days, weeks, or even months. Your first try at getting your ideas down is just that—a *first* try, a decent start. No one will judge you on how successful or complete it is. When you put the writing process to work for you, a lot of the pressure is likely to disappear from your essay writing, yet the work you produce will stand a better chance of being successful.

The Writing Process Makes Writing Less Stressful

Most of us have experienced stress when trying to make a great first impression. Just think about going on a first date, for instance, or interviewing for a job. You realize plenty of things could go wrong: something inappropriate might be said; someone might have a wardrobe malfunction; you could trip instead of making a smooth exit. While mistakes can be repaired in subsequent conversations (usually), sometimes you might get the feeling that you've done or said something that can never be truly "undone." That's probably why most of us find those moments both exciting and stressful—because the stakes seem high and the potential for mishap is real.

Many people think about writing assignments in the same way. Frequently, students get stressed out because they think they are afraid of messing up. They are convinced their writing needs to be aimed at perfection, a home run, as soon as they step up to bat.

Happily, the **writing process** offers you an opportunity to get things right. As a *process,* it involves a series of stages because most writers (even very effective writers) need multiple tries to produce work that they will be proud of—and to produce it with as little stress as possible. Following the writing process won't necessarily make every paper a breeze, but it will very likely make writing more manageable, and maybe even enjoyable. Envisioning writing as a system also will help make it seem more manageable.

Writing is a System

> **For Discussion or Writing:** What do you think of when you hear the word *system*? Can you define it? What sorts of things are systems?

Writing is often thought of as an art, but for the purposes of this book, we'd like to compare it to a system because writing consists of multiple parts working together to create a whole.

Perhaps this comparison will be clearer if we examine another example of a system: a car. A car needs many different parts all working together in order to transport its driver from one place to another. The best engine in the world would be nothing without axles and wheels, and you'd look pretty strange driving around on top of the framework of the car without the rest of the body. Most parts of the car need to be in working order in order for the car to function well. There are, however, parts of the car that are not as necessary. There are parts of writing that are essential for the writing to work—and then, just as with the car, there are parts of writing that just help make it a "better ride" for the reader.

You probably have a pretty good idea of which parts of the car are absolutely necessary. What "parts" do you think are necessary for writing?

> ### >>> Exercise 1.1: What Does Writing Need?
>
> Take a few moments to write down in your journal or in a notebook what you think any piece of writing needs in order to work well.

Working Parts, A Working System

When all is functioning well with a car, it gets the driver from place to place. That's the main purpose of a car: to get people somewhere. Although some cars do end up as well-preserved, rarely driven classics in a garage or museum, people who design a car on a computer or assemble cars on a factory floor usually design the "system" they're creating to take people where they want to go. A good, well-built car will do that, and if things work well, the driver and passengers will enjoy their trip.

Yet countless things can go wrong with a car—from the engine catching on fire to getting a flat tire or running out of gas. That's the thing about a system. All of the parts must *work together*. If one part malfunctions, it can affect the other parts of the system. When a car's tires are new, drivers rarely have to think much about them. As time goes on, the tires start to lose their tread, but the driver thinks, *no big deal*, because the tires are still functioning. Later, the driver finds himself turning the radio up to drown out the noise from older tires. Sometime after that, the driver realizes he has to brake earlier too, and the ride is just all around bumpier than it was before. Even just one part of the system (the tires) is able to affect others (noise-level, smoothness, and braking time).

This same thing happens in writing. One part of the system can affect the other parts, in both good and bad ways. Some people think of the words, the sentences and the paragraphs as the main "pieces" of the writing system; however, we think that way of looking at writing would be like saying the nuts and bolts are the main "pieces" of a car's system. Yes, a car needs nuts and bolts. But what really makes that car go is the engine or the wheels or the gasoline or the driver.

What *Does* Writing Need?

Yes, writing needs words, sentences, and paragraphs. What really makes writing move, though, is its message. The words on the page are often just words on a page unless there is a **purpose**—a goal that the writer aims to achieve by writing the paper, or a message the writer wants to get across to readers. What the purpose is for a piece depends on its writer;

the purpose also depends on the topic, as well as who is going to read the piece of writing. In addition to the purpose, the writing must have structure to it; it has to have a beginning, a middle and an end of some sort. Actual words will be used to fill in that structure, words that without punctuation would all run together. Remember, all of these parts will work with one another to build and run the larger paper.

To think about all of these parts at once is a bit overwhelming. Each of these elements will be talked about individually in this book, but most of the time, we will focus on how specific parts help each other to create the message you want to write. You will be asked to think about which parts of the writing system come more naturally to you and which parts you need to work on with more attention. You will learn to see when one part is affecting the whole system of your essay.

Suggestion Box: Things Writers Might Improve in an Essay

You may be wondering what types of changes writers make during the writing process. The simple answer is: all sorts of changes. We'll list a few examples of changes writers sometimes make:
- overhauling an introduction that wasn't getting the reader's attention
- moving information from one paragraph to another to make it more organized
- expanding on a paragraph that doesn't have much support
- avoiding use of the same word over and over again
- reworking punctuation to help sentences flow better

The list could go on and on. You will not have to think about all of these things at once—only what needs the most attention first. Just as you wouldn't worry about filling the tank of a car that has a busted engine, do not worry about fine-tuning an essay that isn't saying what you want it to yet. Begin with the message, what drives your paper from Point A to Point B. The message is also what helps you figure out what is working in the paper and what is not.

The exercises in this book and the assignments your instructor gives you will help you figure out what you want to say in your paper, and you'll learn how to shape the paper to meet that goal. You'll do some thinking about your paper before you even start writing it. This is called **invention**, and it will help you to articulate your message and get your ideas down. Then, you will get feedback about your paper along the way. Other readers will help you determine what is working and what is not. During this whole process, you will be encouraged to revise, revise, revise! This is when you will do the thinking about the parts of the system and how they work in your paper. You will also eventually do the fine-tuning work of editing.

You Can Gain Control Over How Things Turn Out

Have you ever been behind the wheel of a car that was spinning on ice, or that was pushed about by winds so strong that you weren't sure you could control the vehicle? Few of us enjoy feeling like things are out of our control. That experience is by its very nature a stressful one. People panic when they feel that they don't have much control over how things will turn out—either that, or they grow angry about the situation or simply throw up their hands as though nothing they do will change what happens.

People who do not enjoy writing, or who do not feel that they're very good at it, sometimes feel like giving up. Our experience suggests that desire often stems from the writer believing she can't do anything that will make her writing turn out better. She sees herself as a driver behind the wheel of the spinning car, hoping for—but not having much reason to expect—the best outcome. In a sense, it's only natural for writers to dislike that feeling of not being in control of their writing. They can only *hope* so hard that readers will like what they've written. After a good deal of fruitless hoping, apathy can set in. The writer wonders, "Why should I even try?"

The writing process, however, is an excellent antidote to that problem, for the writing process is all about you making choices about your work. Writers face many, many choices as they take an idea from its seed-like form through a first draft and then through second and third drafts (or beyond). Those choices are important, and yes, that means you will take on a good deal of responsibility. But in those choices you can develop a great deal of control over how a piece of writing turns out, how closely the piece matches your goals for the writing, and how readers—including teachers—react to your writing.

Of course, just because a writer decides, "I'm going to take control over my writing," her work will not necessarily turn out the way she wants it to. Even very experienced writers sometimes make poor choices about their writing. Yet making the essential choice to take a piece of writing through multiple stages—to use the writing process—means that you are claiming your right to make other important choices, such as what you write about, what your purpose will be in writing that piece, what details you will include or leave out, what tone you will adopt, how you will relate to your readers, and so on. Getting into the habit of making—and reflecting on—those choices means that you are taking your position as the person who is more and more in control of your own writing. Ultimately, you will be the person whose hands are on the steering wheel, and most of the time, you will feel like your vehicle has good traction, thanks to your skillful driving.

Even though the writing process involves some hard work, it also gives you much greater control over how things turn out for you as a writer and, more broadly, as a student.

> **>>> Exercise 1.2: Making Choices and Gaining Control**
>
> There is often some risk involved when we make choices. Still, making a choice can often help bring about a good result. Write about a difficult choice you've made (in your education, at work, or in your family life). Discuss either the risks involved or the pay-off from making that choice. In what ways did this choice help you gain better control over the situation? (As is the case with any writing that you end up sharing with others, you will want to decide what you feel comfortable sharing and which details feel too private to share with others.)

What the Writing Process Often Looks Like

You no doubt noticed that this section of the book was labeled as "The Writing Process." We've used that phrase several times already in this chapter, and you'll encounter it throughout the rest of the book as well. Chances are excellent you'll hear your instructor using this phrase as well.

You might reasonably wonder exactly what the writing process involves, what it looks like in action. The writing process generally involves four stages.

Invention

Invention involves collecting ideas and exploring the possibilities that come with those ideas. You might think of invention as similar to a test-drive, or multiple test-drives of different vehicles for that matter. You try an idea out like you might try out a car, seeing what you can do with it and how comfortable you can get with it.

Invention is a time for making ideas visible and putting them out there so that you can choose which ideas you find most appealing. Ask yourself, "Which of these thoughts do I care enough about? Which idea do I want to make the center of my essay?" There are many ways to explore ideas before you actually write the paper.

Drafting

Drafting is the stage in which you write your first version of the essay. It's a good idea to focus on your main idea as you write your first draft; however, if you do end up getting off track a bit, you will be able to re-focus your paper in your next draft or two. Make the first draft as good as you can, but do not tell yourself that it needs to be perfect. It probably won't be perfect. The first draft is often called the rough draft, and there's a good reason it's called that. See Chapter 5 for more about drafting.

Revision

Revision is what many teachers and writers consider to be the real work of writing a paper. This is when you rethink what you tried in the drafting stage. Sometimes, revision may take you back to invention or drafting again. This stage involves questioning what it is you want to accomplish with the paper, if the paper is achieving that yet, and what you as a writer can do to make that happen. See Chapters 6 through 10 for more about revision, also known as redrafting.

Editing

Editing is when writers adjust parts of their papers to make them work more effectively. This may involve rewording awkward sentences or checking for particular grammatical errors you know you tend to make. Sometimes you'll hear **proofreading** discussed as a separate stage of the writing process, but we're including it as the last part of the editing stage. Proofreading is the final, careful rereading to make sure that everything is just as you'd like it to be, without typos or mixed-up page order. See Chapters 11 and 12 for more about editing.

We've briefly set out these stages in the order you see above (and have organized other chapters in this book in a similar sequence) simply because we had to discuss them in some order—not because writers always proceed neatly from one stage into the very next stage on the list. Occasionally, writers choose to jump around; sometimes, they do so for very good reasons. We'll address that situation in just a moment.

The stages of the writing process that we've listed above may resemble a set of rules. However, they are guidelines, *not* rules. All writers—students or not—should be aware of the various strategies and processes that other writers have used to help create effective messages. Strategies and choices are essentially what the writing process involves, but which activities a writer engages in and in what order will vary widely. You will need to discover what works for you and what works in various writing situations.

The Recursive Writing Process

Perhaps you were introduced to the writing process in high school, or even earlier. At that time, your teacher may have expected everyone to engage in a rather rigid, almost rule-based writing process—with everyone brainstorming (for instance) on Mondays, writing a rough draft on Wednesday, revising on Thursday, and editing on Friday. That set-up hides the messiness and creativity that are often real—and really important—parts of the process for many writers. In addition, the approach described above suggests that your teacher is responsible for getting your started on a writing project. The truth is, *you* can choose to set your own pace outside of class. You are free to start brainstorming on your own; you also can decide you're ready to begin revising your work.

You are allowed, as a writer, to jump back and forth during the writing process, no matter what stage you think you're supposed to be "in" at the moment. In other words, you can employ a **recursive writing process**. *Recursive* means working in a loop, going back and forth between various activities, usually in a purposeful way. The opposite of a recursive process would be a very *linear* process, meaning one in which all the steps are taken in a specific order, a straight line, without any "doubling-back."

recursive (back and forth)   **linear** (in a straight line)

There's a certain logic to having an invention "stage" in your writing, as well as a drafting stage, revision stage, and editing stage. We think your writing will be more effective if you do not skip any of these stages. But there's nothing at all wrong with borrowing some of the strategies associated with another stage, regardless of whatever stage you're currently focused on. Below, you'll see some examples of what we mean.

Revision during Invention

In the middle of the **invention stage**, you might decide that you want to "revise" the topic that you're working with. For instance, you might decide to shift your focus from March Madness to women's basketball programs, or from women's basketball programs to the pick-up basketball games you played outside your apartment building. In other words, often a topic evolves during the invention phase; your focus changes the more you interact with your topic. Your invention process does not always have to go in a straight line.

Invention during Drafting

During the **drafting stage**, you might decide that you don't have a good grasp on what you want to do with your topic. Perhaps you've just discovered that you're not yet sure what you find most interesting about your topic, or you realize you're experiencing **writer's block**. Those are great reasons for returning to the invention stage. Why not brainstorm some more questions that readers are likely to have—or questions you yourself have—about your topic? Why not explore, through freewriting or clustering, how your experience in the emergency room is connected to the larger problem of people facing frustration when seeking medical care? Or maybe, even though you're half-way through writing your first draft, this is a good time to call a friend and have a conversation about the topic of your paper.

Suggestion Box: Debate as Inspiration

Finding a friend who disagrees with your thinking can be a great strategy for kicking a draft into gear. Once you have had the opportunity to exchange some ideas with a friend, you can return to invention or drafting.

Invention and Drafting during Revision

The **revision stage** involves making plenty of large and medium-scale changes to your draft, with lots of rereading built into that process. Some of those changes will likely involve adding new examples, new explanations, and new questions to the paper. Sometimes an idea jumps into the writer's head in the middle of the revision stage, nearly fully formed. Just as often, though, the author may need to do a bit of freewriting to put some muscle on an idea that currently is pretty skeletal. Or the writer may end up rethinking the connections she initially pictured in her essay. Even if she goes "back to the drawing board" (the invention stage), she probably will not have to scrap her entire paper. But she does have the right, as does every writer, to jump back and forth between the stages of the writing process.

Editing during Drafting and Early Revision

We encourage our students to save the **editing stage** for the end of the writing process—as much as possible. Still, we recognize that most writers will sometimes feel compelled to stop and fix a misspelled word, or find a better way to end a clumsy sentence, before they tend to the next big challenge during the drafting or revision stages. If you are truly preoccupied with making some quick, small change in your essay, sure, go ahead and do it; clear it out of your brain so you can concentrate on the big stuff. But don't get into that habit too often. Don't go hunting for mistakes and rough patches during the drafting stage and the earliest part of the revision stage. Yes, mistakes are out there, but paying too much attention to them too early may lead you to short-change yourself on even more important matters—your ideas, for instance.

While it's okay to fix the occasional error when rereading, editing is one activity we advise you to keep mostly in its own stage.

Suggestion Box: Ignore the Typos for Now

Take care to keep editing out of your invention strategies. The part of your mind that looks for errors needs to be put on pause, as much as possible, while you are busy piling up new ideas and new details. That's true even if you type slowly or misspell every fourth word. Getting plenty of ideas down is worth the typos.

We hope you'll see the writing process as a practical, rather than rules-based, way of finding and developing ideas that you care about. Feel free to be recursive. Use the strategies that work for you wherever and whenever you find them most useful.

Why Trying Something Different Can Help

As you've probably noticed, this chapter never tells you what you *have* to do or what you *must* do in order to improve your writing. One-size-fits-all advice does not work when it comes to writing. Rather, we want to introduce you to some important issues that writers think about when they are communicating with an audience.

Of course, you will find plenty of specific suggestions in this book, strategies for getting your point across and coping with some of the challenges you may face in your writing. Even as you consider those strategies, you should understand that not every strategy will be right for you. That's fine. Respect what you know about yourself as a person, as well as a student. Use the approaches that you have strong reason to believe will probably work for you. We want to ask one more thing of you: Keep an open mind. Try a new approach occasionally. Experiment here and there. Develop an essay using a strategy you've never tried before—especially if the approaches you've used in the past no longer seem to be paying off. Try playing around with one of the revision strategies you'll find in chapter six, even though you've never done anything like that before. In fact, maybe that's a good reason to try a new strategy—specifically because you have never done anything like that in your paper, and you're wondering how that new approach might change your writing.

Suggestion Box: Give It a Try—and Then Another Try

Sometimes an experiment deserves to be repeated a few times. Your attempt to use a writing strategy for the first time might be only partially successful, but the second or third try may bring much better results. This is even more likely to happen if you experiment with new ways of organizing an essay, a new tone, or even a different type of sentence pattern. For instance, writers sometimes find semicolons to be clumsy tools the first few times they use them; however, they later realize that the semicolon, like every tool ever invented, is extremely effective in some situations and less so in others.

A new writing strategy may prove a perfect fit for you. On the other hand, you should feel free to drop a strategy that just doesn't match your writing goals or your personality. One student might do her best writing while listening to heavy metal (with the volume cranked up, obviously), while another may try this with lousy results. It's not a strategy the latter student feels obligated to use again, and there wouldn't be any sense in doing so; it works well for some writers, but not for him. Writers also might use a strategy in one type of writing situation (a timed, in-class essay, for instance) and not another (a complex, semester-long research project).

People who become effective writers think about what they're doing, try new approaches when necessary, and stay practical. Many of them also find a way to have some fun with their writing. That never hurts.

Beyond the Essay: Writers at Work

VAN ALLEN PLEXICO, Science fiction and fantasy writer

Van Allen Plexico's science fiction and fantasy stories have won him plenty of fans, many of whom show up at various pop culture conventions to hear him speak about his work. His novels include two separate series (Sentinels and Hawk); in addition, he has also edited several works that analyze comic books. He is also a professor of history and political science at Southwestern Illinois College.

Van started reading science fiction in grade school. By eighth grade, he reports, he had begun writing his own novels. "They were handwritten on notebook paper and were terrible, I'm sure, but the desire was always there." Along the way, however, he experienced doubts. "I would write something, decide I wasn't quite 'ready' yet, and stop writing for a couple of years. That probably wasn't the best thing I could have done, but . . . trying to write something very long can be an intimidating task, especially if you've never done it before."

While he enjoys hearing from readers, Van has an even deeper motive for writing. "What keeps me going is simply the overwhelming desire to get the stories in my head down on the page—to work through them and make them click, almost like puzzles to be solved."

Van's website is **www.plexico.net**. We asked him to describe his writing process.

Where do you get your ideas?

Ideas for books and stories come to me naturally, organically, by absorbing bits and pieces of everything story-wise around me. Because I read (tons of) books and comics and watch movies and TV shows, all kinds of neat ideas go into the hopper of my brain, there to bounce around randomly. Eventually little pieces of story ideas and characters stick together in unexpected combinations and suddenly—bang!—a new idea. So the first trick is to just keep scooping up all the good ideas that come along. I call that stage the "idea-gathering" stage, where I have the basic concept and maybe the characters but I'm still looking for inspiration for interesting and exciting things that can happen during the course of the story. Once that conglomeration of ideas comes together as a single story seed, the next trick is to create a summary or outline that gets the best parts and pieces together on one page and allows you to begin weaving them together into a whole—into something new and different.

When you're busy writing a first draft, what does your writing process look like?

I constantly re-read what I've just written and look at each new section in the context of what's already done and where I'm planning to go. There's a lot of scrolling up and down. Only when I'm really on a roll with a set of scenes do I go purely linear—typing frantically, trying to keep up with what's playing out in my head—and even then I'm still looking back up the page at what I just did, every so often, to make certain it's working. Of course, when it's done I carefully go back over the whole thing, finding the inevitable spots where I left something out or didn't write it as elegantly as I could have. At that point, though, a lot of the story has been accomplished in a hurry. There's something to be said for not messing with momentum when it gets going in a big way.

What goes through your mind during the revision process?

I try to push myself to ramp up the 'sense of wonder' when I am constructing my story's basic concepts. In other words, my first idea is usually serviceable but rarely as big and bold and exciting as it could be. I challenge myself to take it up another notch, with a bigger sense of wonder, trying to make the reader's eyes pop out.

For Writing or Discussion:

1. Van mentions that writing sometimes "can be intimidating." Is there any part of the writing process that you find intimidating? What can you do to make the experience less nerve-wracking?

2. Van describes the invention or "idea-gathering" process that leads him to a good "seed" for a short story or novel. In your writing class, you most likely will focus on writing essays. How might your invention process be different from Van's? In what ways might it be similar?

3. Explain what you think Van means when he advises writers to "not [mess] with momentum when it gets going in a big way." What might this advice mean for you, in practical terms, when you are working on the draft of an essay?

What Works For You?

How would you describe your writing process? Refer back to your high school writing experiences. If it has been a while since you have done any writing for a classroom, write about how or where you think you would start and what you would try to do. Do you think it will be difficult to try new approaches or techniques? Why or why not?

What do you find most challenging about writing? What, if anything, do you find most rewarding about writing—or what do you most like to write?

Looking for a Challenge: Keep a Writer's Log

We use writing in our personal, academic, and professional lives so often that we might not even notice when we're doing so. For the next week, keep a writer's log—a written record—of every time you use writing or see anyone do so. Does a waiter write down your order on his pad? Do you receive a text from your friend about meeting later? Are you taking notes in this class? All of these examples count. In your log, note what, when, and where each writing experience happens—and consider whether, why, and how the act of writing contributes to the situation. If you're the one doing the writing, describe in a sentence how that type of writing works for *you*.

Chapter 2: Reasons to Write: Everyday Life and College

At a Glance...

- Writing can play an important role in everyday life, as well as in college and your future career.
- Writing that you produce and share, no matter its length, is built around a sense of purpose you have in creating that document.
- The rhetorical triangle is a useful tool for thinking about your message and your readers.
- In the early stages of the writing process, audience may not be important to the writer; in the later stages, however, audience is very important.

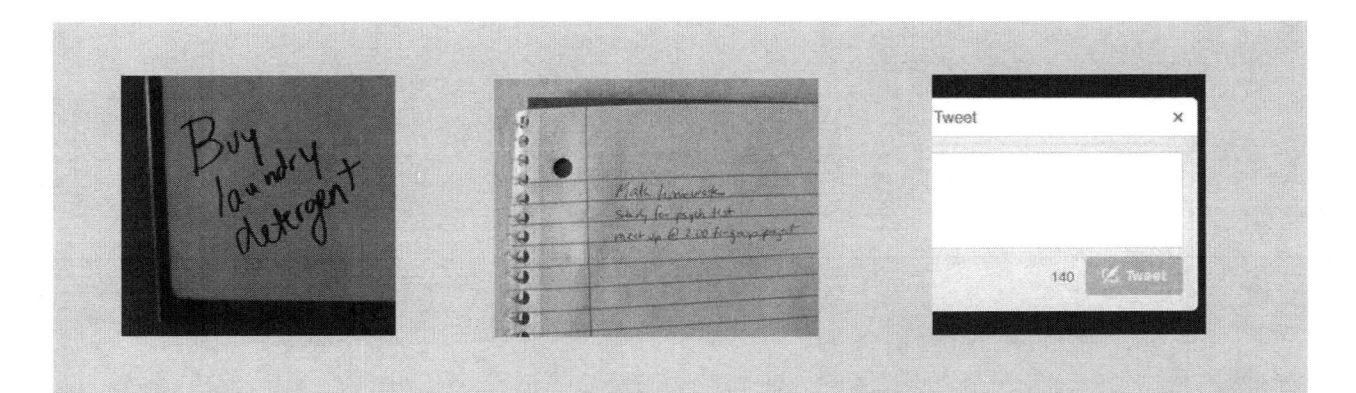

For Discussion or Writing: What sorts of everyday activities in your life involve writing of one sort or another? Think especially of the quicker messages you write. Is there still some thought involved in what you write, how you write it, and how others may react to what you've written?

Why Bother to Write?

Writing can seem like a lot of work -- at least some of the time. It's an activity that takes time, time you could spend watching television or shooting hoops or talking with friends. Frequently, writing requires hard thinking and careful rereading of your work.

Sure, some writers (particularly those who write about wizards or vampires) manage to become wealthy from their writing. Most of the time, though, writing will not make you rich or famous, nor will it automatically make you the center of attention at a party next Friday night.

Given those facts, why should you bother to write? The answer has everything to do with human beings' need to communicate. Humans communicate for practical reasons as well as compelling social reasons. Practically speaking, employees need to let their employers know that they are doing their jobs and deserve to be paid; they use writing to document their work. If you share an apartment, you might send your roommate a text begging her not to buy the most expensive brand of peanut butter because it's way *too* expensive, plus it doesn't taste as good as the cheaper brand. Your roommate, for her part, might post a question on Facebook, asking friends about alternatives to cable television and satellite services. That's the practical side of writing.

Most people find that writing sometimes makes their social lives easier or more fulfilling. Imagine, for instance, that you need to write a short note of apology or let someone who lives far away know that you're grateful for a gift. In either case, you'll want to communicate your main point clearly--and in a way that is likely to be received well by the person receiving the note.

Yes, you could skip writing those notes; but sometimes you value the relationship enough to invest your time and energy in putting your thoughts into writing. Obviously, most things that you write could also be spoken aloud, and sometimes talking with someone makes more sense than writing a note. Yet as Facebook, Twitter, and text messaging all demonstrate, many people feel a need to communicate in written form (even if spelling rules and sentence structure are put on hold in a Facebook post or a text message). Writing is a way of putting your stamp on things, and it often feels more permanent than words spoken out loud.

One More Reason to Write--You're in College

College classes provide you with one more reason to write. If you want to earn a degree or complete another type of college program, chances are excellent that you will be expected to write numerous pieces--some of them quite lengthy, some of them only a paragraph or so long. College involves writing partly because employers who hire college and university graduates expect that students will be able to express themselves clearly, and with a reasonable degree of correctness, in the workplace. Yet there's another reason college classes frequently require students to write: Writing is a great tool for learning a new subject or for digging more deeply into a topic that you have previously explored. In other words, writing is a great way to stretch your thinking--which is definitely part of the college experience.

Writing is about communicating about your experiences and ideas, as well as other people's ideas and experiences. Sometimes writing boils down to telling a good story, a story with a point or a message, something a reader might want (or need) to hear. You can learn how to write effectively for college and for your life beyond college. This chapter will show you that you already know more than you think you know about communicating in writing.

>>> Exercise 2.1: Situations Where Writing Skills Come in Handy

With the help of a partner, choose one of the situations listed below and make notes about how the situation might turn out for a person *with strong writing skills*. Once you've finished with that part of the activity, make notes about how that situation might turn out for someone who *lacked good writing skills*. Be sure to consider long-term, as well as short-term, consequences.

> 1. Requesting a refund of your security deposit when your former landlord mistakenly claims you left your apartment a mess and damaged three walls in the living room.
> 2. Applying for a job (your dream job) that is situated two states away from where you currently live.
> 3. Seeking volunteers, as well as funding, for a new group that rescues stray animals.
> 4. Writing a six-page paper and a bunch of one-page "mini-themes" for your U.S. History course, where more than half of the grade is based on writing assignments.
> 5. Sticking up for your child when his or her special needs are not being addressed at school.

Writing Essays and Writing Short Pieces

This book focuses largely on writing for college classes. For that reason, the book discusses the writing of **essays**: that is, pieces of writing that are multiple pages and which explore a main idea or situation. Essay assignments are common in college and university courses (and not just in English classes).

There will also be times when you will need or want to write briefer pieces: chunks of writing that are a paragraph or two long. Your psychology instructor, for instance, may ask you to write short responses (perhaps two paragraphs) as part of an exam that also includes multiple-choice questions or fill-in-the-blank items. Or you may wish to add a brief, personalized note that you include along with a longer, more formal message in your workplace.

Just about any type of writing that you produce and share with other people—long or short—will be built around the sense of purpose you have in creating that document. For instance, if you share a funny story on Tumblr, you *do* have a sense of purpose: You're trying to get people to laugh. (Maybe you're also hoping friends will share your post with others.)

The tips and suggestions in this book can be applied to essays as well as shorter pieces. No matter how brief the writing is, you will want to ask questions about your purpose and how the people to whom you are writing might react. Thinking like a writer—someone who communicates with others through writing—will help you build up skills that are useful in hundreds of different situations. The ability to adapt is an important skill for writers.

What Rhetoric Is: Something You Already Do

Your reasons to write have a good deal to do with rhetoric. **Rhetoric** is the study and practice of using language—your words—to communicate with an audience for some purpose. Although rhetoric is a new word for most college students, it's not a new concept. It's been around for a few thousand years, and it has likely been a part of your life since you first learned that words (spoken or written) could be useful in helping you persuade the people around you to do something, to grant you an opportunity or let you off the hook, or to just take your point of view more seriously. Rhetoric is about making decisions that make your words more powerful.

When a writer makes choices in an essay in order to reach the readers, we say the writer is making **rhetorical moves**. If you're a fan of an organized sport, you realize that players and coaches think through their moves—their strategy—all the time. They adjust based on whom they're playing and how the season or the game is going. They review game tapes. They swap out one player for another.

Writers who think about their rhetorical moves do something very similar. For instance, a writer could decide to begin a paper with suspense in order to surprise the reader. Or a writer could opt to rearrange his paragraphs to allow an argument to build in strength. More simply, a writer could replace one word with another to be more specific and accurate. Some of these moves may have a bigger impact on the whole essay than others, but they all have one thing in common: the writer chooses each move for a reason.

Suggestion Box: Read Plenty—Plenty of Different Things

If you want to become a stronger writer and do so faster, get in the habit of reading lots of different types of writing. You'll notice that writers use different strategies, different approaches, to discuss a particular topic with a particular audience. In other words, you will educate yourself (in a painless way) on the large assortment of rhetorical moves available to you.

Read first for enjoyment. But somewhere along the line, take the time to notice the ways in which a blog entry about the Orange Bowl on ESPN's website is different from the way your local newspaper describes a flag football contest. Notice how different both of those pieces are from the campaign website of someone who is running for office, or the letter sent out by your local superintendent of schools to explain why the district is enforcing a zero-tolerance policy on bullying. (Does the superintendent try to soothe the fears of parents who are worried their child's rights will be violated by such a policy? Dealing with that concern, rather than ignoring it, is a rhetorical move.) Keep your eyes open and ask yourself which approaches seem to work best and which approaches seem ineffective. You can learn from all of it.

Some choices are better than others, and other choices are just a matter of preference. Rhetoric matters because if you understand the ways in which language works to communicate an idea, you can see the options you have as a writer. These options mean that you can take greater control over the writing you are doing, just as a coach who has many strong plays to choose from can alter the way the game ends.

Rhetoric is about communicating ideas to an audience. You have your own ideas. Some of them are already front and center in your mind. Other ideas will emerge after you do some exploratory writing. Even if you have yet to determine which of your ideas deserve to be written about in essay form, you definitely have stories to tell, positions to convey, and something worth writing. Rhetoric is not just about people who made speeches hundreds and hundreds of years ago; it has everything to do with you and the messages you want to get across to readers and listeners today.

>>> Exercise 2.2: What Rhetorical Moves Do You Make?
Think of a real-life situation when you had to work with others to accomplish a goal—like the organized sport example. Describe the situation. How did you adjust your strategies to

> accomplish your goal while anticipating the needs or objections of the other people involved?

How the Rhetorical Triangle Works: Writer, Purpose, Reader

In the first chapter of the book, we explained that writing is like a system. When writing teachers talk about this system, they refer to it as the **rhetorical triangle**. As shown below (Figure 2.1), the rhetorical triangle is a way of thinking about how three items (purpose, writer, reader) work together when creating meaning. This is at the core of what rhetoric is about.

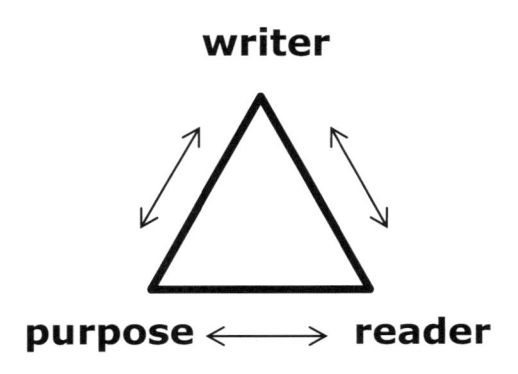

writer

△

purpose ⟷ reader

Figure 2.1: The Rhetorical Triangle

As mentioned in Chapter 1, the purpose/message of a paper is what makes it worthwhile to readers. It is the main reason that we write. The purpose is deeper than the main idea and it goes beyond just being a topic. For the moment, however, if you find yourself thinking of the essay's main idea and the essay's purpose as being close to the same thing, that's fine.

Examples of the Rhetorical Triangle Applied to Two Writers

To see how the rhetorical triangle comes into play, let's examine two writers at work on a paper with an assigned topic. The whole class was told to write about "Class attendance in college," a general enough topic. This topic does not yet specify what the message of the paper is. The message for the paper would need to be something specific to the writer. Different writers would have different reasons to write about the topic, depending on their experiences with class attendance. Writers have their own perspectives, or viewpoints. These perspectives allow them to see the topic in their own way and create a paper that is unique to their views.

Sometimes a writer will have very strong views about a topic. She or he will have ideas to express about the topic that will need to be gathered and harnessed. Let's say that one student, Andrew, has attended college before and was dropped or withdrawn from a college course because he missed too many days of class. Andrew, because of his personal experience, has much to say about this topic, and frankly, he's angry about it. Andrew can voice that anger in his invention for the paper, but at some point, he'll need to decide what his main message is (beyond just that he's angry and something is wrong). He will also have to decide who needs to hear this message: that is, who are the people that make up his **audience**, or readers.

Andrew's Invention: Freewriting

Note: Andrew's freewriting, like much of the other freewriting you will see in this book, contains some typos. Freewriting typically is messy writing, and that's fine. Writers do not need to worry about good editing at this stage in the writing process, since the invention stage focuses on finding good things to write about.

> Man I hate this attendance stuff! Why do teachers have to take attendance anyway? I thought I was finished with this high school stuff but now its here all over again. I can't believe they can drop you from classes just for missing what they think is too many. I paid for thiese classes. Shouldn't I get to decide if I can come or not and besides sometimes it is hard to come to class. And that teacher just dropped me she didn't say anything. She just dropped me. It felt like nothing I did mattered. didn;t matter why I missed didn't matter what I said didn't matter what I'd done in class. Just done. Dropped. Stupid! All that money was wasted. All that time I'd put in was wasted too. I mean I know I missed some days— okay a lot of days...but I was here a lot of days to. And I'd done some writing to. So mad. Can't believe she gets to just drop me. It's not right. Why does she get to make that decision? What was I supposed to do? Sick work court. work again. sick again. can't win. I thought college would be different. I thought I'd get to do what I wanted. Less rules. Less stupid s*#! WTH? man, it's just dumb. And here I am again in the same place. Same school. Same class.

>>> Exercise 2.3: Examining Andrew's Invention Process

- What are some messages that Andrew has worked into this freewrite?
- What do you think the purpose of his essay should be? Who should he be writing to?
- Identify one good point you think Andrew is trying to make.
- Identify one point he makes that you think distracts from the main issue.
-

In the early stages of the writing process, you should concentrate on piling up lots of ideas (possible writing topics and details). As you pile up those experiences and ideas, you can begin to focus on the message that you want to send. Realistically, your message—your main point or reason for writing—will not always jump out at you. Frequently, though, you can "tease" it out of your invention material by asking yourself, "Why am I so interested in this? Why is this topic or situation important to me? Why might it be important for other people to read about this?" By focusing on the three parts of the rhetorical triangle, you, like Andrew, can figure out what your main message is and how you want to achieve it.

Let's look at another example for the same topic. This student feels the exact opposite way from Andrew. Her perspective means that her rhetorical triangle (and the paper she will write) will look much different from Andrew's. Sondra does not plan on missing a single class ever. She lists her reasons below.

Sondra's Invention: Brainstorming

> **Why I don't want to miss class:**
> --I will succeed. I cannot succeed without being here. I need this.
> --I am paying for these classes. I want to get my money's worth!
> --My kids need me to have a better job. I need more education in order to get a higher paying job.
> --If I'm not in class, that means I am somewhere else taken [sic] care of someone else. Classtime is "me time."
> --I know I need to learn this stuff. I've put it off for too long. Now is the time to do it.
> --I can't rely on anyone else to do it for me.
> --I'm behind enough as it is. Feels like I have to relearn so much. To miss a class puts me even more behind.

Andrew and Sondra are not only different people—different writers—but they are also going to communicate different messages to their readers. These two writers are operating with different rhetorical triangles. Both of the essays they end up writing have the potential to be interesting and thoughtful.

>>> Exercise 2.4: Examining the Rhetorical Triangle

Refer back to Figure 2.1 and Andrew and Sondra's invention material. Write brief responses (a few sentences) for each of the questions below.

1. Keep in mind that these two students were asked to write about the same topic. Do you ever worry about writing the "same paper" that another student is writing? Why or why not?
2. Who do you think Andrew and Sondra will be writing to? Something in their writing made you think that. Which parts helped you draw a conclusion about their audiences.
3. The writer's perspective changes the message of the paper. What else can it affect? How else did Sondra's writing differ from Andrew's?

What Audiences Expect

Fulfilling a Reader's Needs

Of course, if you want to communicate your message to an audience, you have to, at some point, show some respect to your potential readers. We don't mean you need to flatter your audience, or make them feel good about something that they should not feel good about, or pretend that you agree with some idea with which you do not agree. None of those approaches is necessary. In fact, readers are likely to reject tactics they are regard as insincere or "fake." Showing respect to readers means, ultimately, that writers can do certain things to make the reader's job easier and more enjoyable, and the writer should care enough to want to do that.

Suggestion Box: Strategies for Thinking about Audience

Here are a few ways in which writers can help fulfill the reader's needs in an essay:
- Focusing on a topic that the writer is interested in and trying to make that topic interesting for readers as well.
- Organizing the essay in a way that will seem logical to readers, including readers who do not know as much about the topic as the writer.
- Giving the reader a main idea that the reader can continue to think about when the essay is over.
- Editing the essay with enough care that the reader is not distracted too much from the good ideas and interesting details in the essay.

Probably there are other things that you could add to this list. However, this is not a bad set of expectations to keep in the back of your mind as you work on essays this semester. But please notice that we said the *back* of your mind. During the early stages of the writing process—for instance, during the invention stage and the first draft stage—it is not crucial that you spend much time (if any) on editing. During those early stages, your ideas may seem very disorganized, which is fine. That's just how early writing comes out, at least for most of us.

Being Your Own Audience

Thinking about *yourself* as an audience may help you to get into that mindset. After all, when you listen to something or read something, you have expectations. Your expectations vary according to what the event or medium is that you're interacting with; for instance, you bring different expectations to a Jay-Z concert than when you watch a program about financial aid on CNN. Still, you have expectations. You probably expect (or at least hope) to have your expectations satisfied: you want the acoustics to be good in the concert venue; you want the bass to pump through your body. Maybe you're hoping for a surprise; perhaps Jay-Z will have a special guest star who appears that night and that night only. In terms of reading an essay, your audience may enjoy being surprised as long as the surprise is not completely unrelated to the essay's main focus. In other words, the surprise should make sense and fit (as strange as that may sound) with the audience's expectations and hopes. For instance, you wouldn't want Jay-Z to surprise you by canceling the second half of the show so that he can project a CNN report on the screen. At least we don't *think* you would welcome a surprise of that sort.

Looking for a Challenge: Find Some Rhetoric, Ask Some Questions

Rhetoric is all around you. Or, to put it another way, you are surrounded by people's attempts to communicate with an audience for one purpose or another. Some of that rhetoric takes a written form: for example, essays and Twitter posts and letters to the editor. Yet rhetoric can also be found in speeches, song lyrics (if the song has a point to make), and advertising.

For this challenge, you will need to find advertising for a product or service of your choosing (e.g., hybrid vehicles, snack chips, electric razors). You may want to look for print ads in magazines or newspapers; in addition, you can find commercials on television, in YouTube, or through a search engine such as Google (example search: *commercials electric razor*).

Watch or read several of these ads for the product or service you've chosen. Then narrow your focus to one ad. Pay careful attention to the images (pictures, graphic design elements, and descriptions) employed in the ad. If you're working with a commercial, listen carefully to the background music, the announcer or actor's voice, and any special effect noises.

Ask yourself the following questions:
1. What audience does the ad target? What types of consumers or potential purchasers do you think this ad is designed to reach? (For instance: Women? Men? Both women and men? Older or younger consumers? People from a particular income group or lifestyle?)
2. What rhetorical moves or strategies does the ad use? That is, how does the ad go about trying to appeal to its target audience?
3. Which of those strategies seems most effective? Do any of the ad's strategies or moves strike you as potentially ineffective? Why? (For instance: Is the ad's appeal based on a stereotype about the targeted audience? Is it outdated? Does the advertiser assume something that should *not* be assumed?)

Write two or three paragraphs discussing the ad from a rhetorical standpoint. Use your responses to the questions above, as well as your own observations, to flesh out your discussion. Be sure to mention where you found the ad. (You may even want to attach the ad or include a link to it.)

What Works For You?

Think of a situation in the past week or two in which you had to think through *how* you were going to communicate your thoughts or feelings to someone. What, if anything, did you end up changing in your approach to that person? (If you had a chance for a do-over, what would you change this time?)

Can you imagine any situations in the coming week—either in terms of a writing assignment or a face-to-face conversation—where the concepts from the rhetorical triangle (writer/speaker, message/purpose, and reader/listener) will come into play?

Chapter 3: Writing and Reading Strategies: What an Essay Could Look Like

At a Glance...

- An essay is a focused piece of writing that explores a theme or main idea in a thoughtful way.
- You can create an effective essay by working through the choices you have as a writer.
- Readers expect final draft essays to include good beginnings, middles, and ends.
- Good essays come from good ideas, not formulas or recipes.
- Critical reading strategies can help you as a writer and as a college student.

For Discussion or Writing: Houses come in all shapes, sizes, and styles, but they share some basic traits. When you think of what a house is—what it's made of, how it's put together, and what types of living spaces it contains—what are some aspects that would be true of almost any home? What are some small or large variations from house to house? How might you compare houses to essays in this respect?

What an Essay Is and Why It's Important

An **essay** is a composition that develops one main theme: essentially, one main idea. Usually an essay involves multiple pages of writing, and the essay's theme is present throughout those pages.

You may have heard someone use the terms *topic* and *theme* when discussing an essay. Although these terms are related, they mean somewhat different things. The essay's **topic** refers to the subject matter you are discussing: *what the essay is about*. The essay's **theme**, however, is *what you have to say about the topic*. For instance, you might write an essay about the topic (subject) of pollution. Your theme, however, is more specific and purposeful: perhaps you wish to argue that most pollution is the result of people's laziness, or maybe you hope to show how the effects of pollution have contributed to people's health problems, including your nephew's asthma.

The essay's possible **thesis** is the essay's theme stated succinctly—that is, in a sentence or two. A good thesis will seem like an important sentence in the essay (in other words, readers will remember the idea), but it will also sound like it fits into the essay in a natural, comfortable way (in other words, it won't seem like you've jumped out of your chair and started shouting at your readers). In an essay that argues or persuades, the thesis will typically include a claim with which a reasonable reader could, in theory, disagree. Other types of essays—an essay whose purpose is to tell a story that has a point, for instance— will not necessarily offer a claim or argument in the thesis, but will instead drive home the essay's main point in a way that goes beyond simply stating the obvious.

The essays you write in college will normally involve multiple **drafts**—more than one version, in other words. Your first draft is not supposed to look exactly like your last draft. Some of the basic parts of the essay may be present in your first draft of the essay, or they may not show up until a second or third draft. It's perfectly conceivable, for instance, that your first draft of an essay might not contain a clear, natural sounding thesis. Often writers get a much clearer sense of what they want their main point to be as they work through their first few drafts.

Most of the time when teachers use the term *essay*, they are referring to a paper or composition. However, the word can also be used as a verb. To "essay" means to explore, to attempt something in a spirited yet open way. It may be helpful to think of your papers or essays as explorations of the topic you have chosen or been given. Your explorations will need a clear structure in order to be understood by the reader, but these structures can take a variety of forms. As we suggested earlier in this section, some essays *argue*; others *explain*; yet others *tell a story*. Some essays manage to do all three of these things or something different altogether. Your essay needs to have a point, and that point needs to be recognizable to readers.

There are many ways to accomplish these goals and many choices that you as the writer must make along the way. Whatever strategies you choose, your readers will expect to see certain elements in each essay you write.

How the Parts of an Essay Work Together

No two essays should be exactly alike, or even very similar to each another. Your instructor is interested in seeing *your* take on the child's birthday party from hell, or your observation about the effect that campus budget cuts have on the music program at your school. With each issue or experience you write about, you will create a fresh essay. Even if the topic has been written about before (it's hard to avoid that entirely), you will bring your own views and your own perspective to the essay. The relationship you establish with your audience will also influence the direction the essay takes. The rhetorical triangle will help you create an essay that is not exactly like everyone else's essay on that topic.

As we noted in Chapter 2, audiences do have expectations. By the time they see the final draft of your essay, they will expect to see several standard essay components—or, for lack of a better word, essay "parts"—built into the essay. Each part should help express your ideas to your readers. We'll tell you a little about these parts here. It's important to remember, though, that your earliest writings on your topic will not necessarily include all of these components. This is a peek ahead at how a final draft of an essay is typically set up.

The Early Parts of an Essay

Title

Purpose of a title...
- A good title will get the reader's attention and make the reader curious about the essay.
- The title also often gives the reader some sense of the essay's tone (e.g., serious, humorous, sarcastic, thoughtful, etc.).

Myths about titles...

- A good title needs to be chosen before the essay is written. **The truth**: The title can be the very last thing you place on the essay if you wish.
- A good title will give away everything important about the topic. **The truth:** A good title is one that does not ruin the essay for the reader.

> **Sample titles for an essay about family vacations:**
> The Perils of Piling in the Car Together
> Jammed Together for Hours and Hours—Wow, Isn't It Great?!
> Families, the Open Road, and Lots of Gadgets
> Five Soundtracks in One Car
> What is Your Sister Listening To?
> Stuck in the Middle of the Backseat: The Technology Question

Introduction

Purpose of an introduction...
- A good introduction will draw the reader in and make the reader want to read the rest of the essay.
- An introduction is also a common place for bringing the essay's main idea into play. That idea (which is more focused than simply an announcement about the essay's topic) is often called a **thesis**. Another name for the main idea is *controlling idea*.

Myths about introductions....
- The introduction needs to announce all of the essay's major points, all of the supporting details or reasons. **The truth:** An introduction that does that is giving away far too much of the essay's content too quickly, which means the rest of the paper could bore the reader. In most essays you will write in college, you can calmly lead your readers toward those supporting details. No need to throw them at the reader all at once.
- The best way to present a thesis is to write, "In this paper, I will prove..." **The truth:** You could probably get that idea across more effectively by starting the sentence with whatever was going to come *after* that introductory phrase.)

> **Sample introduction for an essay about family vacations:**
>
> Family road trips have been main features of movies and sitcoms for a long time. The Simpsons learn to not get along in brand new ways every time they climb in the car together. Flipping through a shelf of old movies at the public library, one might stumble across *National Lampoon's Vacation*, in which the Griswold family makes an error-filled trek to visit Wally World. Every so often, a family trip seems to take on deeper significance, as when a family makes a trip to visit a loved one freshly arrived home from a war. In most classic depictions of the family road trip, siblings fight, parents get aggravated, and boredom sets in during the first fifty miles. But technology is changing the nature of the family's journey by car. Often these days, one sibling is watching a DVD in the backseat while her brother scrolls through his mp3 player or plays a video game—

> with sister and brother both wearing headphones—while the people in the front talk on the phone or find the perfect satellite radio station that the kids won't even hear. In other words, each person is in his or her own world, all of them missing out on the shared miseries and pleasures of traveling through twenty-mile long construction zones and beautiful mountain ranges as a family, all in it together.

>>> Exercise 3.1: Thinking about Introductions

What techniques for writing introductions have you used in writing papers? Have you ever started a thesis with the phrase "In this paper, I will prove..." or similar? Why do you think the myth of this approach appeals to many writers, and why is it ultimately ineffective?

The Middle of the Essay

- **Body Paragraphs**
  Purpose of the essay's body...
    - The body paragraphs are the place where the essay's main idea is brought more fully to life. You can use a variety of development strategies to accomplish this.

  Myths about body paragraphs....
    - The body of the essay should consist of three supporting branches/paragraphs/reasons. **The truth:** There is no magic number of paragraphs for an essay's body. We would certainly encourage you to develop the body with multiple paragraphs, but you do not need to limit yourself to *only* three body paragraphs. Make the middle of the essay as interesting and convincing as you can.
    - Each body paragraph needs to be the same length. **The truth:** The length of paragraphs will vary according to what you are trying to accomplish in different paragraphs. Some paragraphs develop more complex ideas than other paragraphs or fill the reader's need for more description in that part of the essay. Each paragraph should be developed fully enough to support the paragraph's main purpose.

The End of the Essay

- **Conclusions**
  Purpose of conclusions...
    - A good conclusion will give the reader a sense that the essay is coming to an end. Often, a conclusion will lead the reader to consider the ideas in the essay even after the essay is over.

  Myths about conclusions....
    - A conclusion should always sum up (repeat) the major ideas that were mentioned in the essay. **The truth:** The essay's main idea should show up again in the conclusion, but each of the supporting ideas from the body does not necessarily need

to be reviewed in the final paragraph. A good conclusion normally will not feel like a rerun.

> **Sample conclusion for an essay about family vacations:**
>
> Is the common experience of taking to the road together—and experiencing a trip as a group, a family with common memories and gripes—completely a thing of the past? Not necessarily. Some families still manage to tune out technology (at least for significant parts of the trip) and talk with one another, even if some of their time is spent bickering and fighting for leg room and french fries. Other families accept entertainment options as a welcome relief to the boredom that can set in on even the most meaningful long trip. (Boredom is one of those things that gets over romanticized in movies. In reality, boredom is just plain tedious, something everyone just wants to get past as quickly as possible.) No one forces parents to pop in videos or allow non-stop texting on a family vacation. Just maybe teens can learn to wean themselves off twelve-times-a-day photo uploads to Instagram. It is still possible to take a vacation from technology in order to spend more time face to face, elbow to elbow in the sometimes disgustingly cramped quarters of the family car. Very likely, there's some benefit to doing just that: memories each person will share, with greater or lesser degrees of fondness, for years to come. Different families, however, will make different choices. The movies don't offer any answers here. People need to talk to their neighbors in the car—their families—to figure out what they want their next trip to look like and how they can best set themselves up for memories worth having.

Essays Are About Ideas, Not Formulas

It's easy to see an outline of a typical essay format, such as the one above, and end up with the impression that writing an essay is about putting "parts" together with other "parts." Students sometimes try to put essays together that way; they are looking for a formula to follow, a recipe that tells them to add two spoonfuls of this and one spoonful of that and half a cup of shredded cheese. There is comfort in having a recipe, especially when it's a dish you haven't cooked before.

But formulas—simple, highly predictable recipes—are not usually the best way to create an essay. Your ideas and how they get delivered to the audience are more important than following certain steps to writing. Yes, eventually you will need to make sure the essay has a beginning, middle, and an end. But you will be doing something more exciting than just following a formula. You will see where your main idea takes you and figure out, as well, where you want to take your readers. Good essays are about ideas that are important to you and your readers.

Getting Past the Paint-by Number Approach to Essays

At some point, perhaps you have worked on a paint-by-number picture, the type you occasionally find in a dollar store. The idea with a paint-by-number picture is that you don't have to think much about a process; you just paint the parts of the picture that are numbered *3* with red paint, the parts that are numbered *4* with black paint, and so on. You end up with a picture when you're finished.

The picture may be complete, but you don't really get a sense that the "painter" put his or her heart into the piece. By the time many students enroll in college writing classes, they have learned the writer's equivalent of a paint-by-number picture—namely, the five-paragraph essay. We want you to feel free to step beyond formulaic writing, including the five-paragraph formula.

However, since you may not be familiar with the formula that we're encouraging you to step beyond, we'll explain it briefly so you'll know what it looks like.

The Five-Paragraph Essay Formula

The five-paragraph essay formula is based on a rigid format: one paragraph of introduction; three supporting paragraphs in the middle, with each one focused on a different reason or example; and a one-paragraph conclusion. This is a formula that may have been taught to you in middle school or high school because your instructor wanted to ensure that each student would write more than one or two paragraphs, plus the instructor wanted to remind you that an essay needs structure. It's also a formula that many state-mandated tests seem to value at the high school level.

Now that you're in college, there are still a *few* occasions where such a formula can come in handy—for instance, when you have a timed essay exam in your history class ("Discuss three major causes of the Civil War") and there is not enough time to come up with a creative way of developing your essay. For the most part, though, college professors expect a more complicated and sustained structure. The way you organize your essays in college should be more thoughtful. The paragraphs you write and the way they relate to one another in your essay will be based on the point or message you are trying to get across to your readers. In addition, what you know about your readers and their expectations will help you determine how to organize your essays.

Complex Topics Demand A Wide Range of Forms

A great many situations in life do not break down into three tidy parts. A writer's recent divorce, for instance, may have had three causes—but perhaps it had one cause or seven causes, or maybe the writer can't figure out exactly what led to the divorce and wants to explore that question in his essay. If you are willing to set the formula aside, you may find you will have an easier time dealing with complex topics in your essays. Your readers are also likely to feel that the essay you're writing is more interesting (less predictable) than the five-paragraph version that someone else plans to write.

If you feel that you are already in the habit of using a formula to write your essays, there's no need to feel bad about that. You may have written some pieces that were interesting not because of the formula, but in spite of it—essays in which you used the formula as a foundation, and then built beyond it.

The rest of this book will equip you with techniques to help you write even when there is no formula available. In college and beyond, you are going to face assignments for which the five-paragraph-essay formula will not serve your needs. When this happens, you will need to have some good rhetorical moves—effective choices and development strategies—in your approach to writing.

>>> Exercise 3.2: Beyond the Five Paragraph Essay Formula

Consider what you know about the five-paragraph essay format. How might that come in handy as you experiment with other ways of organizing an essay? In your journal or notebook, note what is useful about having worked with this particular formula; be specific. Now note several disadvantages of learning the form or of working within it.

Writing for a Variety of Assignments

When our students receive instructions about a writing assignment, inevitably one of their first questions is, "How long does it have to be?" While length is one item a student should consider when beginning a writing assignment, it is just one part.

When you receive a writing assignment from an instructor, you should ask yourself many questions. Begin by reading the assignment sheet carefully. Underline or highlight anything that is particularly important. If you do not understand part of the assignment, ask your teacher about it either in person or in an email.

Ask yourself:
- What is the main topic? What are the expectations for that topic? What should I do with the topic?
- Does the assignment say what sort of approach I should take? (Examples: Explain something, Give an opinion or argue, Explore the topic)
- Who is the audience for this writing assignment? What will this audience already know about the topic? What will need to be explained to them?
- What is the scope of the assignment? How much depth will I need to go into? How should I fill the length that is required for the paper?
- When is it due? How much time will I need to come up with ideas? When is the first draft due? When is the final draft due? Do I have any other major deadlines that will conflict with these deadlines?
- Does this course or course teacher have different requirements than other classes I have written for?

You will soon discover that courses in different disciplines have a differing set of expectations for written assignments. Some disciplines will require more formality. Others will expect more personal observation skills. Most will want critical thinking in papers. Sometimes, these expectations are clearly explained in an assignment. Other times, especially in more advanced classes, it is assumed that you as the student are familiar with these unspoken rules already. The best way to prepare for these different expectations is to pay attention to the changes between your classes and your class assignments. One way to do this is to become a more strategic reader.

> ### >>> *Exercise 3.3: Actions and the Writer/Reader*
>
> On a piece of paper, divide the page in half by drawing a line down the center of the page. On the left side, write "Writer." On the right side, write "Reader." (If you are doing this activity on a computer, just write "Writer" and then space down before typing "Reader.") Under each category, create a list of actions you associate with each word. Write down *anything* you do as you read and write. Be prepared to compare your list with your classmates.

The Importance of Being an Active Reader

So far in this book, we've focused on the choices that you will need to make as a writer. These choices will not only make your papers stronger, but they will also help you to grow as a writer. In this next section, we would like for you to start thinking about the decisions that you make as a reader, and we'd like to show how reading is another way to help you evolve as a writer. This requires an **active reading** strategy, not a **passive reading** method.

To read passively is to merely read the words and let them slide into your mind as you go over them. The problem with this (as you probably already know) is that the words often slide right back out again once your attention moves to something else.

Your instructors want you to read actively. This means that as you read, you are expected to do something more than just read over the words: there should be a complementary activity or action.

HOW TO READ ACTIVELY

Engage with the material by asking questions
- What is the most important idea?
- What from this reading is relevant to this course?
- What is most relevant to my life?
- What experiences do I have that reinforce or oppose the reading?

Annotate the text

Create a system for note-taking as you read. Find a system that works for you.

- Write in the book or handout:

  ✓ **Highlight important sentences or paragraphs.** Avoid over-highlighting, though, or you'll end up having to reread *everything*. Ask yourself what is most important to remember and only highlight those parts.
  ✓ **Write marks in the margins.** Create a shorthand system that works for you. Maybe put stars next to important passages and question marks next to paragraphs or sentences you have questions about.
  ✓ **Write your thoughts and reactions in the margins.**

- Record your thoughts in other ways as you read:

  ✓ **Use sticky notes.** If your school has a textbook rental service, try using Post-It notes (or something similar) in your book to tag important sections. Take notes on the Post-It notes. (It's a good idea to put the page # on the Post-It note just in case it falls out of the book.)
  ✓ **Keep a journal.** Some students like to have a notebook or a binder for each of their classes. Notes from the textbook can be kept here too. Other students prefer to work electronically. Notes can be maintained in a blog or a journal that is part of the class. Some students type their notes and save them in a folder on a USB drive.

- Ask: *What should I write?*

The short answer to that question is to write down whatever will be most useful to you and your coursework. The longer answer is that you are writing to learn and to make meaning of what you are reading. You can write about what you understand by summarizing the important lessons. You can also write about what you don't understand by writing questions about the reading. This can be taken a step further—you can also look up what you don't understand.

Use Reference Materials to Help You Read Actively

- **Glossaries:** When you encounter a term that is in bold or underlined in a text, that means that it is located in a glossary at the back of the book. This is a sort of like a dictionary for terms that will be important in that textbook. Flip to the back of the book and locate the term.

- **Dictionaries:** Some of the words used in a textbook will be new to you without being vocabulary that is specific to the text's main subject. When this happens, consult a dictionary. It is a good idea to own a dictionary, but you may be able to find a trustworthy online dictionary to consult.

- **Search Engines:** Sometimes a concept may still be unclear to you even after reading the definitions in a glossary or a dictionary. Use your favorite search engine to look up the information on the Internet. Just make sure to use what you have already learned from the dictionary to help you expand that knowledge.

These strategies will take more time than just passively reading your text, but the end result will be that you will remember the reading much more effectively. Much more important than just remembering what you've read, though, is understanding what you have read and learning from it.

The Importance of Reading as a Writer

In addition to reading actively, we would like to encourage you to read *rhetorically*. You'll recall from Chapter 2 that to write rhetorically is to think about the relationships among the reader, the writer, and the message. It is possible to read with the rhetorical triangle in mind as well.

HOW TO READ RHETORICALLY

Ask preview questions. Before you begin to read an assignment, ask yourself a few preview questions. These are questions that you can explore before even reading the first lines of the text.

- Who is the author? What do I know about the author? What do I expect from this author based on that knowledge?
- What is the title of the work? What can I assume the text will be about based on that title?
- If there are subtitles or subheadings, what do they indicate about what the reading will be about and how it will be organized?

Read the introduction.

- What expectations do you have for the text now that you have been introduced to the topic?
- Has reading the introduction changed your assumptions? Why or why not?

Read the rest of the text.

- Take note of any time your assumptions shift or change. What made that happen?

- Also notice any time the writer was able to surprise you.
- How did the text conclude? Were you left wanting to hear more? Were your expectations fulfilled? Why or why not?

Dig deeper by rereading the text.

- How was the text structured? What was the focus of each paragraph or each section?
- How was the text supported? Which support was most effective in communicating with you, the reader?
- How did the writer transition from one part of the text to the other?
- Were you the intended reader for the text? If not, how do you think the intended audience reacted to the piece? Why?
- Did you believe the writer? Why or why not?
- How did your own life experiences and your own knowledge as a reader influence how you interpreted or responded to the text?
- How is this text similar to other texts like it that you have read? How is it different?

In the beginning of the semester, you may struggle to answer some of these questions. You will find that just as with writing, the more practice you have with reading, the more readily you will be able to answer these questions and notice the deeper elements of both reading and writing.

Looking for a Challenge: Reading Blogs and Creating Your Own Blog

You may already be familiar with **blogs**, personal or professional websites featuring frequently updated short-form content (posts) that often link to other online spaces or articles. Some blogs are more like online journals or diaries, while other blogs are less personal; some are free-standing, and others are arms of larger websites or online publications. Some blogs are one-sided conversations, but many allow visitors to remark on a post by submitting comments.

You can find a blog on just about any topic by using Google or similar search engines. Type in your topic plus the word *blogs* (for instance, *Harry Potter blogs*). Once you've found an interesting blog, follow it for at least a few weeks. Figure out what sort of rhetoric is at play in the blog—that is, what ideas are explored in its posts, how the author or authors present(s) a voice and identity, and what type of relationship each author has with the audience. If you feel so inclined, join the conversation by leaving comments when a blog post grabs your attention.

Consider starting your own blog if you feel that you need more space in which to express your thoughts. You can set up your own blog by using a free blogging service such as Blogger (blogger.com), WordPress (wordpress.com), or Tumblr (tumblr.com). In order to set up a blog, you will need to provide the blog service with your email address and name. However, you can prevent your name and email from appearing on your blog if you wish to protect your privacy.

If you do start your own blog, consider how private or public you want your posts to be. Typically, you can make your blog "public" (meaning that anyone on the Internet can view it) or "private" (in which case the only people who will be able to read it are those to whom you give the address). Think carefully about how much information you should share on your blog about the people in your life. Writing about a coworker's behavior may be fine—but you probably should not use that person's real name or mention precisely where you work. Treating others with respect is as important a rule in the **blogosphere** (the wide world of blogging) as it is in face to face communication. Remember, too, that words published on a blog remain and can be found weeks, months, and even years after you write them.

What Works For You?

Think about a reading assignment that you have coming up this week (in any class that you are taking). What is the assignment? What kind of reading? Which strategies will you use and why do you think they will help?

Chapter 4: Invention

At a Glance...

- Invention is anything you as the writer do before writing your draft.
- Time spent on invention activities will help you to write a better essay.
- There are many ways to invent material for an essay. Choose what works best for you. Try a variety of invention techniques.
- Invention can be done with low tech or high tech methods.
- Invention is a time for the writer to explore ideas without thinking about the reader yet.

For Discussion or Writing: Think about a product you use on a regular basis—more specifically, an item that involves technology, something that had to be engineered into existence. How did that product get invented? Take a couple minutes to speculate about what sort of conversations or writing or planning or diagram-making or testing had to occur long before the first version of that product was shipped out of a factory.

Now answer this question: Why are you being asked to think about this scenario in a writing textbook?

What Invention Means and Why It's Important

Have you ever found yourself staring at a blank piece of paper or a blank screen, wishing the words would come, but all you get is frustration instead? This tends to happen when writers have not given themselves time to think about what they will write about before attempting to write. (Perhaps you're thinking, "But I've sat down and written pages before without doing any of that invention stuff!" Yes, it is possible to just sit down and write; however, when this occurs, chances are you are already very familiar with the topic.) Some writers even prefer to discover what they think by writing about it. All of these reasons are why you should invest time in invention activities. They are meant to help you think through your topic or "test drive" your ideas.

The best ideas usually do not come to a writer fully formed. They develop over time; frequently, they change a good deal in the process. Even when a writer is convinced she knows exactly *what* she wants to say, invention activities often will help her figure out *how* to say it. Occasionally, the "very certain" writer ends up changing her mind and ends up with an approach she likes better. Invention really means not slamming the door shut too soon. Good things happen when writers keep their minds and their eyes open.

Many instructors use the term *prewriting* instead of *invention*. Those two terms mean essentially the same thing. We'll call it invention here, partly because we want to remind you that you can use the invention techniques from this chapter during any stage of the writing process. Which name you call these strategies is not important: what matters is that you're willing to try them.

Thinking by Writing: Freewriting

Freewriting involves writing down your thoughts in a quick, non-censoring way. It's a technique that will help you get past the part of your mind that says, "Hey, that's a stupid idea—don't write *that* down!" Many writers find that freewriting is an essential tool for collecting all sorts of ideas—strong ideas, confusing ideas, ideas that at first are only half-formed.

Why would you want to collect ideas that aren't all great? Writers need choices. The more ideas you can pile up during the early stages of the writing process, the better. You'll have more ideas (more topics) from which to choose, and when you have lots of choices, you're less likely to find yourself stuck with a topic that doesn't work for you. Also, it's often difficult for writers to decide immediately which ideas are worth keeping and which can be discarded. Freewriting is a way around that problem. Collect the ideas and experiences that run through your mind. Save the sorting out (the quality control part of the writer's job) for a later stage of the writing process.

Suggestion Box: How Do I Freewrite?

- Start writing. Sometimes your teacher may give you an assigned topic to write about (for instance, "college" or "education"). Other times you may need to work with an idea off the top of your head, or something that's happening in your life or something that's in the news. But the main thing is, once you have a topic, start writing.
- Do not stop writing until time is called (either by you or your instructor).
- If you run out of things to say, write "I can't think of anything to write about" until something (*something* . . . anything, really) pops into your head. Then write about that topic (whatever it is). And keep writing. Do not stop. (Not even to gaze out the window as though a good idea might walk by in a minute or two. We call that waiting, not freewriting.)
- Do not pause to worry about spelling, grammar, or finding exactly the right word. Fake it. Misspell the word if you have to. Skip over your uncertainty for the moment.
- If you find yourself backspacing or hitting the delete key, try turning off the monitor—or place a sheet of paper over the screen—and continue to type that way.
- Get thoughts on the screen or your notebook paper. They won't be perfect. They won't all be perfectly connected to each other. They won't all make sense together. That's fine.
- Remember that this is not an essay you're writing. It isn't even the first draft of an essay. You're simply trying to pile up ideas—or figure out where an idea might lead you. That's a very important skill for writers.
- Do not backspace. Do not cross things out. Do not erase. (Seriously! You need to go forward with your thoughts, not backwards.)

What does freewriting look like? Here's a sample, about five or six minutes' worth. This freewriting is rough. During the invention stage, rough writing is normal; it's almost to be expected, in fact.

> I was talking with my friend yesterday. Talked about a lot of stuff. Her sister is getting married, but that's the sister I don't like, so I'm not going to write about her. Another thing my friend mentioned — her dog is sick, could be diabetic, maybe something else. Talked about how expensive it is to take dog to the vet but she wants to help it, doesn't want Tough Pup to suffer. She said...at first I thought she was joking — she said there's heaalth insurance you can get for pets. Helps to pay pet bills...vet bills I mean... when they go thru the roof and you're not expecting it, you don't have the money this month to pay for it. So you pay a little each month for pet insurance health insurance for Tough Pup. Just seems really weird to me. I don't want to judge my friend...I love animals too, would do almost anything for my cat, but you got to remember there are people out there, lots of people who don't have ANY insurance! any health insurance. So now we have health insurance for dogs and cats (and what about hamsters and goldfish, can you get it for them too? okay so i'm sarcastic) but I know five people off the top of my head who don't have any insurance when they want to go to the doctor. Well, they need to go to the doctor, it's not that they want to go. And if I told them (wonder if they already know) that some people buy health insurance for dogs so the vet can run thousnand dollar tests on it....I don't know how they would react. Maybe they would be would feel insulted by it. Because they really need to go to the doctor or they want to take their child to the doctor but where's the insurance for them, they can't afford it.

You'll notice there's some rambling in this example, but that's okay. Freewriting is one place where you're welcome to ramble. (You may, in fact, stumble across a great essay topic or supporting argument when you ramble in a freewrite.) Typos (such as *thousnand* instead of *thousand*) also pop up in this freewrite. Again, that's not a problem. Freewriting is *not* about writing neatly. Freewriting is about collecting possible topics and exploring ideas.

Freewriting will cost you nothing (other than a bit of your time). It's usually painless. It often leads to some good seeds that can be grown into something stronger at a later time. The more rough material you write down—the more you pile up—the better your chances of success once you start writing the actual essay.

> ### >>>Your Work Now: Practice in Freewriting
>
> Choose a topic to freewrite about. Any topic could work, but in case you're stuck, we'll offer a few possibilities:
> - your workplace and the things that happen there
> - your toughest class or the class you have enjoyed the most
> - challenges parents face
>
> If you end up veering off topic, that's okay. You may end up writing about something even

> more interesting than the topic that got you going. Whatever you do, though, keep freewriting until time is up. (If this is your first time freewriting, we'll encourage you to keep at it for at least seven minutes. If you have previous experience with freewriting, you may want to aim for ten or fifteen minutes. Set the alarm on your phone and keep writing until it goes off!)

Looping is a method of freewriting that builds on an earlier session of freewriting. After taking a break from the freewriting, you should reread the freewrite. If the freewrite was typed, copy and paste the good part(s) of the earlier freewrite into a new document. If it was hand-written, rewrite the good portion on a new page. Then begin freewriting again, using the good part of the old freewrite as your inspiration for this new freewrite. This same technique of rewriting something and trying to remain focused can be used more generally by rewriting a prompt or a quote or any other material that catches your attention. That type of freewriting is usually referred to as **focused freewriting**. Even though this freewriting is more focused, the prompt is still just a jumping off point for your own ideas.

> I don't want to judge my friend...I love animals too, would do almost anything for my cat...Well, the truth is, I feel like I am kind of judging my friend, but that's not my intent. I get that people care a heck of a lot about the animals they spend their time with, pets who are there when they get home from work, pets they will spend days searching for if they manage to get loose, and then if...when...a pet dies, well, that's a tough time. But I have to ask, is it possible to get TOO attached to a pet? Too attached. I mean can you put so much emphasis on your dog, your cat (in my case) that you neglect the people around you, your family and friends. Have to be honest—in my family, the cat and the dogs (my nephew's dog, my brother's dog, big mangy dog) are members of the family, they have birthdays, my mom gives them presents. Wonder if we put more emphasis on our pets than generations that went before us. Maybe because we spend more time around the house (many kids don't go out to play, they stay inside with the dog or cat and video games, etc.). Or maybe it's because most families are smaller today. Fewer kids in the house to play with. Animals become more important as playmates and friends. Plus in that case maybe parents have more money they can spend on spoiling their pets. Varies from family to family I'm sure. Is it ever WRONG to spoil your pet? Can you go overboard? How do you know you're going overboard, spending too much, making the cat the center of your life? Don't want to guilt trip myself here—no way am I going to stop treating my cat like she's part of the family. But the way we treat her, maybe there's something deeper going on. Although she is just plain awesome as a cat.

Sometimes you may find yourself freewriting about a real-life event. In that case, you may want to spend your first round of freewriting trying to capture the event on the page: for instance, who was there, what happened first, what happened next, and so on. During a second round of freewriting (particularly if you do some looping), you could explore the deeper significance of one or two of those details—for instance, why you grew nervous when your neighbor got out of his truck. Give yourself a chance to explore not just what happened, but why it happened and what you thought about it.

Aural Invention: Talking It Out, Recording, Instant Messaging, Voicemail

Some students wonder, "Why can't I just talk out the paper instead of writing? I'm fine when I'm talking about something." To this, we respond, "Why can't you?" Not all invention needs to be in written form. Some students find great success with recording themselves talking out the paper. They then play it back as they write down some of what they've said. Sometimes, they don't have to play back much of it at all but are able to continue writing because they have the initial ideas in place now that they've talked it out.

Another way to accomplish the same task is to chat with a friend or a tutor. One way to do this is to just naturally talk about the topic as the friend or tutor jots down some notes about what you are saying. A benefit of this invention strategy is that you have immediate feedback. This is a real audience who can ask you questions about what you are saying and also help you to keep going. Some students turn to social networking sites like *Facebook* or *Google+* when they are stumped. If this is you, then you can use the chat feature there to chat about your topic with a friend. Just make sure once you have a good idea going, you end the chat and begin writing the paper!

Even if you are not a particularly chatty person, it is possible that you've experienced a moment of getting a wonderful idea for a paper topic but being unable to write it down at that moment. Moments of brilliance may strike as you are trying to sleep or taking a shower. Another favorite inspiration place might be the car or bus. The ride home from school or work can be a great time to come up with ideas. If you're not the one driving or you have a hands-free device, use your cell phone to call your voicemail or text yourself, leaving as many ideas for yourself as you can. When you check your messages later, you can recall that idea once more and then get it down in writing.

>>> Exercise 4.2: Practice in Aural Invention Technique

Come up with a topic that you can imagine yourself writing an essay about. (If you're stuck, you might want to skim the topics you discussed in your freewriting during the previous exercise. Which of those topics deserves further exploration?)
Get together with two classmates. One of your group members will record what you say (as best as he or she can capture it); the other group member will have the job of asking you some questions that are designed to serve as a nudge in case you sound like you're running out of things to say about your topic. (Remember those key question words: *What....? When....? Where.... Who....? Why....? How....?*) When your turn to talk is over, the note-taker will supply you with notes about what you said. Then it's time to rotate roles until each group member has a chance to be the talker. (Each of you should work with a different topic, unless your instructor wants you to focus on the same topic.)

Each person in the group should plan on talking—without long pauses—for about five minutes.

Brainstorming

Brainstorming is truly a mental free-for-all. List any topic that comes to mind, even if you're not sure you could turn it into an essay. Nothing is too silly at this point; it's only a list. (A student once wrote, "Annoying habit: toenail clippings left all over the house." She later handed in a good paper about how couples can learn to cope with each other's annoying habits. The essay had its origins in a seemingly trivial item on a brainstorming list.) To help organize this list, you might try typing very general topics (TEXT MESSAGING, for instance) in capital letters. List possible subtopics beneath the general topic in lowercase letters:

TEXT MESSAGING
- popularity of texting
- legality/illegality of texting while driving
- teachers' irritation with in-class texting
- texting as a necessary activity...e.g., emergencies
- texting etiquette
- texting vs. phoning/e-mailing
- thumb damage from texting (read article on...)
- novel recently published...made up entirely of text messages
- how language changes in texting

Brainstorming is most often used to help writers come up with a main idea for a paper, but it can also be used to generate ideas for support.

TEXT MESSAGING...WHY TEXTING IS BETTER THAN CALLING
- why call when it's just a quick simple question?...texting more efficient
- phone call interrupts what the other person is doing (but they can read a text while multi-tasking)
- texting feels more modern...calling is what my grandparents do!
- calling means all that background noise is heard
- you could accidentally end up on someone's speaker phone if you call—text message is not likely to be accidentally shared with others (but what if they forward it...?)
- maybe I can sneak in a text message while my prof is lecturing...not so with a phone call (ha! hope she doesn't see this on my list!!)

Your Work Now: Practice in Brainstorming

Let's try two rounds of brainstorming. For round one, your assigned topic is "problems in my community." (You're welcome to define "community" as you wish. You could focus on your hometown, or a neighborhood within that city or town; or you could focus on what's happening on your campus or at your job or in some club or organization to which you belong.) List as many problems as you can. Include things that others see as problems even if you don't consider them as problems yourself.

For round two, you will want to pick a problem from the list above and focus strictly on that issue. (Try to pick a problem that seems complex, rather than one that seems to involve an easy solution.) Now your job is to make a list of everything that comes to mind that is somehow related to that problem—for instance, the potential cause(s) of the problem; the solutions that have been suggested or tried; the "stakeholders" (that is, the people who have "stake" or interest in how the situation turns out); the things that might happen if the problem is not addressed; etc. You are not responsible for coming up with the perfect solution during this brainstorm session. (But who knows, maybe you'll come up with it anyway!) What you do need to do is brainstorm a long list of details related to this problem.

Questioning

Writers frequently ask themselves questions about topics that they're fuzzy about. It's a very normal, even healthy, thing to do.

You don't have to have even a vague sense of what the answer might be, particularly if your assignment is a research paper—that's what research is for, after all. Or you could list questions for which you *think* you know the answers; in that case, the research you conduct later will either reinforce or disprove what you thought was correct, and by the end of the process you should end up with a solid, defendable thesis. Or (perhaps better still) make a list of questions you think the audience will have. (If, on the other hand, you've already written a first draft, make a list of questions about that draft.)

At this point, though, concentrate on questions, not answers. Try to go beyond simple yes-or-no questions whenever possible. One set of questions on a topic about which I currently know very little:

> **EARTHQUAKES**
> - How do you go about preparing for an earthquake? (Can you REALLY prepare for one?)
> - Are most people in earthquake-ridden areas (California, etc.) prepared for an earthquake?
> - How do contractors in earthquake-ridden areas deal with this danger when designing buildings? Do they do a good enough job? (If they don't—will they get sued?)
> - Is this region prepared for an earthquake? What if that earthquake in April (think it was a 5.8?) had been stronger? What sort of damage would have resulted?
> - What's the likelihood of a major earthquake in this area in the next five or ten years? (Wonder how they figure that out...)
> - Are people too relaxed about the possibility of an earthquake?
> - How much does "earthquake-proofing" add to the cost of a new bridge or building? How do different building materials (e.g., wood, brick, stucco) hold up?
> - How would a major quake affect the local economy? What would I do if my workplace was out of commission for six months—no paycheck? Is there quake insurance on my home, my car? Does renter's insurance cover belongings ruined in an earthquake?

Once you have a topic and need more support, try a different form of questioning. Ask yourself questions such as those in the following box, and jot down your answers in a quick, almost freewritten way.

Suggestion Box: Questioning for Support

Who—who would need to hear more about this? who is affected by this issue? who is involved in this incident?
What—what is the most important part of this topic or situation, in my eyes? what would other people not know about this unless I told them?
Why—why does this matter? why did it happen this way? why does it work or not work?
How—how did the situation get this way? how could it be changed? how am I hoping to change it?
Where—where did this occur or where will it occur? where is this not likely to occur?

Clustering

Clustering is sometimes referred to as "concept-mapping" or "spider-webbing." The instructions for using clustering as an invention strategy are pretty simple.

- Draw a circle (not too large) in the middle of a blank sheet of paper. Write a general topic (for example, SOCIAL MEDIA) in the circle.
- Create branches for possible subtopics, and list details, issues, events, names, terms, problems, or examples for different aspects of the topic. Try to keep similar items on the same branch.

- Write down as many details as you can, even if some of your details seem to contradict one another.

Figure 4.1 is an example of clustering; the main topic for this cluster is social technology.

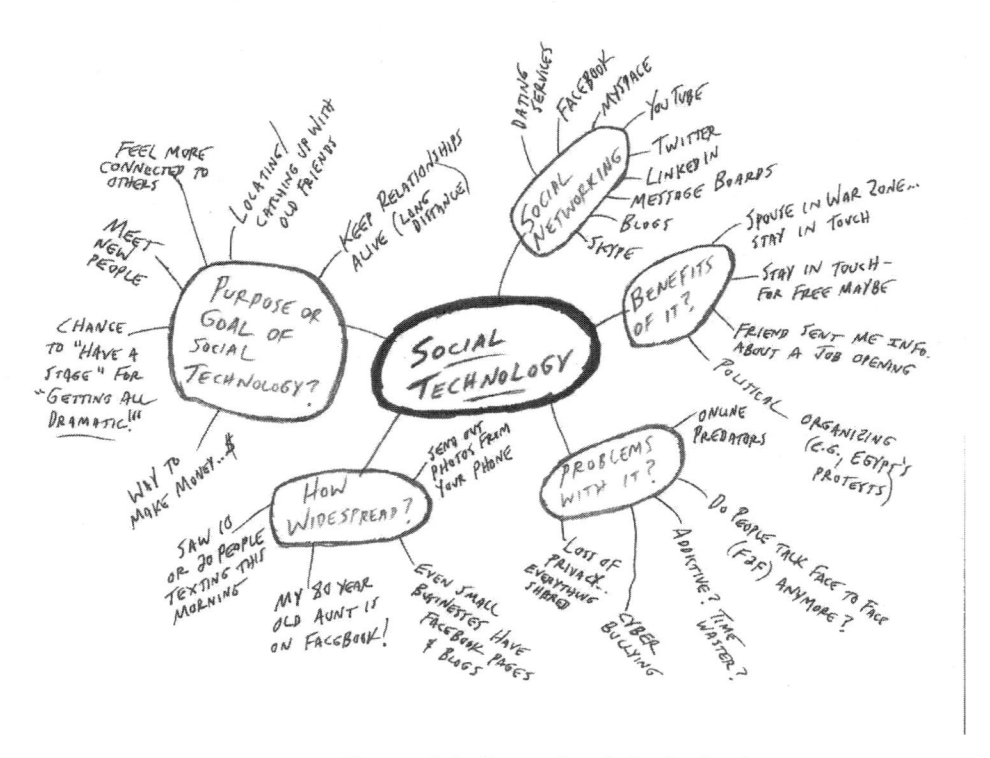

Figure 4.1: Example of clustering

Later, go through the cluster looking for the strongest focus—the issues or event that you could spend several pages trying to explain or argue about. If you wish, you can then use some of the other invention strategies from this chapter to explore that part of the topic in greater depth.
(For a digital version of clustering, try Prezi.com. You'll need to set up a free account.)

Drawing

You do not need to be a fabulous artist in order to use drawing as an invention method. When you use drawing as part of your invention process, your goal is not to create a great picture; it is instead to visualize some of the details that will go into your paper. This is especially helpful when you already have an idea of the things you should mention in your paper but do not know how much to go into each item.

In our classes, we've discovered that some students can more easily mentally picture what needs to go into the paper than they can verbally explain it. Taking the time to draw a quick sketch (stick figure people are fine!) may help you figure out which details deserve to be included in an essay. If you are a visual learner—or someone who really likes to draw—this invention method deserves a try.

Figure 4.2: a student drew what comes to mind when he thinks about his family

Storyboarding—drawings in a sequence—combines drawing with outlining. The result looks like a comic strip and puts a few images in the order they will be described in the essay.

Looking for a Challenge: Take a Topic for a Spin—Using Several Invention Strategies

You've been reading about various invention strategies and trying out a few of them along the way, possibly with a different topic each time. Now is your chance to test out each invention method by applying it to the same topic.
Put the topic at the top of the page and then try each method for five minutes. Your teacher may ask you to try this with a topic that you will be using for class. If, however, you do not have a topic in mind, try one of these topics:
- What family means to you
- The difference between high school and college
- The first time I _____[fill in the blank]_____.
- Technology and education
- Something happening in the news, either locally or nationally

---

How to Use the Internet for Invention

Most of the assignments in this book are designed to be written without research; however, sometimes students like to investigate a topic online before they begin writing about it. We truly think you should try plenty of other invention methods if you feel you're stuck. However, if you do want to look for writing topics online, you need to know how to do so responsibly—so that you're still the one who creates the writing that ends up in your essays.

48

You should ask yourself why you are looking online. For instance...

> ### Is it because you know absolutely nothing about the topic?

We doubt that you know nothing about it. Consider writing a list of what you do know and going from there. Then write down a list of what you would like to know or think you should find out. If you really want to investigate the topic online for more information, go ahead, but...
1. Keep a record of the sites you have visited so you can mention them in your paper and a Works Cited page. Either bookmark the sites or copy and paste them into a document that you'll save.
2. Keep track of your reaction to what you've learned. Don't just read and collect more information— stop and write after you've done some reading. This has multiple benefits, the greatest of which is you'll have material for your paper *and* that material will be your own writing.

> ### Are you looking online because you want to know what others have said about the topic?

This is tricky. First of all, if you go to a search engine and type in the topic and hit "search," there's no telling what results you'll receive. Maybe it will be the world's most interesting article on the topic, but it is much more likely that the results will be more generic than that. The search terms you use will make a difference. The more specific and unique the words or phrase, the narrower your results will be. Try using something from your list of what you would like to know.

Part of the dilemma with trying to explore ideas by looking at others people's ideas is you really need to know what you're looking for in order to get the best results quickly. Students who do not get good search results at first can end up clicking away indefinitely, further postponing the writing they are supposed to be doing. This is the one thing you do not want to happen when in the invention stage. This can lead to desperation.

> ### Do you really want to find a jumpstart for your own ideas, or are you hoping to find your ideas already written perfectly?

If you answered "yes" to the first half of the question, then you are using the internet to assist your own invention process, which sometimes works out okay. However, if you answered "yes" to the second half of the question, then you are trying to replace invention with plagiarism.

Plagiarism is presenting someone else's work as your own. There are many ways to plagiarize, some of them accidental. Any time you start to look elsewhere for ideas, you risk plagiarizing. And plagiarism (even the accidental variety) can result in very serious consequences in college classes.

Suggestion Box: What Can I Do to Avoid Plagiarism?

1. Continue looking for what you have to say about the topic instead of looking for what others have said.
2. Do some writing of your own.

3. If you find something interesting online (or elsewhere) and think you might want to use it (or some of it) in your paper, then copy and paste it into a new document AND copy and paste the web address (or URL, usually begins http://www...) into that document as well. Write down other pertinent information, such as: the title of the article, the author(s), the date it was written, the date you found/read the site, if the article was published in print anywhere.
4. Make sure that you place anything you use word for word in quotation marks and that you explain where that information came from. (Example: Nathan Joseph's article claims that "America has turned into one big reality show where everyone is a contestant and everyone is a viewer and we are a little bit confused.")
5. If you use ideas from the article, make sure you put those ideas completely IN YOUR OWN words and also explain where that information came from.

How to Determine Which Invention Activity Will Work Best

Which strategies will work for you in general, and which will work best when you have a specific writing dilemma? The answer will differ for each of you, and for the best results, you may want to experiment with multiple methods.

> **Freewriting** can be done at any stage in the writing process. Have an idea? Don't have an idea yet? Try freewriting just to see what you think. **Focused freewriting** should be done when you have an idea and just want to "play around with it." You can also freewrite after you discover you need more information or support in your paper.

> *Benefits:* Freewriting can help open your mind to new ideas you didn't realize you had or discover ideas that were there but buried below the surface. You can also find new ways of saying something when you freewrite again and again on a topic.
> *Drawbacks:* It often has to be organized into something with more structure. You need to be able to select what you should use and discard the rest.

> **Exchanging ideas** with another person (**aural invention**) is a way to work with others during the invention process.

> *Benefits:* Discussion is a great opportunity to bounce ideas off someone while getting the other person's take on the topic as well.
> *Drawbacks:* You'll need to exercise self-discipline in order to know when to stop exchanging ideas and start writing.

> **Brainstorming** is another good way to generate ideas for a paper when you don't really know what to do yet. It can also be used once you have an idea and want to explore some possible support.

> *Benefits:* Brainstorming helps you to see the possibilities spread out on the page and allows you to organize the ideas into similar groups/paragraphs.
> *Drawbacks:* The drawbacks are similar to those associated with freewriting. Brainstorming can also become too narrow; in other words, you may find yourself resistant to new ideas.

- **Questioning** is a way to find more details and support once drafting has been done.

    Benefits: Questioning can help you identify the "holes" in a paper or help fill them in once they've been identified. This strategy can help you relationships between your ideas and strengthen the support in your essay. Asking yourself thoughtful questions about your topic may help you develop a good conclusion for your paper or help you build stronger transitions (idea bridges) in the body of your paper.
    Drawbacks: The questions and answers you generate may end up looking like a checklist. Be sure to use those raw materials to build a thoughtful essay rather than a bunch of separate ideas.

- **Clustering** is a good way to explore support for a paper before or after some drafting has been done.

    Benefits: If you are a visual learner, clustering can help you "see" how the paper might take shape. Clustering may also make it easier for you to organize your ideas before drafting, since it may reveal connections you'll want to develop in your paper.
    Drawbacks: Clustering sometimes leads to superficial ideas. Be sure to challenge your own thought process; push yourself to go beyond the obvious.

- **Drawing** is a useful tool for easing your way into a topic while exercising another form of creativity.

    Benefits: What we picture in our minds is often more vivid than what might capture in a brainstormed list. If you spend time drawing an important scene in your mind—for instance, how an idea plays out—you may improve your odds of bringing many of those details into your paper.
    Drawbacks: You could spend so much time on a detailed, precise drawing that you leave yourself too little time to write a draft of the essay. Remember that the drawing you produce is a means to an end, not an end in its own right.

- **Browsing the library or searching the Internet** is a way to see what topics and support already exist.

    Benefits: Brief research may give you the start you need in order to get going.
    Drawbacks: There can be so much out there that you don't get started *or* may be tempted to turn over the control of your paper to someone else's ideas. You'll want to try another invention method after this one in order to explore your own thoughts more fully. Sometimes, more in depth (and academic) research will need to be done before you can truly make the topic your own. Other times, outside research may prove counter-productive. More often than not, your own ideas will need to serve as the heart of the paper.

How to Make Invention a Critic-Free Zone

For some people, writing for an audience is the most awkward and intimidating part of the writing process. What is it about writing for an audience that sometimes makes us think someone's just zapped us with a stun gun, causing us to freeze up? Probably it has something to do with the fears all of us have from time to time about people judging us based on what we've written or how we've written it.

Audience matters to writers, but it shouldn't be something that overwhelms you, especially not in the earliest stages of writing anything. We encourage you to push the voice of the critic out of your head for a while. Try to make the invention stage a critic-free zone.

The writer and teacher Peter Elbow advises writers to turn down the volume on critical voices in their minds. He argues writers need to do that in order to capture their ideas during the invention stage and the first-draft stage without worrying what people might say about the paragraph just written.

How to do that? The writer Anne Lamott (in her book *Bird by Bird*) suggests that you'll probably want to list the various critics whose voices are likely to pop into your head (people who might include, for instance, your English teacher from last year, or your aunt who is unbelievably strict about grammar, or your next door neighbor who never has liked you much). After you have a list of your would-be critics, Lamott advises, you should picture each one as a field mouse or an insect. In your mind, you can place each of these critics in his or her own jar (throw in an oxygen tank if you're feeling especially kind), then seal the jar so that you won't hear the critic's voice while you're working. This is an amusing notion, but it just might be the kind of mental trick that will allow you to get your words and ideas out.

We really hope you'll do yourself—and your writing—a big favor by temporarily muting the critic's voice. Write freely; brainstorm without a censor on your shoulder; write down things that may or may not end up working out. You can always play censor later if you need to. Writers rarely use every thought or example from the invention phase in the final draft.

Remember: Your only commitment during the invention phase is to get your ideas out. This means getting out as many ideas as you can, as fully as you can, no matter how rough those ideas seem. Get as many sparks lit as you can. Chase an idea and see where it leads you. That's all you're responsible for in the invention and first-draft phases. Thinking too much about audience at this phase will likely have the effect of making you timid, afraid of offending this group or that group, or afraid of the criticism you suspect some readers might heap on your favorite idea. This stage of the writing process is about you determining what it is you really want to say. Your ideas will evolve; you can change large or small details later. For now, just see what ideas you have, and worry about the audience another day.

What Works for You?

In your journal or notebook—or blog, if you keep one—write about which invention techniques you've tried and which seem to work best for you. If you have not done much invention before, write about which techniques you think would work the best for you and why.

Chapter 5: Your First Draft

At a Glance...

- The first draft is your first time trying to write the paper the way you want it to look.
- It is *just the first draft*.
- The most important step is to start writing.
- Use writing you have already done to help get you started with more confidence.
- Figure out what writing environments will work best for you.
- Focus on your main idea and give yourself permission to use various strategies to develop that main idea.

For Discussion or Writing: Artists work with lumps of clay and shape them into something greater. You will work with your ideas to do the same. Like the artist and the clay, you have some rough material already (your invention work). In what ways will shaping it be like what this artist is doing to the clay?

What Drafting Means and Why It's Important

Drafting is teacher-talk for *writing a version of the paper*. You may wonder why we don't just call it "writing a paper." Sometimes we will refer to drafting in those terms. Still, it's important that you understand that your first draft is *just the first draft*. In other words, there will be at least one more draft beyond this first draft—and it's likely that you will write several drafts of the paper. This idea of writing multiple versions of the same paper might take some getting used to. Many students are used to being given an assignment and finishing it as a single process: they think about it, start writing, keep writing, finish writing and then reread and fix the writing all in one day. This is not what we mean by "drafting the paper." What we are asking you to do is take all of the invention material you've created and all the pre-thinking you have engaged in and now *start* writing the paper.

The main point of this chapter is only three words long: "Just do it." When the time comes to write the first draft of a paper, just sitting down in front of a computer or a notepad is a simple yet essential step. Remember that the draft will not write itself. All the talking about writing a draft, all the freewriting, all the questioning, all the procrastinating in the world...it all helps you get ready for drafting in its own way (maybe not the procrastinating), but the drafting stage needs to occur.

How to Start Writing

Even the words "start writing" are deceptive because, really, these words imply that you will start writing at the beginning. And this is deceptive in two possible ways. First of all, the beginning. You do not have to start the draft at the introduction. An introduction will need to be there eventually, but it does not have to be the very first thing you sit down to write when you do finally sit down to write. Sometimes, you will have a great introduction idea, and writing it down will help the rest of the paper just flow forth in a natural way. Other times, your topic may be complex or controversial enough that the essay requires an especially tactful introduction. In that case, you may want to come back to your introduction after you've gained traction by developing some of the body paragraphs.

Anything that makes you doubt your ability to keep writing should be postponed until after you have done *some* writing already.

If you have done some invention, you *have* done some writing already. Look at it now as you are about to write. Either use it to give you a game plan or framework of sorts in order to help you know where you want to go with the writing, or actually use pieces of it and start writing new material around the writing you have already done.

How to Use Invention Material as a Framework

If you have clustered or outlined or engaged in some other visual means of pre-writing, then you should now have a mental picture of the possible structure for your paper. This is your plan. Some students gain great confidence from having a plan. It helps them to know that they have some idea of where they are going. If this is you, then pick the part of the plan that you have greatest confidence in and start writing that portion of the paper. Keep going for as long as you can. If you need to, refer back to the plan, but don't let the plan completely rule you either. Remember to use the plan and not let it use you. Perhaps you'll discover that what you are writing is better than the original plan; in that case, set the plan aside and follow the new direction your essay is taking. Be willing to keep an open-mind about both your plan and the essay you are writing.

Assuming you have done some freewriting or another type of invention activity where you already have text written, reread that writing now. Better yet, reread it with a pen or highlighter in your hand. Underline the parts that stand out as being particularly good. If you like color-coding, then use a highlighter to underline the parts that are all on one topic and then a different color highlighter or pen to underline all of the good writing you've done that is on another topic. An electronic way of doing the same thing is to copy and paste the writing from one document into a new document. (For further help with copying and pasting, refer to the "Twenty-First Century Writing Tips" section.)

Maybe you've shared some of your freewriting or brainstorming with your classmates. If they reacted positively to one of your ideas or to a particular example, be sure to mark that material as something that may be worth including in your first draft. Perhaps your classmates wanted to know more about a situation you mentioned only briefly during the invention stage. Again, mark that material for potential inclusion in your first draft.

Once you have all of your good pieces identified, start writing around them. If you are working electronically, start filling in additional sentences before and after sentences as needed. If you are working by hand, start rewriting the sentences you identified and add new ones as needed. If all goes well with this method, then you should have taken some writing from your invention and transplanted it into a new document from which point you may grow it into longer, more focused writing.

Suggestion Box: How to Use Invention Material to Assemble Your First Draft

Most of us have had the experience of putting together a jigsaw puzzle. What's the best way to start? With the parts you know you can put together, of course. Most people choose to do the sides first or the parts that are most interesting or easily identifiable. It shouldn't be much different with beginning your writing. Start with the parts you enjoy or at least know how to write. When you begin with those sections, it becomes easier to "fill in" the rest later on. In the same way that it is easier to identify where lots of little tree pieces will belong on the puzzle after something else has been completed, it is easier to see the "holes" in your paper once you have something committed to paper already.

Do not worry about whether or not your first draft is complete or if it is the best it can be. In the beginning drafts, you should concern yourself with committing writing to paper. And why not start with the items you really want to say? No one will yell at you for eating dessert before dinner here. If you are having trouble getting started, then it just makes good sense to start with whatever makes it easier to get started. For some writers, that will mean writing an introduction. For others, it will mean bypassing the intro and skipping straight to a body paragraph. Go where your instincts lead you for the time being. This will make it easier to write the paper *you want to write* instead of the paper *you think you're supposed to write*.

What a First Draft Is—And Isn't

It should be emphasized that this writing you are doing is *just the first draft*. You do not have to have a fully realized paper right now. Sometimes, writing will flow naturally from beginning to end as you write your first draft. Other times, you will feel like you keep meandering and jumping from point to point or feel like you are writing in stops and starts. Occasionally, you'll wish you could just give up on the whole thing because you don't think what you have right now is very good. These are all possible reactions to the writing of the first draft. And it is possible for the same student to have each of these reactions throughout one semester.

The important thing to realize is that whatever happens, you should give every effort to write this draft of the paper. Nothing can get accomplished with your writing if you do not sit down and actually commit words to paper. Without that step, your paper just exists in theory. It's all kept locked away in your head. Once it is down on paper or screen, then readers can begin reacting to it.

Let's return to those words: *just the first draft*. Read them matter-of-factly. Just the first draft. Now, read them with emphasis on the italicized word: just the *first* draft. Remember that whatever you write today is fine because it gets those ideas out on paper. This is your test run. If it works out, great! If it doesn't, no problem! Now, you may be thinking, "That's easy for you to say, but if it doesn't work, then that means I have more work to do." And this is true. But what is also true is that you would have work to do either way. Even if it "works," we want you to examine it to make sure that it is the best writing you can put forth on that particular subject. If it doesn't "work," then you'll be able to figure out from your test run what does work and what needs to be fixed or adjusted.

Now return to the words: just the first draft. What we do not want you thinking is that this is *just* the first draft. Do not make the mistake of thinking this is a completely throw away draft and you can slack on it because it is, after all, *just* the first draft. The first draft lays the foundation for the paper that will follow. People in construction never say, "Oh, I don't have to be very careful with this first part of the house. It's *only* the foundation that the house will rest upon." Students who do the minimal amount of work on first drafts just to save the "real" work for later in the drafting process often cheat themselves out of writing the strongest paper they could write.

How to Avoid Common Writing Traps

Frequently, writers trick themselves into not writing. This phenomenon is especially common when a writer needs to write the first draft of an essay. The writer never actually comes out and says, "Whatever I do today, I'm going to be sure to put off starting that first draft I have to write." Still, the writer manages to push the writing task away—which means, obviously, that it will need to be done a day or a week later.

Arm yourself against traps that writers often fall into. Here are some lies writers sometimes tell themselves about writing. We have also explained why each lie, or notion, below is a trap you should—and can—avoid.

I need the perfect schedule (or the perfect room, or the perfect computer, or perfect weather) in order to write. NOT TRUE!

Waiting for the perfect writing conditions to come along can be incredibly frustrating. Actually, that approach usually leads to the writing not getting done. While it's great when writers are able to set aside large blocks of time to write, having huge blocks of time shouldn't be a requirement for getting some writing done. Those perfect days are pretty rare. After all, the day when you don't have any other assignments to do may never come; the day you take off from work might be the day the power goes out, taking your computer with it. Can you make something of those twenty-minute pockets of time you find in your schedule? (Several twenty-minute writing opportunities can add up to a draft.) Can you get some ideas down on notebook paper if the computer isn't cooperative? We encourage you to try hard to do so. Getting ideas down on paper, even in a very rough form, is a much more productive activity than dreaming that a perfect writing day will someday arrive.

I'll just take a quick break before I start. One more break won't hurt. NOT TRUE!

Sometimes breaks are warranted, even necessary; however, if a small miracle occurs and you find a large span of time available in which to do your writing, do not sabotage it by taking multiple breaks. Instead, if you already know you are prone to procrastination, gather up any supplies you need before you begin (writing supplies, snacks, music, caffeine), so you won't be tempted to take too many breaks. (In later advice about writer's block, we may somewhat contradict this advice, but it holds true for the most part).

I do my best work under pressure; that's why I wait until the last minute. **NOT TRUE!**

Often writers tell themselves they'll pull off miracles at the last minute, or they convince themselves they function best under pressure. For some writers, pressure does help. Far more writers, however, write better when they are able to grow a paper over time, rather than hoping that something incredible will come together at the last moment. When writers run out of time, they tend to produce one-draft papers which usually read like last-minute efforts; in a sense, such writers cheat their ideas out of all the attention and energy they deserve. Waiting until the last minute is indeed a choice that some writers make, but often it's not a choice that brings about the results the writer hopes for.

My work will be so bad that I'll be embarrassed to show it to anyone. **NOT TRUE!**

Maybe you will be embarrassed; it's certainly possible. Most people who dare to write end up embarrassed occasionally by something they've written. However, we don't think you should consider a rough draft a tool that someone will use to judge you. Remember what writing a rough draft is all about — mostly it's an opportunity to sort out ideas (in words) and start to trace where some of those ideas are headed. In a sense, a rough draft of an essay is a map that you're making up as you go along. Some parts of the map will work; some parts probably won't work; some parts may confuse your readers and steer them in the wrong direction. Your rough draft (like a half-finished map) may look . . . well, pretty rough. As long as your readers understand that this is your rough draft (not your final version), you shouldn't have to feel too embarrassed by your draft. Besides, what's the alternative? Not writing a rough draft, and turning in—a few days or weeks later—a final draft that ends up looking like it's a rough draft? You might as well write the rough draft and figure out which roads work and which do not, and then produce a final draft that looks like a much clearer, more effective map of your ideas.

I don't know what to write. There's just no way for me to get started. **NOT TRUE!**

The real answer to this question is to dig once more into the invention activities from Chapter 2. You *can* find something to write about. You have ideas. Take the leap and begin writing something. Your instructor and peers will help you move forward once you've committed some writing to the page or screen.

It's great when writers can find huge chunks of time in which to write. But really, we don't know many people who can actually do this. You shouldn't give up on your writing simply because you don't have big blocks of time to devote to it all at once. Yes, good writing usually takes plenty of time—just not all at once.

Many people who need to write (for college assignments and in the workplace) write in short sprints—coming back to a task many times rather than expecting that one draft will do the trick. You might be surprised to learn, for instance, that an early draft of this textbook was written in sprints ranging from ten to thirty minutes at a time. Of course, we've had to invest lots of time in order to turn out something that we're proud of, yet it was the rare occasion when we were able to spend hours and hours on the book at any one time. We kept digging into our project as best as we could when we could, over and over, because that's one very good way to get words on the page.

>>> *Exercise 5.1: Pick a Trap to Avoid*

Just about every writer faces traps that get in the way of completing work. This exercise asks you to spend five to ten minutes brainstorming and freewriting about the traps that you most frequently fall into as a student. These should be the problems or situations that interfere with your doing your best work. Focus especially on situations that are at least partly within your control. (For instance, you likely do not have full control over your schedule at work or in class, but you do have a say about how some of the rest of your time is spent.) Narrow your list from three or four situations to just one.

For the time being, tackle just one situation. But tackle it hard. Take ten to twenty minutes to make a specific plan that spells out what you plan to change—in that one area—in order to give yourself a better chance of success as a student, especially when it comes to writing a first draft of an essay. Of course, you may discover that your plan will prove useful with other assignments. If that happens, all the better. Your ten to twenty minutes of figuring out how to side-step a trap will really have paid off.

Where and How to Draft

There are many different ways to write the first draft. Any approach is correct if it allows you to write a successful paper. That said, if you notice that some ways help you to write more material more often, then you should probably get in the habit of working that way to maximize your potential. Some things to consider:

- Handwriting vs. typing vs. doing some writing by hand before going to the computer
- Silence or music in the background; dim lighting or bright lighting
- Time of day
- Location: at home, quiet room, library, near a window

What Works for You?

In your journal, write about what writing conditions you prefer. Under what circumstances have you found it easier to write? What environment or materials make writing more difficult for you? Was there anything from this chapter that you might try to do to help you with your next writing assignment?

Suggestion Box: Free Noise (Potentially Helpful Noise!) from the Internet

The Internet is a source of much knowledge and plenty of entertainment. Have you ever considered, though, that the Internet has plenty of potential for helping you block out distracting conversations, blaring commercials, and the jack hammer that's been tearing up your street since seven o'clock this morning?

"White noise" is a term for fairly routine, peaceful noise that drowns out the more annoying noises that surround us. People who work in office cubicles, where sound travels all too easily, have been known to buy expensive "white noise" machines so they can get work done.

Here's a cheaper solution. If you have access to the Internet and either a good set of ear buds or really loud speakers, go to an online video site (YouTube is a good bet) and search for videos using phrases such as the following:

- white noise
- peaceful sounds
- sounds of nature
- weather videos (thunderstorms, rainstorms, windstorms)
- relaxing city sounds or traffic sounds
- ceiling fan or electrical fan noise
- washing machines or dryer sounds

No need to watch the video, of course. You can listen to it even when the video is minimized at the bottom of your computer screen. (Choosing a longer video means you'll end up with a longer stretch of uninterrupted work time.) Just be sure the sound you've chosen is one that will help you to work, rather than put you to sleep!

Essay Strategies to Consider (Common Development Strategies)

As you write the first draft of your essay, your most important job is to keep your eye on your main idea and bring it to life as best as you can. First drafts are all about main ideas. Any technique that helps you communicate or support your main idea to your readers is a useful technique. There are plenty of techniques that can help you do just that. We suspect you will stumble into some of those techniques on your own, perhaps as a result of your invention activities.

Still, we imagine you may feel stuck at some point during the writing of your first draft. Maybe you have described some situation that is designed to get readers thinking about your main idea, but you're wondering what else you can do in the essay. Perhaps you feel as though you are about to run out of steam and end up with only a few paragraphs instead of a complete essay. It's normal to want to hit the panic button at moments like that. But what's even more effective is to keep in mind that there are some common development strategies that many writers before you have used as they fleshed out main ideas that were important to them. We'll list several of those development strategies here.

- **Narration** Narration involves telling a story that has a point. It has to have a point—that is, an idea that it illustrates, or an understanding that the writer gained after living through the experience she's relating. Sometimes, the story is long and complex enough that it takes up most of the essay. Other times, however, the story is brief and is just part of the larger essay. A brief story within an essay is sometimes called an anecdote.

- **Argumentation** Argumentation involves building a case on behalf of—or in opposition to—some idea or proposal. When an argument is used as part of a college essay, the argument is usually not the ugly, mean-spirited type of argument one sometimes hears on talk shows that are trying to score high ratings. Instead, an argument in college writing is usually built on respect and logic. As is the case with any argument, the person doing the arguing has to supply readers (or listeners) with reasons that might lead them to change their minds. Frequently, argumentation is just one part of a larger essay. On occasion, an entire essay may devoted to one central argument.

- **Explanation** Sometimes readers do not need an argument to see the writer's point, but they do need some careful, thoughtful explanation of a key point or two. In order for an explanation to be helpful to readers, it must be presented in clear language and clearly related to one of the essay's main points. It shouldn't seem like useless trivia, in other words. Sometimes, a key concept will need to be explained if the audience is not likely to be familiar with it already.

- **Comparison and Contrast** Actually, this development strategy is really two strategies, but they are so closely related that they're often discussed in the same breath. A writer may compare two or more things (or people or events) in order to make a point; that is, the writer points out similarities that somehow related to the essay's main idea. Or the writer may choose to emphasize differences among two or more things (or people or events) because those differences have something important to do with the essay's main idea. Again, the essay's main idea is of central importance here. Sentences that compare or contrast something without making a connection to the essay's main idea will probably strike readers as lifeless filler and a major distraction.

- **Cause and Effect** This development strategy usually involves showing readers what caused an event or phenomenon to occur (for instance, how Event A led to Event B, which then led to Event C). Sometimes, this strategy is used to examine what the effects of an event might be—for instance, the effects that a city's hosting of the Olympics has on the city's residents.

We've described these development strategies very briefly here; our intent is to suggest different approaches you may want to try as you write the first draft of your essay. Unless your instructor gives you more specific instructions, you should feel free to try any of these strategies in your essay. If you try a development strategy and it doesn't work out, you can always cut it from your next draft.

Multiple Strategies

Often, these development strategies work best when they are used in combination with one another. That is, the writer does not limit herself to a single strategy but puts to work as many different strategies as seems helpful and purposeful. These strategies are similar to different vehicles you might jump into as you chase after that important idea. Picture yourself behind the wheel of a two-door sports car, but then you discover that an all-terrain vehicle, or even a plane, might get you across an especially rough patch of land. The whole time, your eye is on that very important main idea which is at the center of the essay. (If you've seen Matt Damon's portrayal of Jason Bourne in the Bourne movies—*The Bourne Identity*, *The Bourne Supremacy*—or read the Robert Ludlum novels on which the movies are based, you probably understand what we're talking about here. Jason Bourne will use any vehicle that is handy in order to get himself where he needs to go. Good writers know how to do that, too.)

Student Example: Development Strategies at Work in a Draft

Let's take a look at an essay in which the writer uses a handful of different development strategies to explore his main idea. *One quick note:* This is the third draft of the essay. The first draft of the essay, like most first drafts, was much rougher and less complete than the version you see here.

Stuck on Celebrities—For a Reason

A couple days ago, one of my friends mentioned on Facebook that her acquaintances paid much more attention to the death of a well-known British singer than the deaths of nearly one hundred people who were killed in a terrorist attack in Norway. (Both events occurred on the same day.) As soon as I saw her post, I realized my friend was right. In some circles, Amy Winehouse had received more attention by dying in her own home, at the age of twenty-seven, than all those people in Norway who were the victims of a terrible act of violence. In fact, I was one of the people who was spending more time focusing on Winehouse than on the people in Norway. That morning, for instance, I had posted on Facebook about Winehouse and written a brief post about her on my blog. I had not written anything, up to that point, about the victims of the terrorist attack.

Why do so many of us get all caught up in the lives—and the deaths—of celebrities? What is it that leads us to spend time talking about them, tweeting about them, reading gossipy pieces about them,

Strategy used in this passage: **NARRATION**

Strategy used in this passage: **CAUSAL ANALYSIS**

61

and then asking our friends, "Did you hear what Kanye West (or Tom Hanks or Bono) said last weekend?" None of us is born knowing what a celebrity is or what one looks like. We pick the idea up somewhere along the line, perhaps starting with the first time we begged our parents to take us to a movie starring a teen idol or saved up money to buy the latest music from our just-discovered Favorite New Artist. Which celebrities we pay attention to and which we lose track of most likely changes over the years; still, the habit is there. Without realizing it, we've brought celebrities into our lives as though what they say or do or don't do really has something to do with how our own lives unfold.

Strategy used in this passage: **NARRATION**

When I was fourteen, I managed to shake the hand of the then-current president of the United States. The experience meant something to me, though I'm sure it meant next to nothing to him. (He lost his re-election bid a week later. I'm pretty sure shaking my hand had nothing to do with his bad luck.) I bragged to my friends about this event the next day; just possibly, even those friends who didn't like the president were slightly impressed. But why should they have been impressed? I did not save anyone from a burning building; I hadn't rescued a small child from the path of a speeding car. I simply stuck my hand into a crowd of hands during a campaign event and—just by chance—it was my hand he shook. Yet at least a little of the president's celebrity status rubbed off on me, at least for a few days. Now that I'm an adult, I was glad when one of my friends recently got the chance to shake President Obama's hand. He's famous; he's admired by many; a handshake brings a little of his fame home to our neighborhood. Some things don't change.

It's easy to convince ourselves that we have something in common with those celebrities we read about or manage to see up close. We think we know something about their lives—their crushes and marriages, their break-ups and triumphs, their addictions and legal problems and even their money problems, although the money problems are usually in a different league than our own money problems. Anyone who goes on Twitter has a chance to catch up with the latest thoughts of Serena Williams, Paris Hilton, and Ashton Kutcher. A visit to YouTube might show Beyoncé stopping by the ABC program *The View* to discuss a new song or the latest news from her personal life. Thanks to modern technology and celebrities' tendency to live so much of their lives in public, we feel we know these people. Maybe we think we know more about them than we know about our relatives or next-door neighbors. At a certain point, many of us find ourselves identifying with a celebrity. We feel a connection with the celebrity. [Strategy used in this passage: **CAUSAL ANALYSIS**]

Of course, there are other occasions when we do just the opposite: We come down hard on a celebrity who seems to constantly make poor choices. Some of us enjoy criticizing celebrities who act out in obnoxious ways or who dare to make several bad movies in a row. If a celebrity is arrested for driving drunk, we might take it personally. ("She made twenty million dollars last year, and she couldn't afford to call a cab?") A celebrity who is revealed to have cheated on his significant other is definitely lower than low—or at least that's what the morning radio programs tell us as we're driving to work. If we find ourselves immersing ourselves so deeply into celebrity culture, why is it that we enjoy thinking we are better than the celebrity whom everyone is inclined to trash today? Perhaps it's because we need to convince ourselves that our lives still matter and still amount to something—even if we are not famous, even if we are neither rich nor powerful. After investing plenty of our time in paying attention to celebrities, we still find a way to tell them, "Go away. You're annoying me. You're not even as smart or responsible as me. I'm pretty special in my own way. You would be lucky to be as special or as good as me!"

Yet perhaps there's another reason many of us pay so much attention to what happens with celebrities. It could be that people paid so much attention to Amy Winehouse's death because they saw [Strategy used in the passage that begins here: **COMPARISON & CONTRAST**] something of themselves in her very imperfect life. Winehouse struggled with her addiction to drugs, and although she was very talented, she often did things that seemed to make her life worse rather than better. When we watch her story play out in the news, we see a bit of ourselves, but in a distant way, as though it's all on a screen and she's just an actor playing a part rather than a real person living out her life. It's a safe (if sad) thing for us to watch. Meanwhile, the people in Norway seem even closer to how we envision ourselves. We see them as normal, everyday, life-size people. They are people like us—or they remind us of our siblings or our sons and daughters—and something tragic has just happened to them. As much as I know I should pay attention to them and learn their story, perhaps I'm scared by the idea that what has happened to them could happen to me or to my loved ones.

Those people in Norway weren't celebrities. They didn't have recording contracts or booking agents working to get them on talk shows. They had text messages they were about to send, books they wanted to read and movies they wanted to watch, and dreams (small and large) they hoped to accomplish. It's much easier for me to focus on a celebrity than people who seem very average and very vulnerable. During my occasional visits to TMZ's website, I never feel traumatized. The news about the victims in Norway, in contrast, has the potential to make me feel anxious. In a sense, TMZ is the safer choice—even if I know it is not the better choice.

For Writing or Discussion:
1. What was the writer's main point in this essay?
2. If this were your essay, what would you add? What development strategies might come in handy if you were to revise this essay?
3. The writer implies that a friend's Facebook post got him started on this topic. What have you seen in traditional media (newspapers, magazines, television news) or in social media (Facebook, Twitter, blogs, and so on) in the last day or two that could serve as an idea, a starting point, for an essay of your own?

Development Strategies Are Tools

In the essay above, the author used at least three different strategies for developing his main idea. There's nothing magic, of course, about the essay making use of three strategies. The writer could have used two strategies, or four or five. If he had wanted to, for instance, he could have included some **description** to make his point—perhaps by including a paragraph describing Bill Gates' high-tech luxury home. The writer used the development strategies that fit with what he wanted to say in each moment of the essay.

The choice to include such a description, however, would depend on whether that information would help support the writer's point about the fascination many of us have with celebrities and their lifestyles. That's the important thing about using development strategies in any essay: the writer's choices should be in service to some point the writer is trying to make, or a question the writer is trying to explore. College writing is mostly about making and supporting a point.

To put it another way: No development strategy is more important than the idea you're trying to develop. A good idea is the heart of any good essay. Development strategies are simply tools—very useful tools—for bringing your best ideas to life.

Looking for a Challenge:
Wait! Don't Do It! Hold Off on Reaching Closure!

Closure is one of those words that pops up often these days. Daytime talk show hosts such as Dr. Phil encourage guests to "reach closure" or "attain closure" (that is, come to terms with, or even "close the books") on difficult experiences or relationships they've endured. In some contexts, perhaps, reaching closure might be a very good thing.

Frequently, however, we've noticed that developing writers often try to wrap up their thinking about a complicated topic far too early in the writing process. Instead of digging into a tough question in a deep way, they opt for plugging in a bumper-sticker style slogan that doesn't really do the topic justice. Or maybe the writer chooses to overlook aspects of an issue that make the subject a challenging one, even though readers will be aware that those problems are out there somewhere. Both of those approaches are tempting; as writers ourselves, we too sometimes want to take the easy way out. But if you dig in rather than closing the books too early—if you write your way *into* the challenging questions, rather than dodging them—you stand a much greater chance of earning your readers' respect. Essays that deal with tough questions are often the most compelling reads.

Chapter 6: Rethinking Revision

At a Glance...

- You need to know what *revision* really means if you are to do it effectively.
- Creating a revision agenda can make revision more manageable.
- Look for the "good bones" that might be in your first draft.

For Discussion or Writing:

If you were fixing up your kitchen and discovered a major plumbing problem, simply painting or retiling wouldn't solve the problem: you'd have to get in there and mend or even replace pipes. Or if the cabinets you found on Craigslist don't fit in the allotted space, you might have to order new ones or rethink the current arrangement of your appliances. Why are these appropriate metaphors for the writing and revision process?

This chapter deals with an essential, substantial part of the writing process that many writers somehow skip. We hope you will come to see **redrafting** (also known as **global revision**) as an important opportunity to accomplish what you want your writing to do—namely, to communicate something important to your audience.

>>> Exercise 6.1: Picture People Revising Their Writing

Most likely, you have come across the words *revise* and *revision* many times over the years. Jot down your impression of what those words mean. When you see them or hear them, what sorts of activities do you picture people doing? Create a list of 10 definitions and/or activities.

What Revision Means and Why It's Important

Revision is a term that people frequently misuse. Some writers say they're going to "revise" their paper, but what they really mean is that they are going to give it a final run-through for clarity, grammar, punctuation, and spelling. These kinds of changes are more accurately called *editing*, not revision. (See Ch. 11 for more on editing.) Fixing mistakes and switching a few words around can make an important difference in the overall quality of a paper, and we always encourage our students to devote a good chunk of time to editing a final draft before it "goes public"—that is, before it is submitted to be read by a wider audience or graded by an instructor.

However, as important as editing is, it's no substitute for genuine revision. **Revision** refers to large-scale changes that affect the overall purpose or structure of a piece, as well as changes that alter the way an idea is supported or developed. Revision also includes the changes a writer makes in order to adapt the piece for a particular audience. We would encourage you to think of the root word that's at the heart of the term *revision*: *vision*, meaning "sight." When you revise something, you're really taking the time to *re-see* or *re-envision* its possibilities.

To summarize, editing involves smaller, more localized changes. Revision involves larger, more global changes in the paper's content, purpose, or structure. Revision usually takes the form of purposefully adding, deleting, or moving chunks of text.

When an Instructor Asks You to Revise

Why revise? Does the request to "please revise" a paper mean that you've done the assignment wrong? Why do writing teachers ask you to redo your work?
Mostly the answer has to do with hope. Few pieces of writing are completely thought-out, or as well-developed or well-organized as they may eventually end up, at the rough draft stage. But writing teachers are always on the lookout for signs of hope, and often, real potential is evident even in a rough draft. A teacher who asks you to revise has recognized something worthwhile in your paper—something that deserves to be fleshed out, brought to life, clarified, toned down, or tuned up. Revision is an opportunity to help a promising idea reach its promise.

While we hope you'll appreciate the compliment your teacher pays you when he or she asks you to revise, we think there's a better reason to revise, one that goes beyond simply pleasing a teacher. Revision is a chance to find the heartbeat in your paper, the pulse that is vital to your essay's effectiveness and, really, to its existence.

When *You* Decide That Revision Is Needed

When you can't quite hear the paper's heartbeat—that is, when there is plenty of body in the essay, but nothing that makes it feel like it's alive—the paper probably needs some heavy-duty revising. Or perhaps there is a heartbeat, but the paper is incredibly out of shape: bloated beyond recognition, with obvious flab. Or maybe you've noticed the opposite problem—an essay that is too thin for its own good, a paper that needs some muscle added to the bones of its main ideas.

These are all occasions when you may decide you owe it to your work to perform some serious revision. People who become good writers eventually begin to develop a sense about when a project would benefit from revision. In other words, they don't need to wait for the teacher to nudge them to revise.

How to Work from a Discovery Draft

Revision happens early in the paper writing process, often after the writer has produced a discovery draft. A **discovery draft** is an early draft of an essay in which the writer (on purpose or by accident) searches for the topic she really wants to write about. For example, when LaKeisha was writing her first draft, she focused on describing the busiest month she's ever experienced: last July. She wrote an entire six-page rough draft about that month, devoting approximately a page and a half to each week. However, rereading her draft, she perceived that the events of some of those weeks wouldn't be of much interest to her readers. At the same time, she realized that the strange experience she had between 9 AM and 1 PM on July 17 was exciting and complicated enough to deserve its own paper; not only was it more interesting and life-changing than everything else that happened in July, but it was also more interesting than simply having a busy month. LaKeisha discovered her real topic—a better, narrower focus—during the course of writing her very first draft and then rereading it. In other words, she looked at her potential topic and re-envisioned its possibilities.

>>> Exercise 6.2: Giving Feedback on Your Classmate's Discovery Draft

Sometimes writers have an easy time "re-seeing" the potential in their own discovery drafts. Still, there's nothing wrong with providing this type of feedback for a classmate or friend. Take a few moments to carefully read your peer's draft. Point out to your peer one idea from this draft that you think deserves to be developed into an essay all of its own. Explain why you think that idea or experience deserves to be the main focus in a new draft. If the essay already feels focused on one topic, point out the most interesting part of the current draft.

Some questions you could ask yourself:
- What is the main idea that the writer has in this draft?
- What main idea do you think the writer meant to write about (if different from your first answer)?
- What part are you most curious about?
- Are there any parts that confused you or that strayed from the main idea in a bad way? Which parts? Why?
- If you were the writer of this paper, what would you do for the next draft?

How to Create a Revision Agenda

If you ever attend meetings at work or as part of an organization, you may have noticed that the ones that run the most smoothly and efficiently are those in which the person running the meeting has drawn up an agenda, or a schedule of things that need to be discussed or acted upon. Frequently, writers who believe their work needs to be revised will draw up a plan for the work that needs to be done; that list is called a **revision agenda**. Revision agendas are tools that can help you save time, as well as needless frustration.

You will need to reread your discovery draft to get started. In fact, you may very well want to read your draft out loud, or even ask a classmate to read your draft to you while you follow along on your own copy. As you read, put aside (for the time being) any problems you notice with grammar, punctuation, or spelling. Try hard to focus on the paper's content and how that content is organized in the current draft. After you've read the draft (or had it read to you), ask yourself some important questions about the draft and write down your answers to those questions.

Suggestion Box: What is the Process for Creating a Revision Agenda? How Do I Get Started?

1. **Start by asking yourself what works well in the paper.** What trait do you see in this essay that you really like? What section(s) of the essay seem like they definitely belong in the essay? Write yourself a note about those traits and/or those sections, so that as you revise you will be sure to keep "the good stuff" in the paper.
2. **Next, ask yourself what your purpose was in creating the essay.** (That is, what was the main message you were trying to communicate in the essay? Or what effect were you trying to bring about in your readers?) Write that purpose at the top of your draft.
3. **Reread your essay one more time.** Look for places where the essay may have strayed from the purpose statement you jotted at the top of the draft. Perhaps there are several places where the paper strays. If there are, pick out the two or three places where the essay takes the biggest "detours." Mark those sections of the paper, and indicate (probably by number) which of those sections seems to be the biggest problem.
4. **Jump to the "What are Some Purposeful Changes I Can Make?" section in Chapter 8 and consider what type of change seems most appropriate for that section of the essay.** Write a note next to that section, indicating the action you wish to take there.
5. **Look at the other "detours" you've marked in this draft. Which one is the next priority?** Repeat step 4 for that section. Repeat the process for other parts of the paper that seem to stray from the purpose note you wrote at the top of your draft.

Does Your Draft Have "Good Bones"?

If you've ever watched a series such as *Flip This House* or *House Hunters*, you may have heard a prospective buyer—often someone who is looking for a house to rehab for profit—say that a particular house has "good bones." In that context, "good bones" usually means that the most basic elements of the house are in good shape and the floor plan mostly seems to work. The house's "skeleton" is good enough that it will hold up pretty well, even if some of the stylistic details (moldings and flooring choices, for instance, as well as paint or wallpaper) will have to be changed in drastic ways.

This is not a bad question to ask when you're in the early stages of the revision process: *Does the current draft of your essay have "good bones," or not?* If it does, then the essay's topic is appropriate for the assignment; in addition, the essay's core idea is well-thought-out and seems substantial. Sure, some of the examples may need some "rehabbing" (or may in fact need to be replaced), and the style of the draft's sentences may need some attention (just as flowery wallpaper may need to be stripped from a house's well-constructed walls). A draft with good bones will hold up nicely as its details undergo renovation.

If, however, you decide upon rereading that your current draft does not deal with a topic that you really care about, or your chosen topic does not seem relevant to the actual assignment, you would not want to invest time in making changes around the edges of that essay. In such a case, the essay's core is not yet strong enough to make the smaller changes worthwhile. Instead, with plenty of hard work, you would focus on reworking the essay's core. After strengthening its bones, you could then justify changes in style as a good investment of your time and energy.

What should you do if you decide you like one of the draft's paragraphs, perhaps an example or two, but not its bones? Do what home rehabbers everywhere do. Figure out what can be salvaged—that is, what can be put to better use in some future project, where it won't seem at all like it's been wasted. Pull that material, save it to a scrap file of good ideas for future use, and walk away from this particular draft.

Looking for a Challenge: Putting Invention Strategies to Work Again

Flip back a few chapters to Chapter 4: Invention. Skim through the invention methods and decide which could work the best for you at this stage of the writing process. If you feel like you have strong ideas but poor organization, try clustering or outlining the work you've already done. Use the cluster or outline to reconsider your organization and possibly add more support to your paper. If you wrote an organized paper that is too short, consider a different form of invention like questioning, freewriting, drawing, or aural invention. Use one of those methods to generate new material to add as new paragraphs to your paper or to discover new details to add to the paragraphs you've already created. You may even discover new and improved ways of saying something you already have in the first draft.

What to Do If You Don't Like Your Draft

We hope you'll enjoy writing at least some of the discovery drafts you produce this semester. On occasion, however, you may reread your draft and have a very negative reaction to it. It may look so awful to you that you want to crumple up your hard copy and delete the draft off your flash drive. We know what that feeling is like. Still, we hope you won't get rid of the draft—at least not before you've given yourself a genuine chance to work with it to see whether at least some of the draft can be salvaged and improved.

1. Save It.

The first thing you should probably do with a crummy draft is to save it in more than one place. We realize this suggestion may sound illogical (after all, isn't one copy of a bad paper enough?). The back-up copy needs to be there just in case you get carried away at some point and decide, on impulse, to scrap the draft. Though purging a draft you're unhappy with can give you a satisfying feeling, having a back-up copy means that you will be able to change your mind later and perhaps follow the advice below. Then, if at all possible, print out a hard copy of the draft so that you can lay out all the pages in front of you at the same time.

2. Find Something You Like about the Draft.

Your next step should be to go through the draft and find one sentence that you like. Maybe the draft is a mess; perhaps it doesn't look much like an essay, or at least not a logical essay or a well-organized one. But we're betting that there's at least one sentence in there that will look good to you. It might be a sentence in which you manage to capture an important idea in a clean, crisp way. Or perhaps you have a great sentence of description, or a sentence that introduces a perfect example for the point you were trying to make. Underline that sentence with a straight line. (Maybe even double-underline it. Yes, that sentence is important enough to deserve such treatment.)

3. Return to Freewriting.

Now, copy that sentence into a new, blank document or onto a blank sheet of notebook paper. Use that sentence as the starting point for a fifteen minute freewrite. (Break the fifteen minutes into two halves if you like, but make sure you manage to get in a full fifteen minutes of writing. Yes, that sentence you chose is indeed that important.)

4. Find a Passage You Dislike, and Figure Out Why You're Unhappy with It.

Go through the draft again. This time, look for one passage (ranging from one to five sentences) that you dislike. Your job now is to write some detailed notes to yourself about what it is you don't like in this passage. (If you're working on a computer, you can use the insert comments feature to do this. If working from a hard copy, use any and all margins that are available—side, bottom, top—and draw arrows back to the passage as needed.) Why are you not happy with this passage from the essay? Do you think readers would find it confusing? Are you confused by it yourself? Did you lose track of the essay's main point while writing this section? Is your tone off? (Does it sound, for instance, very sarcastic even though that's not the tone you were aiming for?) Does the passage sound vague? Or maybe the passage says something that you don't actually believe, and you feel like you were "faking" this part of the essay. Whatever your reasons for disliking this material, explain your thinking about the passage in detail.

5. Repeat Steps 3 and 4.

Next, repeat the two steps above—that is, finding and freewriting about another good sentence, as well as picking out a problem passage and figuring out why it isn't working—at least one more time. (If you have time to repeat the process a couple times, that's even better.)

6. Prepare to Write a Fresh, New Draft.
Review your freewriting and your notes. Do you have some ideas about how you may be able to write a new, fresh draft of this essay? Your new draft would grow at least partly out

of the freewriting you've just done; that is, you would be building on the essay's strongest material.

Your notes on weaker passages, meanwhile, should give you some insight into what it is you do want to accomplish—as well as what you'd like to avoid—in your next draft.

A very rough draft—even one that makes you cringe—doesn't have to be thrown away. If you work at, you can use it as a learning tool to figure out what you want your next draft to look like.

What Works For You?

In the last chapter, you were asked to take a chance and write without worrying about where the writing would go. In this chapter, you've been asked to re-evaluate the choices you made in the first draft and make a new plan. Before you work on that plan, however, you should take a moment to reflect on what is working in the draft. What do you feel you are doing well? (This could be anything from coming up with topic ideas to organizing the essay to completing the assignment on time) Take a moment to jot down a list of what you have accomplished in the assignment so far.

Beyond the Essay: Writers at Work

THE REVEREND JEANNE M. HANSKNECHT, Episcopal priest in Ann Arbor, Michigan

People often think of a religious leader as someone who presents his or her message orally—presiding at a church's or synagogue's weekly religious services, for instance. According to Jeanne Hansknecht, however, writing that she does behind the scenes plays an essential role in her career.

Jeanne's ministry is focused largely on families and children. Her church in Ann Arbor, Michigan, is attentive to people on the fringe of society—especially the homeless. In addition to working in her church's free breakfast program, Jeanne does her best to stand up for the rights of the people in her community, and she sees writing as a tool that can help bring about positive changes: "I write letters to my representatives on all levels of government in order to advocate for the poor and disenfranchised."

What, specifically, do you write for your job—and how often does your work involve writing?

When I am not working directly with people, I am writing. I am writing homilies [sermons] for one to three services a week as well as for funerals and weddings as they come up. I write articles for the parish newsletters and annual reports. I write faith formation curriculum for all ages. I write liturgies. I write emails and posts on social media in order to be accessible to and remain in contact with my parishioners. I also write thank you notes and words of encouragement the old-fashioned way. If I actually clocked the hours I put into writing or the writing process, I would exhaust myself!

What anxieties or fears—if any—do you harbor as you write?

I used to stress about writing for a grade especially when the criteria were not clear. When I was in seminary as a woman in her forties with a family I decided that I didn't have the time to worry about pleasing a professor. I still tried to follow directions fully but mainly my goal was to write to learn. I wanted to get something out of every paper I put sweat equity into. That shift in thinking did wonders in reducing anxiety.

What advice do you have for people who need to write about controversial issues?

The key to breaking through social, religious, economic, and racial barriers and prejudices is to connect with another person's story and to risk the vulnerability in sharing your own. When you write, put forth your authentic self. Even when something you are writing isn't about you, claim your voice in the work. Write something that only you could say.

What role does revision play in your writing?

Nothing gets published or preached without revision. Revision for me can mean complete rewrites and taking the homily in a totally different direction. Sometimes this takes place during the homily!

For Writing or Discussion:

1. "Revision for me can mean complete rewrites." What do you think would compel Jeanne to start a homily over again? Think of the work she described in the first paragraph. A "totally different direction" would surely take more time and effort. What could make this time and effort worth it?

2. In her answer to the question about writing anxiety, Jeanne uses the term "sweat equity." What do you think she means by this? Have you ever thought about writing/homework in that way before?

3. Jeanne says that the way to break past social barriers is to "risk vulnerability." Are you more willing to listen to someone who has taken that risk? Do you plan to use this advice? Why or why not?

Chapter 7: Getting Feedback

At a Glance...

- Feedback involves hearing what other people think about your paper.
- Feedback helps you as the writer to consider the needs of your reader.
- Peer feedback (hearing from your classmates) is an extremely useful tool in a composition class.
- There are many ways to do peer review and many reasons to do it.
- Conferences with your instructor or campus tutors can also help you improve your paper.

For Discussion or Writing: Writing often feels like a solitary activity because writers typically do most of their writing when they are alone. For a moment, consider what would happen if writing were like rock-climbing or climbing a mountain. What happens when the rock-climber is alone versus when he has a fellow climber with him? How might having another climber nearby change the experience? How might you, as a writer, benefit from having access to another writer's take on things?

What Feedback Means and Why It's Important

When a writer revises without receiving feedback first, it is similar to when a writer drafts without doing invention work. It can be done, but the time and work spent on revision will have more direction if useful feedback is received first.

Feedback is when writers ask others to read their work and respond to it. The responses can be informal, like asking someone at home to read over your work. When feedback is required in a writing class, it is called **peer review**. Writers—all writers—need to know what's working in their writing, what's not working, and what could perhaps be reworked so that it will work better. We encourage you to do what all good writers do: get as much thoughtful feedback on your writing as you can.

Writing is, most of all, about communicating effectively. Writers need to communicate an idea or experience to their readers. The readers—the audience—are real people, whether they are teachers or not. The sooner you begin thinking of your audience as real people, the better your chances of connecting with them and impressing them.

Suggestion Box: Asking a Friend or Relative for Advice

It is convenient and natural to ask someone you know and like for advice, especially if a class peer review session was missed. Keep in mind that though these people want to help, you will need to show them the best way to help you. Because they do not know what's been going on in your class or what the writing assignment is, you will need to take some time to explain to them what your paper is supposed to be. We've seen some students' friends or relatives who mean well give bad advice because their idea of what the paper should be was different from what the student was learning in class. We've also seen cases where the person helped *too much* and ended up forcing his or her own style or personality on the paper or changing the writer's message too much. Taking the time to talk about what kind of help you need before getting the help can make a huge difference in the kind of help you receive.

What Peer Review Is and Why Writers Use It

We encourage you to get feedback from your peers at some point during the writing process. The timing of that feedback can be up to you or assigned by your instructor. It can happen early in the process as you are testing out ideas or later on when the ideas have a firmer foundation but you're not entirely sure the order or support are working out well. You could even get feedback multiple times as you work on the same paper.

The Purposes of Peer Review

In most writing classes, the instructor asks students to participate in peer review activities. During a good peer review session, you should be able to:
- see what readers think about your writing
- get feedback before your instructor grades the paper
- get a better sense of the strengths and weaknesses in your writing
- see what other writers did with the same assignment
- get a better idea of what you like and dislike as a reader
- empathize with your audience and their needs

The discussion below, however, focuses on working with one or more students in your writing class as you improve your writing.

The Advantages of Peer Review

> ***You and your classmates are in the unique position to do each other a favor.***

These students are in the same situation that you are in and know the assignment you have been working on. If you ask a friend or relative or even take the paper to a tutor, then you'll need to explain the assignment to them. Also, those tend to be one-sided conversations where the other person offers you advice and you have nothing to offer them.

> ***You are equals.***

You and the other peer reviewers are writing at roughly the same level. This allows you to give and take. Someone reviews your paper with both positive and negative comments, and you do the same for them. At the end of the peer review session, you get to decide what to take away from the advice that was given.

In our classes, it is not unusual to hear someone ask, "Why can't we just get feedback from you [the instructor]?" It is understandable that students want feedback from the teacher. After all, your professor has studied the subject and has years of experience to pull from when responding to papers. The thing about teacher feedback is that no matter how kind-hearted and well-done it may be, it is still given from a position of authority. Students feel more obligated to take that advice because the teacher has the experience and *is the grader*.

The peer situation is different. Because you are working with a group of equals, you have more control over the decisions you make about the feedback you've been given. The fact is that after peer review, you have decisions to make. You have to evaluate the advice that was given. Do you accept what you have been told about your paper? Why or why not? What will you do with this advice that has been given to you? Students are more comfortable asking these questions regarding their peers' advice than they are feedback given by an instructor. These questions help you to grow as a writer, as you contemplate the strategies you have used and will use in your paper.

> ***You will learn from others.***

Much can be learned about writing from reading the papers your peers have written. As you review their work, you'll discover more about what you like and dislike as a reader. These opinions are what make you a capable peer reviewer. As you read the papers, you have a gut reaction as to whether or not you like a sentence, paragraph, example, or so on. Questioning why you liked or disliked a part of a paper helps you to think about writing on another level.

You will also no doubt compare your writing to that of your peers. You'll notice their strengths and weaknesses just as they'll notice yours. As long as you and your peers are trying to help one another, this can be a very helpful way of learning about yourself as a writer. In most writing classes, there are a variety of different strengths and weaknesses. What you struggle with, someone else may do very well. Likewise, the part of writing that comes most easily to you is probably a struggle for someone else. It is in this way that you can help one another positively.

Good Peer Reviewing Does Not Happen Accidentally

Often, students need to practice how to peer review. It can feel a little uncomfortable at first. After all, you are sharing your coursework with someone else who is in the class. That goes against the rules of what you are often told to do in other courses. Not only that, but the very essence of peer reviewing is to ask someone else to critique your writing. This does put you in a vulnerable position, but keep in mind that the other people in your group are in the same position and probably feel the same way that you do about it.

The best peer review happens when the reviewers know what kind of feedback to give. Your instructor may ask you to talk about where you are with your paper right now and what you would like help with. Maybe this will be a written assignment. Another possibility is that everyone in the group will have the same questions to answer about each paper.   No matter what the focus of the peer review is supposed to be, the best thing you can do as a reviewer is to be specific. A bland statement that the paper is just okay, or something to that effect, is unhelpful, when the writer is seeking advice.

Suggestion Box: Making the Best of the Peer Review Situation

As a writer: Don't be too modest or too shy. Or, to put it another way, do not slam your own paper before your share it with others—but *do* be honest and specific about what you would like help with. Try not to act defensively. Listen to what your peers say with an open mind. Remember, you are all in the same situation of having your papers reviewed. If you don't like the advice, then you don't have to apply it to your paper. If you don't understand their advice, be sure to ask what they meant before leaving the peer review group.

As a reader: Do not over-advise. Your peers do not want you to rewrite their papers for them. They just want to know how it is going and to be told some things they can do to improve their papers. Do offer specific information about which areas need to be improved and give ideas of how to do so.

As a group: Peer review works best when everyone contributes. If members of your group are not participating in an assigned peer review activity—either by not bringing a draft for others to read or by not supplying comments when a group member shares a draft—it's in your best interest to help get your group back on track. If your group doesn't take its work seriously, your instructor may intervene.

How Different Approaches to Peer Review Work

We'll give you a snapshot of several different approaches to peer review. Your instructor may favor one approach, asking you to use that approach each time. On the other hand, your instructor may choose to use Approach One this week and Approach Three next week, or assign his or her own peer review activities.

Approach One: Traditional Small Group

This type of peer review is the most common. It is often considered to be the most personal type of peer review feedback.

- This group consists of approximately three students.
- Each writer needs as many copies of his or her draft as there are members in the group (3 members= 3 copies of the paper). The writer gives each member a copy and keeps one.
- The group chooses someone to go first.
- The writer is welcome to say what kind of advice he or she is seeking. The writer then reads the draft out loud as the other group members follow along on their copies of that draft.
- Once the writer finishes reading aloud, reviewers take a moment to make some quick notes on the draft. They might, for instance, focus on

- o any questions the writer posed before the draft was read aloud
  - o what impressed them most in the draft
  - o what (if anything) confused them or seemed to need further development
- The group discusses the draft. Someone acts as time-keeper so that the group will be able to repeat the peer-review process for each student's draft within the time frame given for the review.

Approach Two: Pass the Paper Around in a Circle Within a Small Group

This method is much the same as the traditional small group. The difference is that this approach conserves both time and paper.

- Each writer brings one copy of his or her paper. The writer may leave a note for reviewers at the top of the first page.
- The papers get passed to the person to the right so that each student has someone else's paper in front of him or her.
- The papers are read silently. Each reviewer answers the peer review questions on a separate sheet of paper.
- When all students are finished with their review of the first round, the papers get passed to the right again. This process repeats until all papers have been read and reviewed.
- The papers are returned to the original author.
- All writers review the comments left for them. Time should be allowed for discussion. Each writer can ask questions about the comments left on his or her paper.

Suggestion Box: Providing Feedback to Your Classmate(s)

This activity is designed to make your peer review both efficient and helpful. After reading your classmate's essay, write your responses to the questions at the end of the essay or on the reverse side of the draft.

1. Explain what you think the main message of the paper is. If unsure, indicate that you are not sure and then give your best guess.
2. What was the best part of the paper? (May be a whole paragraph or a sentence or two. Do NOT say "everything." That doesn't help the writer know what <u>not to</u> change)
3. What was the weakest part of the paper? What element should the writer spend the most time on before turning in the next draft?
4. What overall change would help the paper the most: reorganizing the order of information, adding material to each paragraph, changing the way the sentences sound, punctuation, adding a better introduction or conclusion?
5. Go through the paper again. Underline the parts that you think are *really good*.
6. Read through the paper again. Put a question-mark next to any parts of the paper that are unclear. THEN state why it is unclear (for instance, you did not understand a sentence) or explain what that section made you wonder about.

Approach Three: Whole Class Workshop

- One paper gets shared with the whole class for feedback.

- All students offer suggestions. The instructor may assist with comments as well. This is often most helpful with discovery drafts or other papers where the writer needs assistance with purpose, organization, or support.
- This workshop is often led by the instructor with the use of a projection system. This may also be done by posting an electronic copy of the paper to a course management or file sharing system if the class is using one.
- The writer may tell the class about his or her paper and the kind of feedback desired.

Approach Four: Popcorn

- Each student places a copy of his or her draft on the desk (or more if specified by the instructor).
- On the top of the first page, the student writes a note to the reviewers to explain what sort of feedback would be most welcome.
- The student then moves to another desk and begins reviewing the paper left there. Reviewers read the comment left by the writer and try to help specifically with that concern as well as respond to other things they notice (both good and bad) in the paper.
- When the student is finished reviewing a paper, he or she moves to an open desk. If no open desks are available, the reviewer should wait at for an opening.
- Reviewers should also respond to comments left by previous reviewers. Review continues in this manner until all papers have been reviewed multiple times or time is called by the instructor.

*An alternate method for this peer review: Students print more than one copy. Put all copies in a central location in the classroom. Students pick up papers, review them, and then return them to the pile to repeat until time has been called.

Looking for a Challenge: Interview a Classmate

For this challenge, you will need to find a partner from your class or a friend who is also writing a paper for a class.

1. Interview the writer about his or her paper. Ask questions about the message. Allow the writer to talk for a while uninterrupted. When the opportunity arises, ask a question that will help him or her to continue to talk about the paper's topic or its support. When the writer is finished speaking, write down the most important messages you heard during the interview. Give those notes to the writer.
2. Trade roles and allow your friend or classmate to interview you, following step one above.
3. Use the experience to assess your paper. Did your interview information match up with what is actually in your paper? Was the interviewer able to understand your message? Which parts interested your interviewer the most? Are those parts supported with details in your draft?
4. Use what you learned from interviewing your partner to think about what you could improve in your paper too. Which parts of the other writer's paper did you find most interesting and why? Could you use a similar strategy in your own paper?
5. Reread the notes you received. Did your interviewer write down anything that was said better while you were being interviewed than it is written in your current draft?

Approach Five: Tasks in Timed Rounds

- Each student places a copy of his or her draft on the desk.
- On a sheet of paper below the draft, the student writes a note to the reviewers about what he or she was trying to achieve in this draft of the paper.
- The student then moves to another desk and begins reviewing the paper left there.
- The instructor will announce a specific task for each round of peer review and will set a timer. Students should read the paper in front of them, perform the task, and then wait until time is called.
- For the next round, students should move to the next desk to the right and follow the same procedure as the previous round but with a new task announced. This process continues until all rounds are complete.
- Suggested tasks:
    - Focus on main message: Write down what you think the writer's main message is and why.
    - Introduction: Read only the introduction. What do you expect the paper to be about (based only on the intro and the title)? How could the writer improve the introduction?
    - Order: Outline what you think the main points of this paper are.
    - Encouragement: Read through the whole paper and put stars next to (or highlight) any words, sentences, or paragraphs that you really like. Write an encouraging comment at the end of the paper.
    - Proofreader: Circle any words or sentences that you think might need to be changed because of errors.

Suggestion Box: What Questions Should Guide My Peer Review?

Your instructor may furnish you with questions for your peer review. If not, here are some questions that may come in handy.

When reading a paper that contains lots of NARRATIVE:
- Describe what happened in the paper in just a sentence or two.
- Why do you think the writer wanted to tell this story?
- What was the most interesting part (a sentence or a paragraph)?
- What does the writer need to work on the most to improve this paper?
- Were there any parts that felt too long? If so, which topics or paragraphs?
- Were there any parts that were confusing or that you wanted to know more about? If so, which topics or paragraphs?

When reading a paper where the writer is ARGUING:
- What do you think the writer was trying to get you to believe or do?
- What was the most convincing part of the paper? The least convincing?
- What support could be added?
- How effective was the conclusion?
- Could the paper be stronger if organized differently? Explain.

What Peer Review Might Look Like

The draft below shows what peer review sometimes looks like on the page. As you'll see, two of Karlos Martin's classmates commented on his first draft. A portion of the first page is provided below:

This draft was placed on an online discussion board for feedback:

1   The beginning of this whole situation started back in Hawaii with my little family. The only problem was getting the ticket, because once I got my check, I didn't have enough money to get them a ticket, which was a major setback. So, I let her know that she would have to wait until I got a good job in the states.

> *Student 2 Feedback: What do you mean by your little family?*
>
> *Student 2: Where was your family and where did you want them to be? I'm confused here.*

2   Later the following day after work, I decided to come home relax and watch some television, but just when I thought things were going good my ex-girlfriend Stephanie called. She was explaining to me that she still loved me, which made me fill really mushy inside.

> *Student 2: It seems like we just jumped in time here. I don't know what is happening.*
>
> Student 1 Feedback: Oh, no way...you KNOW that's not going to end well. LOL!

3   I thought about my son every day, but the only problem was that I was just too deep in love. Then there was one Monday I came home from school and Stephanie called me crying telling me that she might be pregnant, but she didn't want to talk about it. Two days passed by and I still hadn't received a single phone call from Stephanie. *Not one.* I'm thinking to myself: "what is going on?" I'm at home minding my business

> *Student 2 Feedback: It sounds like your son is really important to you. I'd like to hear more about him.*

Karlos's classmates reacted as real people, readers who wanted to know more. Their suggestions and questions led Karlos to sharpen his focus in his next draft by adding more information.

>>> Exercise 7.1: Your Advice for Karlos

You've read the first half of Karlos's first draft as well as comments from two of his classmates. What other advice would you offer Karlos if you were in his group? Write a paragraph in which you discuss your reaction to his draft and/or suggest ways in which he might improve his essay.

Checklists for Peer Review and Redrafting

Try using one of the following checklists to guide your peer review process. The lower numbered checklists are for early in the writing process; the higher numbered checklists are for later in the process.

>>> Review Question Bank 1

These questions may be used during a conference with a teacher or a tutor or used with a peer after a discovery draft has been written.
- What is the main idea that the writer has in this draft?
- What main idea do you think the writer meant to write about (if different from your first answer)?
- What part of the paper were you most curious about?
- Are there any parts of the paper that confused you or that strayed from the main idea in a bad way? Which parts? Why?
- As a reader, what would you like to see in the next draft?

>>> Review Question Bank 2

- From memory, outline the main points of the paper. Do you feel that these main points all belong in the same paper?
- Who do you think needs to read this paper? (Who is the audience?)
- Were there any places where the paper jumped or felt off-topic?
- Did you believe the writer? Which parts were most believable or interesting?
- What was the weakest part of the paper? What suggestions do you have for that part?

>>> Review Question Bank 3

- Which ideas (or sections) in the draft are the best developed?
- Which sections seem to need further development?
- Do you see any idea (or experience) in this draft that you think deserves to be the focus of its own essay? If so, which idea? What would you like to see the writer do with that idea?
- What questions do you still have after reading this essay that you would like to see the writer discuss in the next draft?

>>> Review Question Bank 4

After rereading your classmate's paper, answer these questions by using a scale of 1 to 10, with 1 meaning *absent* and 10 meaning *great*. Be as honest as possible.

- How well did the first paragraph or two introduce the topic?

- How interested were you in reading the paper?
- How effective was the conclusion?
- Was the paper long enough? Did it have enough support?
- How well did the paper flow from one topic to the next?
- How did the paper sound to you?
- To what extent did the paper feel like it was written by a real person who cared?

>>> Review Question Bank 5

Rate the following items for effectiveness. Use a 1-4 scale with 1 meaning *needs to be a top revision priority*; 2 meaning *needs some attention*; 3 meaning *pretty good but could be changed a little*; and 4 meaning *excellent*.

- Paragraph length
- Paragraph focus
- Sentence variety
- Sentence correctness

Review Question Bank 6

Respond to at least two of the items below to complete your response to your classmate's paper.

- What do you think was the most important part of the paper?
- What was the strongest paragraph? The weakest?
- What grammar issue do you think the writer needs to work on the most?
- Tell the writer if the paper "jumped" at any point.
- Underline any sentences that were hard to read or understand quickly.

>>>Exercise 7.2: Workshop/Peer Review Report

Following a workshop or peer review activity, answer each of the following questions as fully as possible.

1. **Workshop preparation:** How did you prepare for the workshop? What kind of help did you want from the workshop? Describe how confident you were about your preparation.

2. **During the workshop:** What did you learn by listening to other people during the workshop? What did you learn about your own paper topic?

3. **Peer review feedback from others:** What has been the most helpful peer review feedback you have received? How has it helped you change your writing?

4. **Peer review feedback you've given:** What have you noticed about other people's writing as you've done peer review? Has it helped you to identify your strengths? How effective of a peer reviewer do you think you are? What could you do to be a better peer reviewer?

How Conferences and Tutoring Can Help Writers

Many people think of writing as a solitary activity—something that involves only the writer, his or her own ideas, and the computer or loose-leaf paper where the writer is capturing thoughts. In reality, though, audience awareness plays an important role in most successful writing. So does the feedback that writer receives from early readers.

You'll probably receive some brief, written feedback from your instructor from time to time. Most instructors may provide additional feedback in the form of a conversation about the draft you're currently working on. If your instructor invites or requires you to participate in such a conversation—often referred to as a **writing conference** or simply a **conference**—we would strongly urge you to take full advantage of this valuable opportunity. Even if your instructor does not explicitly invite you to sit down and discuss your writing, our experience tells us that most instructors are glad to help students who ask for a conference, assuming that the instructor has office hours or a few extra minutes between classes. *Note:* You may want to ask a few days in advance, especially if your instructor has a tight schedule.

Preparing for a Conference

What will you and your instructor likely talk about during this conference? That depends on a number of things, including the following:

- where you are in the writing process (e.g., is this a discovery draft? a second draft where you've worked on developing your thoughts further or clarifying your purpose? a near-final draft in which you are interested in discovering error patterns?);
- the amount of time available for conferencing; and
- what you and your instructor hope you will get out of the conference.

Participating in a Conference

Most instructors who conference with students want the student to be a full participant in the conference—alert, familiar with the draft (reread it just before the conference if possible), and interested in asking and answering questions about the draft. Participate with an engaged attitude—without, for instance, text-messaging a friend under the table while your instructor offers advice. Also avoid showing up to conferences with the expectation that a teacher will tell you exactly what to do in the next draft. As you can imagine, neither of those approaches would help you gain more control over your writing, nor would they allow you to start making more effective choices during the revision process.

While your instructor knows a great deal about good writing strategies, the point of a conference is to help you figure out which choices work well *for you* and *in this document you're creating*, and which choices you might wish to rethink. Conferences are opportunities for you to receive specific one-on-one feedback from the instructor, but you will need to be prepared with good, thoughtful questions in order to reap the full benefits of your time together.

Choosing Good Questions to Ask in a Conference

As instructors, we're always impressed when students ask questions that can only be answered by a live, human reader—in other words, questions that the student could not find an answer to by simply looking through a textbook or a website. (Examples of questions that can usually be answered by looking something up: "How do you spell *persistence*?" "What state has the smallest population?") Ask your instructor what she thought your main point was when first reading your draft. Or ask what emotions your fifth paragraph stirred up in him as he read it. Or ask whether she thinks the essay will seem relevant to someone who has not lived through the exact experience the essay discusses. No textbook can give you a thoughtful reaction to what you're doing in your draft, so you can make good use of your conference by asking questions like these. You may also want to consider your own particular weaknesses as a writer and ask your instructor how well your draft is working in those areas. If, for instance, you struggle with organization, why not take this opportunity to verbalize what you've tried to do in organizing the draft and then ask for assistance in that area?

The questions in the Suggestion Box below will help you get ready for a conference with your instructor.

Suggestion Box: How to Review Your Essay Before a Conference

1. How successful do you think the paper is? Does it say what you want to say yet? What is it you think you are trying to say to the reader? Is that message in the paper yet?

2. What kind of feedback have you received so far? Do you agree or disagree with it? Why?

3. What changes have you made to the paper? (You may want to highlight the changes on the paper itself, indicating where you added material, deleted material, moved items around, etc.) Why did you feel these changes were necessary? Do you think they have dramatically improved the paper?

4. What questions do you have for your instructor about your most recent draft of the paper? What specifically would you like the most help with?

As you think about these questions, concentrate on the changes you know you can make. Do those changes. Then ask what questions you have about where to go from there.

Conferencing on Portfolios

Although most conferences are focused on a single draft of a single essay, sometimes instructors will ask students to discuss a portfolio of their work from the first half of the semester or even the entire semester. A **portfolio** is often a collection of the writer's best and/or favorite work, as chosen by the writer; usually, the portfolio also includes some reflective writing about how or why those pieces were created. When discussing portfolios, your instructor probably will ask you to think in broader terms about the various choices you made when you chose your topics, wrote your early drafts, and revised some or all of those drafts. (How, for instance, does your collection of work show your growth as a writer from the beginning of the semester to the current point? Which papers are you most excited by, most proud of? Which papers still strike you as having undeveloped promise? How diverse are your essays; that is, how much variety do you see there? What role has audience played in the way you write and revise?) A portfolio conference may be intended to help you prepare to write a reflective essay about what you've learned up to this point.

On the other hand, some instructors ask students to reflect (in writing) on some of their writerly choices before coming to the conference. As always, check with your instructor to see if there's anything special you should do to prepare for your conference.

How to Use the Campus Learning Center or Writing Center

Most writers benefit greatly from getting multiple opinions on their writing-in-progress. For that reason, even if your instructor and peers provide you with great feedback, you might also want to make good use of the tutors in your college's learning center or writing center (if your college has such a facility). Take a draft of your essay to the center and plan to spend some time discussing the draft's strengths and weaknesses with a tutor. Don't expect that the tutor will "fix" the paper for you, but do ask questions that will give you a sense of what strategies the tutor thinks you might be ready to try in your next draft.

What Works For You?

Which type of feedback do you prefer (a type of peer review, a tutoring session, a conference with the instructor)? In what ways does that type of feedback feel comfortable or useful? What do you do after receiving this type of feedback and what difference does it make in your writing?

Chapter 8: Global Revision

At a Glance...

- Global revision means turning a rough draft into a more complete and connected draft.
- The changes during this phase usually involve adding and removing parts and rearranging portions of the paper.
- During this draft, the writer begins to think more about the reader.

For Discussion or Writing:
Imagine that you are about to invite someone out to dinner—someone you are just getting to know. What sorts of things would you want to consider before you picked a restaurant? How would the other person's food preferences (or other needs) affect your choice? Describe the connection between this scenario and that of revising an essay with your reader in mind.

What Global Revision Means and Why It's Important

Global revision involves making sure the paper works as a whole, on a large scale. Will the "big stuff" make sense to readers? During this phase of revision, writers make changes to help their message come through clearly. Sometimes the writer needs to sharpen or clarify the paper's main idea. In addition, the writer may want to improve the paper's support and organization.

What Are Some Purposeful Changes I Can Make?

Global revision can take many different forms, but most revision actions fall into one of the categories explored in the following box. At various points in your writing process, you may end up engaging in all of these activities, though you won't need to do all in every paper.

Suggestion Box: What Kinds of Large-scale Revisions Can I Make to an Essay?

- **Adding any of the following:** new ideas; new reasons; new questions or concerns; new details or examples; etc.
- **Removing or reducing content:** deleting stray ideas that you jotted down in the first draft so you wouldn't lose them, but now you've decided they don't really belong; deleting a bland introduction so that you replace it with something better; etc.
- **Moving material around:** relocating an idea or point or reason to a more prominent place in the paper (so it will receive more attention) or to a less prominent place (so it will receive less attention); moving a point closer to a point which is similar in some important way; moving a fairly general statement to a place where it seems to fit better (such as the introduction or conclusion); etc.

The revision activities listed here are all related to your paper's purpose. You will only want to add material (or remove it, or move text around) for good reasons—not just for the heck of it. The changes you choose to make should help readers get a clearer sense of the purpose you have in mind. Put another way, your revision choices should be *purposeful*—especially when your paper is due in a few days.

However, if you have plenty of time before your final draft is due, you could try a "let's see what happens" approach to revision. This means playing around with your revision options in an experimental, trial-and-error way. Sometimes inventors—and writers—discover wonderful things when they close the blinds, lock the door, and go a little wild with their projects. In fact, such times are often when writing is most fun, but we recommend this approach only if you have plenty of time in which to reconsider (and fix, if necessary) the results of your experiments.

What If I Ruin the Good Parts?

Change brings with it some degree of risk. Although writers revise their work with the hope of improving it, it's always possible that this change or that change might actually end up weakening the piece. For that reason, we strongly urge you to keep *all* of your previous versions of any paper you're revising. Save each draft. When storing your file electronically, be sure to give each draft a different name (e.g., Minimum Wage Draft 1, Minimum Wage Draft 2, etc.) so that your early drafts will not be eliminated when you save your new draft.

From Discovery Draft to the Audience Draft

The discovery draft that you wrote in Chapter 6 is for the writer. This is when you put any thought down on paper (or on screen) in order to see it all before you. During the discovery draft, you should attempt to banish all worry. This is the draft that no one else needs to see. This is the draft that will be fixed later, so it does not need to be perfect at all. It's your experiment. The writer Bruce Ballenger says that this is the draft the wind blows through. It isn't solid yet. Nothing in this draft is permanent.

Most student writers are comfortable enough with these discovery drafts. The struggle comes in going from the discovery draft to the next draft. How do you shape all of that "get it down" material (the discovery draft) into a stronger "fix it up" draft (the audience draft)?

Identify the Great Material

Read through the discovery draft. Highlight all of the words, sentences, or paragraphs that are incredibly good. This is the material that you love so much that you know it needs to go in the next draft. It just works. You're positive that this material will make it through to the final draft pretty much as is. Next, identify the good material. These are the words, sentences, and paragraphs that are going into the next draft but which need some work.

Move the Great and the Good to a New Document

This process is best done on the computer, but it can be done by hand as well. On a computer, open your original draft. Then go to "File" and "Save As." Rename the paper to show that this is a new draft. Your original material will always be available to return to just in case you don't like the new version. Working in this new draft, start moving the material around. Copy and paste the good stuff into a good pile (page one) and then leave all of the rest of the typing in a "not as good" pile (page two). From there, keep moving the material around until it is in an order that makes sense or flows. Remember, this is experimentation. Keep working with it until it starts to make sense. If working by hand, you might consider the original meaning of the term "cut and paste." Yep, that's right. People used to bring out the scissors and cut their papers apart and then take out the glue and paste the parts in the place they wanted them to end up. It may feel a little elementary, but it does work!

Consider Outlining

Many people use outlining before they begin writing. Another approach involves outlining what you have already written. Take the pile of good material and outline the topics. This will help you to identify possible supporting paragraphs for the paper. After the outline is complete, look at the elements. Do you see any similar topics or groups? Great! You can move those items closer together. This will help the paper to flow more smoothly. Use what you have learned from the outline in order to create a new outline and then work on redrafting from there. (For an example of an outline that was part of the writer's revision process, see Evelyn's essay on military deployments in the student draft collection at the back of this book.)

Redraft

It should be noted here that you may be so inspired by your discovery draft that you know precisely what you want to do next without highlighting, outlining or copying and pasting. If so, let that inspiration take you to the next stage right away. The goal is for you to be able to work on the next draft, the "audience draft." The main difference between the audience draft and the discovery draft is that the discovery draft is *written for yourself* and the audience draft is *written chiefly for your readers*. Think about what your audience will need to know in order for them to understand your message. What order will help the audience make sense of your material? How can you introduce the topic in a way that will get their interest and explain the main topic? How can you transition from topic to topic?

Yes, this is a lot to think about. That is precisely why this work is saved for the second draft. Now that you've written material in the discovery draft that you feel confident about, that good stuff can be used in creating the audience draft!

Keep in Mind That There is Still One More Stage

You may be tempted to fix all of the little mistakes in the paper right now. That's fine; just don't focus on those smaller items so much that you lose sight of the main points. Remember, you'll do at least one more check of the paper for those smaller concerns.

The Need for Connection: Fitting the Puzzle Pieces Together

One of the main tasks you will focus on as you redraft your paper is creating connections. The earlier invention work and discovery drafts that you worked on were to help you think through your own thoughts and ideas. As you move forward, your attention should shift to how your ideas are coming across to readers.

Connect to the Reader

As we've stated elsewhere, you should attempt to write to a specific audience. Many times a paper will remain "just okay" if the writing lacks **audience awareness**, or connection to the reader.

So what does it mean to "connect to" the reader? In part, you will need to see the reader as a real person with real interests. Imagine yourself in a conversation with this reader. What are the things he would want to know? What can you do, in writing about the situation, so that the reader will nod in agreement or think to himself, "Yeah, that's right"?

Connecting to the reader means the reader feels like you are talking to him, and then he sees you as a real person, too. We all know how this sort of connection makes us feel in real life: we feel important and respected and are more willing to listen to one another. This is a tremendous thing to accomplish in a paper. This is what makes good writing great.

Connect the Pieces of the Essay to One Another

Readers cannot connect with your ideas if they cannot follow the sequence of the ideas. Figure out which topics need to be discussed first, which topics would make more sense later in your essay, and so on. At this stage, you may want to print out a draft of your paper and then cut the different "chunks" of it apart, moving them around on your kitchen table or floor in order to better notice relationships among the ideas in your draft.

Imagine these pieces of the paper as pieces of a puzzle. They are complete little pictures on their own, but they only give a very small part of the whole picture. Which pieces should be connected to one another to help the reader see the whole picture in the clearest way possible?

Does that section about protestors at military funerals really belong at the very beginning of the essay? Maybe. But just possibly, it would work much better (make more sense to your readers) if it came near the end of your paper. Play around with order. Remember that you are the one who has control over the order in which your readers encounter this idea or that idea. Use that power wisely.

How Writers Show Readers Connections

Figure 8.1

See that picture (Figure 8.1)? What is it?

It's not much of a picture. It's just a random clump of dots. Some people may be able to make a picture out of that, though, right? Maybe you're the type of person who can look at these dots and say it resembles a bear or an ice cream cone or something else. Some people will work to create meaning out of a random clumping of dots. Most people, however, will not. And those "most people"—they are your audience.

Often, readers do not like to do extra work. They figure they are doing the difficult work of reading the paper and should not have to work any harder than that. Honestly, stop for a moment to think about how you feel when you read. Do you want to have to wrestle meaning out of a text? Or would you prefer that the writer does most of the hard work?

This brings us back to the picture of dots. Do you remember the connect-the-dots pictures you completed when you were a child? What was once a bunch of dots could become a bear in a tree or an elephant at the circus, or any number of things once you drew lines from numbered dot to numbered dot in sequential order. A similar activity can be done by writers for their readers. Writers provide all of the dots in the paper, but they also have to provide the big picture meaning *and* the connections in between.

These simpler pictures need less connection. Simpler topics need less connection as well. The more complicated the picture (or paper topic), the more connection a viewer or reader will need. Many students think that they will be "dumbing down" a topic if they take the time to spell it out for the reader.

Figure 8.2   **Figure 8.3**

Look at the dot pictures right before this passage. Figure 8.2 is obviously a circle. That picture does not require additional explanation. Figure 8.3 requires some explanation, though you could probably guess the general idea behind it.

That is what readers want. They need to be able to know the general idea but be interested enough that they want you to provide all of the links and details for them. In this way, "connecting the dots" is not dumbing down your message; it is providing the reader with what he or she needs in order to more fully understand and appreciate your message. The more complicated the message, the more connections are necessary for the reader.

What happens if the message isn't very complicated and doesn't need many connections? In that case, you as a writer need to provide a reason for the reader to be interested in it. In Figure 8.2, the viewer has no need to physically connect those dots. If that picture were a paper, then the reader wouldn't need to read it; the reader would already be able to predict everything that is in the paper.

You may choose to write about simple topics, but if you do, then you'll need to provide some complication or interest for the reader. Find an original on the topic so that it will not seem so simple, or routine, for your readers.

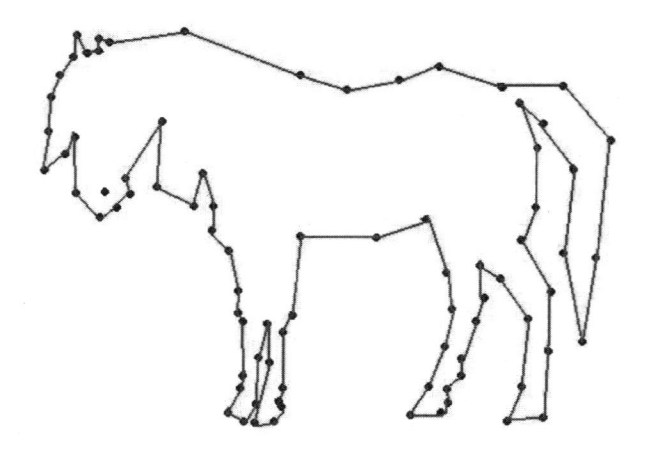

Figure 8.4

The picture here shows what happens with varying levels of connection. In the case of Figure 8.3, a viewer or reader is going to quickly give up on making meaning of just the dots (or if they are creative types, they'll make meaning, but it may not resemble the intended meaning).

The fully connected dots (Figure 8.4) show the picture clearly and in its entirety. The earlier pictures show what happens when writers fail to fully connect the portions of text to the main purpose. It is still possible for readers to figure out the main point of the paper, but it is that much more difficult for the reader. Again, *remember how you feel as a reader*. Do you like it when it becomes difficult to figure out what the writer is trying to say or the point he or she is trying to make? As much as possible, try to *connect the dots for your readers*.

How Can Thinking About Audience Help?

You will probably hear writing instructors talk about audience many times. Repetition usually means something is important; however, you may still be wondering, "Why is audience so important?"

Nicole recalls some of the papers she wrote as a freshman in college. These were papers that she thought were fairly good at the time. The papers made sense to her, but when they were returned to her, the professor had written in the margins that they "need a transition" or "Topic jumps!" Worst of all, there were times when there were just some random question marks. Years later, it occurred to her what those marks pointed out—that she was still writing a paper for or to herself, or to no one at all. She realized that without readers in mind, she was skipping over ideas because *she* understood them. When she took the time to wonder what someone else who hadn't thought about the same topic that way before might need to know, she had more success and received fewer question marks.

How to Fix a "Baskin-Robbins" Problem

Hopefully, you've had the experience of visiting an ice cream store that offers many delicious flavors. (Baskin Robbins, for instance, is even known as "31 Flavors" in some places.) The flavors such a store offers are not always the same and the customer must look at the offerings and choose one, two, or maybe even three flavors to put on an ice cream cone. This is a daunting task made a bit easier in shops that let customers sample flavors before ordering.

Nicole remembers visiting Baskin Robbins as a child and wondering what all 31 flavors tasted like. She sampled a couple here and there; her problem, however, was that she would soon forget what the first flavor or two tasted like. She could only remember the flavor she had just tasted. The little pink sample spoon just didn't have enough in it for her to savor in order to fully remember the taste and texture of the particular ice cream flavor. She was left with a vague recollection that she *kind of* liked the first one and was indifferent to the second one, and so on. It wasn't until she had a whole cone that she was able to fully enjoy a flavor.

This 31-flavors syndrome can happen in papers, too. Instead of allowing readers to linger over one idea, the writer might list topic idea after topic idea, leaving the reader with only a vague recollection: there may have been some good points in there someplace, but it's not clear what an audience should take away from the paper, or what the essay's purpose was. Or a 31-flavor paper might provide details about *all* of its ideas, not just its most important point or points.

Eating a bubblegum scoop after just finishing a pina colada scoop may have been fun and interesting when we were eight years old, but now we need something more sophisticated. As many customers decide after sampling a dozen flavors in a row, there can be real satisfaction in enjoying one flavor—or idea—more fully.

How to Add Details

Sometimes a reader—perhaps your teacher, maybe a classmate or tutor—will write "More" or "Expand on this!" in a paper's margin. Usually, this comment means the reader wants to know more about something specific. She has reacted to what you have written about and wants to hear you explain more of your opinion. Or perhaps he sees an opportunity for you to explain the significance of some fact or idea you've mentioned. (How *is* your cousin's vicious house cat connected to the situation you described earlier? Readers will be wondering about the cat's significance; you should explain the connection.)

At this time, perhaps all you as the writer know is that the reader wants more. That nagging and horribly vague feeling you're experiencing while debating what "more" means is probably similar to the one your reader had when she wrote the word "more." Just as you can't quite put your finger on what it is she wants to know more about and you are left with some questions about what precisely she meant by "more," well, that's how she felt when she wrote "add more" as a note on your paper. Your reader didn't know exactly what more she wanted; she just knew there was probably more to the story or more to your feelings or opinions there and suspected she wanted to hear it.

This is actually a good thing in disguise. Readers are often right about these kinds of things. They can sense when you are onto something good and this "more" response taps into reader interest, something that isn't always easy to obtain. Now that you know your reader is interested and wants to know more, reread the paragraph.

Suggestion Box: What Are Some Ways to Generate More Details?

Rewrite a sentence or two from the paragraph and try to freewrite from it. This works best if you have an idea of what the reader wanted to hear more about. The act of rewriting the sentence can sometimes spark ideas for you to continue in the freewrite.

Talk it out. Sometimes you don't think you have more to say about what's in the paragraph. Having someone nearby to ask you a couple of questions may convince you that you really *do* have more to say about it.

Question yourself. Ideally, we all have someone to "talk things out with," but that's not always the case. It may sound strange, but a lot of writing problems (and problems in general) can be solved by having a conversation with yourself. Write the main questions, "Who, what, where, when, why and how" down on a sheet of paper, leaving space between all of the words for a written response. Then reread that paragraph again. Which questions can you answer? You're not expected to be able to answer all of them, but hopefully one or two will prompt a longer response and give you something to put back into that paragraph.

Leaving Readers Wanting More

We've all heard the adage about how we should "leave them wanting more." There's a certain logic to this idea. After all, writers are wise to not wear out their welcome. A simple idea that isn't developed further will start to seem stale after a while, and every teacher has probably read a twelve page paper that would have been more effective as a four-pager.

But just like any advice, the "leave them wanting more" notion can be applied in the wrong place or the wrong way. Instead of keeping an idea very simple (and letting it get boring), how about showing what that idea—or habit, or situation—might lead to? Or, instead of simply telling a story about something that happened to you, why not make the story so much more meaningful (and interesting) to your readers by showing them how this event changed you, or frightened you, or made you question your beliefs?

An essay that stops abruptly usually leaves readers thinking, "I thought you were building up to something very significant and then you just...stopped." Give them a sense of fulfillment, a feeling that you've followed through on an idea, and they really will be impressed—so impressed, perhaps, that they'll look forward to your next essay.

Sometimes, students get too caught up thinking about page length. They may think they need to stop a two-page paper in its tracks once they hit the bottom of page two or three. Other times, they feel that they must bring the paper to a close, even if the essay doesn't feel finished. If you find yourself in a similar situation, check with your instructor; many teachers would be fine with students going a little beyond the assigned page minimum if it helps them create better essays.

Taking Details Out of the Paper

Perhaps the central purpose of your paper—your main point, your thesis—has changed dramatically during the global revision phase. If so, it's possible that some of the details and examples in your current draft now seem out of place. Watch for such details as you reread the essay and circle them (or put them in bright green font or something) when you find them. Then reread your paper as if those details have been removed. Which version of the paper makes better sense? Go back and delete the details, examples, and explanations that no longer seem to match the paper's new sense of purpose.

It's also possible that all of your supporting examples belong in the paper, in the sense that they do not contradict the essay's main ideas, but perhaps you've ended up with too many examples that are all very similar. If you find redundant examples (that is, examples that seem to do the exact same work as other examples), cut those examples so that your readers will not get that "been there, read that" feeling as they move through your essay.

Deciding Which Details Help—and Which Don't

Earlier we referred to the importance of showing, not just telling. Details are a significant part of a paper's support. There are times, however, when details can get in the way of a reader's understanding of your paper and its purpose.

The beauty of a well-placed detail is that it can answer a question that the reader didn't even know she had. Good details will enhance the writing with specifics that help the reader really "get" the full meaning you as the writer intend for them to get. Weak details are distracting and confusing and sometimes overwhelming.

Weak Details

> There used to be an activity book for kids called *MadLibs*. It was about **half the size** of a coloring book and was full of **unfinished** stories. The stories were finished from beginning to end but had **gaps** in them where the kids would be told to fill in a word.
>
> - **"Half the size..."** > Half in which way? Do the readers really need to know the size?

> - **"unfinished"** > This implies that the stories were missing endings.
>
> - **"gaps"** > What kind of a gap? Readers will likely think of holes.

Better Details:

> On long car trips, I used to play MadLibs with my sister. This was a booklet that had a word game in it. My sister would hold the book and would tell me to come up with a few adjectives, nouns and verbs, and then she would fill those words into the MadLib story where an adjective, noun or verb was missing. The resulting story was always fairly silly. We discovered that the stories were silliest when I came up with really specific words to use as fill-ins.

Avoiding TMI (Too Much Information)

Another type of unwanted detail is when the writer gives too much of a mental picture for the reader about something the reader would prefer *not* to picture. We'll spare you the details from the following "too much information" scenarios:

--incredibly specific details of the pus in a staph infection;
--something incredibly gross that your baby cousin did when unattended;
--a particularly rowdy, unofficial after-prom party and all that occurred (yes, everything) among the various couples in attendance.

These types of details should be avoided because they take the readers to places they really do not want to go. The readers could decide to discontinue their reading of your paper or could be distracted by other things and no longer take your message seriously.

From Writer-Based to Reader-Based Drafts

The first drafts of most essays are **writer-based**—that is, they are full of ideas and experiences that matter to the writer and more-or-less make sense to the writer, but not necessarily to other readers. There's nothing wrong with producing a writer-based draft; in fact, it's kind of hard to avoid doing that sometimes. Yet as you reread and revise your work, it's very important that you start to think more and more about readers who are *not* you. In other words, you'll need to turn your writer-based pieces into essays that make good sense to, and which interest, readers. Once you've done that, you'll have **reader-based** writing. With luck, you will still be able to enjoy the essay. After all, we're not talking about selling your soul—just giving consideration to your readers' needs and expectations, too.

Thinking in Snapshots

Consider this sample problem: A student keeps writing really concise sentences and paragraphs about incredibly abstract things. What she really needs to do is to go beyond giving just a sound bite or snapshot and instead elaborate by giving the background story, much like someone would do while showing a snapshot in an album to a friend.

In a first draft, a sketchy or embryonic section of text may be good enough. After all, you're trying to capture your idea in words and then capture the next, related idea before it vanishes from your mind. Many writers have that experience all the time. But second drafts are great for developing sketchy ideas more fully—providing the background information, or perhaps the examples or supporting details, that will help readers make sense of the idea and understand how it is connected to the other points you're making in the essay. Just as scrapbookers and Facebook users alike may need to caption a photo so that others understand its significance, writers should go back to the "snapshot" ideas from their first drafts and help readers to see the idea more clearly.

>>> Exercise 8.1: Making Your Essay Longer—and More Vivid

If your current draft feels underdeveloped, here's a quick strategy for making your next draft not just longer but more vivid—in other words, more lively, more convincing. (This strategy will probably work best on a printed-out copy of your draft, though it likely could be adapted for on-screen use as well.)

- Locate on each page of your essay one idea or experience that seems vague or unfocused—that is, a passage where readers who have not had that idea or experience themselves will not have a strong sense of what you mean. Circle that vague idea.
- In the margins, jot yourself a series of notes about the additional details that will help readers to get a better sense of what happened or what your point is. Work especially hard at capturing details that are based in the five senses. (For instance, what sounds did you hear when you walked into the manager's office? What scents hit your nose? What colors or pieces of furniture dominated your vision when you walked through the door?) The more details you note in the margins, the better.
- Commit yourself to adding at least three to five new sentences to your essay to develop each of your previously vague ideas. Use the notes from your margins as the raw material for crafting those new sentences. (You may decide to use several of those notes in your next draft, or you could, alternately, concentrate on developing one of those details—for instance, the dirty aquarium you noticed in the corner of the manager's office—over the course of several sentences. Sometimes one detail says a great deal about the situation you're discussing; that detail deserves to be explored in depth.)
- Later, when you examine the "flow" or organization of your next draft, be sure the new material you've added fits in well with the material around it.

Suggestion Box: First, Revision...Lastly, Editing

Many writers overlook revision and jump straight to editing their paper. As writers and writing teachers, we want to sell you on how very important—essential, actually—the revision process is if you hope to give your readers something worthwhile. Beyond selling you on that idea, we'd like to offer you some specific questions to consider when you sit down to revise an essay. These questions are designed to help you figure out what large-scale (global) changes you may need to make as you revise your work. In this guide, revision comes first, and editing (which is also important) comes last.

What's your PURPOSE in this paper?

- Think beyond just "writing a good essay." What do you want your **main idea (thesis)** to be in this essay? (Put another way, what's the main point you're trying to communicate in this essay? "My job" is a topic, but it's not a message. Same for the topic of "college students and stress." What big point do you want to make?)
- If you have several points you wish to make in this essay, **what's the big idea that ties them all together**?

What adjustments will you make for the sake of your AUDIENCE?

- How will you **get your readers interested** in reading this essay? How will you **make it relevant** to them? (Put another way, how can you **show them that this essay should be of interest to people other than you**?)
- What's **your tone** in this essay? What **adjustments (if any) might you want to make** in order to give it a tone that will work better with your target audience?
- What **background information** do you know that your audience also needs to be told? What **confusion** is your audience likely to run into when reading your current draft, and how can you reduce that confusion?

What will you ADD to your paper?

- What do you want to **emphasize more** in your next draft? That section probably deserves additional sentences or even paragraphs.
- What points (if any) could you a **do a better job of supporting**? Add details and examples to those sections. Show **how those details/examples are connected to the main point** you're making.

What will you TAKE OUT of your paper?

- What **ideas or details in this draft are "left over"** from some previous idea that turned out not to be your main idea? Delete those details.
- What do you **need to de-emphasize** in your next draft? (What topic or event receives too much attention in the current draft?)

What will you REORGANIZE or REARRANGE in your paper?

- If you moved section X to where section Z currently is, **would that make your ideas clearer to your readers**?
- What parts of the essay are most in need of **stronger transitions so that readers see the connections** between your ideas?

Lastly, after you've engaged in the redrafting (revision) activities described above, you'll want to turn your attention to the EDITING concerns that are addressed in Chapters 11 and 12.

When Audience Starts to Matter

Once you have explored your ideas and written a first draft, that draft might be extremely well developed; maybe you'll have found plenty to say without running out of steam. More often, though, our own rough drafts are underdeveloped, or undercooked: on their way to becoming a good meal, but not yet ready for the plate. When your first draft is underdeveloped, that's a good time to start using the concept of audience—that is, important readers other than you—in a positive way.

Strategy: What They Might Say

We recommend a strategy called What They Might Say. Read through your first draft and find some idea or situation that is important but not developed as fully as you think it should be. Copy that statement—a sentence or two, that is—at the very end of your draft. (Be sure to leave some blank space between your conclusion and this material.) Expand on this important yet undercooked idea by responding in writing to one of more of the following prompts below. Write several sentences for each prompt you choose; use the words in the prompt as the beginning of your first sentence.
- Yes, what I've just written makes a good point, but what if...
- The situation I've written about above would be different if...
- That may be the way it is for some people, but other people...
- I guess I might feel differently about this issue if....
- One problem with my suggestion above is....

These prompts are designed to help you transition from putting audience on "mute" (during most of the invention phase, and possibly during the writing of your first draft as well) to beginning to think about what an audience wants or needs to read. The following checklists can help too.

Strategy: Questions
You can also ask yourself these questions about your audience:
- Who needs to hear this message? (male/female? old/young/in between? etc.)
- Does your audience agree or disagree with you?
- What will that audience already know about my topic?
- What won't they know about my topic?
- What might keep them from agreeing with me or seeing things my way?
- How might I get them to see it from my perspective more clearly?

Voice and Tone—How the Writing Sounds

Your readers usually hope to get your "take" on things when they read your essay. This is true even if you write about a topic in the third person (*Buying a used car is a challenge for most consumers*) rather than the first person (*I always have a tough time finding the right car*). Most of the time, readers are looking for your perspective on the topic. (Exceptions would include when you need to write a lab report for a class in the sciences or a set of instructions. Every so often, you'll encounter a writing project where your viewpoint is expected to fade entirely into the background.)

In Chapter 2 we discussed the rhetorical triangle. Take a moment to review the diagram of a triangle in which the writer, the audience, and the topic all play a role. When your audience reads *your* take on a topic, the audience may end up hearing the voice of the unique human being who wrote the essay. In other words, the writer's **voice** is the quality in the essay that suggests the writing was not spat out by a computer or a robot. You could think of voice as the slice of your personality that ends up in the paper. If your writing has a real voice, your teacher might be able to guess (at least by the end of the semester!) that you wrote a particular essay even if you did not put your name on the paper.

An individual piece of writing frequently has a **tone** as well. You could think of tone as how that piece of writing sounds, or the attitude the reader thinks the writer has toward the topic. (Don't worry, by the way, if voice and tone sound very similar. The concepts are closely related.) As you think about the large-scale (global) changes you could make in your essay, one thing to consider is how you wish to sound in the paper. How much of your personality—and what parts of your personality—do you want to share with your readers? What attitude do you want readers to hear when they read the essay? As a writer, you have an important role in the rhetorical situation. The voice and tone that readers find in the essay are partly the result of *you* choosing to write that paper.

>>>   Exercise 8.2   What is the Essay's Tone?

Read your draft from start to finish. If possible, read it out loud. How would you describe the essay's tone? (What attitude will readers think you have toward the topic you're writing about?) Write a paragraph in which you discuss what tone the current draft has as well as what tone you hope the next draft will have. (Chapter 11 includes more help with tone. Turn to that chapter if you decide you need to adjust the paper's tone.)

Looking for a Challenge: How Humor and Satire Work

Visit the online edition of *The Onion* [http://theonion.com], an online "news" website that specializes in **satire**, a style of writing that pokes fun at the culture around it while pretending to be a straight representation of that culture. (Satire is also a staple of television shows such as *Saturday Night Live*, *The Daily Show*, and *Key & Peele*.)

At *The Onion*, you'll find a variety of not-quite-right takes on current events and trends that are part of our culture. Enjoy as many of the articles as you wish as entertainment, but also find at least one article that you wouldn't mind analyzing.

Ask yourself a few key questions about how the author managed to create humor in the piece. For instance, is the topic itself funny? Is the topic so inconsequential you wouldn't normally see a full-length article about it? Has the author chosen to emphasize a trivial aspect of an important event? Does the article—or the (perhaps fictitious) person quoted in it—say something that no one would have the guts to say in real life? Which examples or specific word choices contribute to the humor? How do photographs or other visual elements (graphs, color choices, etc.) add to the effect?

Additional follow-up activity: Find a topic that is currently in the news—preferably one that you haven't seen tackled recently in a satirical show or website—and write two paragraphs about the situation: one as straight-ahead, serious reporting and the other from a satirical standpoint, where your main goal is to elicit laughs. Share one or both pieces with readers who know you well and who aren't likely to be easily offended.

Consider whether one or the other of the opening paragraphs could be turned into a good beginning for an essay. Also consider how a change in purpose—for instance, from writing something serious to a piece that is funny—requires other changes in the piece.

Beyond the Essay: Writers at Work

BRIAN DEMAY,
On-air personality and program director at a Delaware radio station

Brian Demay has worked in radio for three decades. He says he has always loved the collaborative teamwork involved in making a radio station successful. He looks out for the people with whom he works and wants to see them be successful in their careers. Strong writing skills, in fact, help ensure that both he and his staff will get their paychecks. Technology means that writing plays an even more vital role in the radio industry than it used to. "Nearly all on-air personalities blog," Demay notes. "What you see—and hear—on our website requires good writing. We obviously don't want to look or sound stupid online." Radio stations are often known for their contests and interaction with listeners. Again, writing plays a role. Brian notes that contests don't come together on their own.

What kind of writing is involved with organizing contests?
We write promotional announcements, along with brief "spots" that describe the contests my station is conducting—how to play and how to win. I also write all online descriptions of my radio station, from who the on-air personalities are to what we might be giving away that week. And in a typical week I answer twenty listener emails, and am required by the FCC [Federal Communications Commission] to file each correspondence in our Public File. [Written records such as these are essential if the station hopes to be allowed to renew its broadcasting license.]

Why do commercials require good writing?
A commercial radio station pays its employees through its advertising revenue, so effective commercials are an imperative. There's nothing to gain from allowing a poorly written commercial on the air. Successful radio stations thrive on repeat business. If commercials don't bring results, our clients [the businesses that advertise on the station] go elsewhere. Proper writing techniques ensure repeat business, so I need to make sure the writing is as good as it can be before a spot airs.

How essential is writing to your own income? What percentage of your time is spent writing?
During a typical week, I spend seventy percent of my working hours writing. Writing has always been a big part of my career, but over the last several years it has become even more important. As a program director, I am responsible for every on-air announcement that is broadcast on WJBR, so it's important that the writing be compelling, concise, and effective—or I will be out of a job!

How much time do you typically have to prepare a piece of writing when you're at work?
Radio is known for its immediacy. I often write a series of promos that air the same day, usually within an hour or two of submitting copy.

What advice can you offer students who are trying to become better writers?
Write crappy first drafts. It helps me to just start writing, and then start revising. Once you have words on the page, it gets easier. Also, be sure to read a lot. You can't find your own voice without experiencing others' voices. What do you like about this author? What don't you like? Read, and become inspired. Take notes, but most importantly: just write. The more you do it, the better you'll become.
As someone who sifts through job applications and resumes in his role of program director, Brian is frank about what strong writing skills can do for a job candidate. "There is no more important or undervalued skill than writing. Being a good writer will set you apart from others, and in this competitive job market you need every advantage."

For Writing or Discussion:
1. Brian mentions that some of the writing he does (for instance, his emails to listeners) become part of an official record that the station must maintain. Think about other professions in which employees are expected to keep careful track of what they write on the job and possibly share it with outsiders. Can you think of any situations in which such records could contribute to the organization's success or failure?
2. The last time you heard about a contest, probably you didn't stop to think about the writing and planning that went into it. What other fun activities can you think of that might involve someone doing plenty of writing behind the scenes in order to make the event happen?
3. How has technology affected writing's role in your current job or future career?

What Works for You

When do you first start to think seriously about your audience? What questions do you ask yourself about your readers? What types of changes do you typically make once you get a better idea of who your readers are and what they're expecting in your essay?

Chapter 9: Redrafting for Deeper Development

At a Glance...

- Writers use a variety of development strategies to bring their main ideas to life.
- Readers often appreciate complex thinking in an essay.
- There are several ways to develop support in your paper.
- More than one development strategy may be used in a single essay.
- Consider adding good complication to your paper.

For Discussion or Writing:
Think about a movie or television show you really enjoyed. Take a moment to review the plot. Did anything happen in the show that complicated things in a good way—that is, made the storyline more interesting? What was the complication? What would the movie have been like without that complication?

What Development Means and Why It's Important

Development is the writer's attempt to flesh out—bring to life—his or her thesis (main idea). Ideally, the further the reader goes into the body of the essay, the more convincing and more interesting the essay will get. Since this does not always happen in the first (or even second) draft stage, it's worth the effort to work on development during the revision process.

This chapter offers you a number of ways to improve the body of your essay, the part of the paper where you develop your ideas and support them. Instructors frequently ask students to work on development, and this is an important part of the revision process. The strategies in this chapter are things any writer can learn to do, and each of these strategies becomes easier to use the more you experiment with it. They will help give you plenty of opportunities to be creative in your essay.

>>> Exercise 9.1: Getting to Know Your Audience

Before continuing to work on the development of your paper, stop to ask yourself a few questions about your audience. This can help you determine what needs further explanation and development and what can be left out. It can also help you decide if any special approach is necessary.
1. Who *wants* to hear your message already? Who *needs* to hear it?
2. What is your audience likely to already know about the topic? Can you leave that information out of the paper?
3. What does the target audience (the people who *need* to hear the message) usually think about the topic? How can you get them to see it from your perspective?

What Strategies for Development Look Like

The best way to write the first draft of an essay is to grab an idea that matters to you and get down some words that will help you make it matter to your readers. In other words, the best technique for developing a first draft is whatever will work for you. Since you've ended up in this chapter, however, odds are good that you already have a first draft and you're looking for ways to improve its development or reinforce the support you've offered for your idea.

Each of the strategies below is presented as a development technique in its own right. However, writers rarely use just only one of these techniques in isolation. Most writers will use at least a couple of strategies, maybe several, in an essay. That's why we've followed up these strategies with a section called "Using Multiple Strategies in the Same Paper."

Explaining to Make Your Point

Sometimes a paper requires plenty of explanation–that is, careful unfolding of an idea so that readers can make better sense of it. The more unusual your idea is, the more explanation it will probably require. If you're trying to help readers see a connection between things that they are not likely to connect on their own, you'll have to explain it to them. If you hope readers will understand why you believe Event A led to Event B, or you want to convince them not to do Y because it might result in Z, you owe it to them (and to your idea) to explain your thinking as fully and clearly as possible. Explaining is a common and often essential activity in many essays.

The trick in explaining things is to give your readers enough information but not more than they really need. By "enough information," we mean the kinds of facts and details that will prevent readers from feeling lost and which will also help them to understand your point clearly. When we caution against giving readers "more than they really need," we want you to avoid something that most writers struggle with occasionally—that is, providing readers with so much information that they feel overwhelmed. Explaining ideas and experiences effectively really boils down to thinking carefully about your audience.

The better you know your audience, the easier it is to explain things in a convincing and clear way. If you don't know your audience well, you'll probably want to spend some time making a list of things that your readers probably do and do not know about the subject you're writing about.

> - Do your readers realize that most families celebrate birthdays in some way? *Sure.*
> - Will your readers know that a Quinceañera is a very special celebration of a young woman's fifteenth birthday, and that the gift of earrings at a Quinceañera often has religious significance? *The answer would depend on how familiar your readers are with traditions that are part of many Latino cultures.*

If in doubt as to what your readers will need to be told, we would encourage you to include the questionable material. Be ready, however, to take it out of the paper if many of your **target readers** (people who are similar to the rest of your audience) tell you that they already knew those things. It is possible to explain too much, just as it's also possible to explain too little.

Telling a Story to Make Your Point

Most people like to hear a good story. Stories have the power to make us laugh, scratch our heads, or exclaim "No way—you've got to be kidding!" On rare occasions, a story can make most of the people who hear it tear up a little.

What Makes a Story Matter?

Any story that you include in an essay, however, has to contain something beyond mere entertainment value. It must make a point. That point could, of course, be funny, or it might be deadly serious. But the only reason for including a story in your paper is because it will help your readers to see your point more clearly. It has to do some work. When you include a story in your essay, readers should be able to say, without hesitation, "Yes, I see why she told us that story. I get the point she's driving at."

Perhaps you have a true story that will help you make your point. Such stories can be immensely useful. (Just be sure to change some of the identifying details—names, workplaces, etc.—if you think someone might resent your including them.) Other times, you won't have a personal experience that is relevant to the point you're trying to make. Still, you can easily imagine a situation that *could* happen to *someone*, a situation that would be a perfect illustration for your point. That type of example is called a **hypothetical situation**; it's a made-up yet fairly believable situation. Hypothetical examples can be used very legitimately in essays, as long as (and this is important!) you are up front with readers and do not try to fool them into thinking the situation really did happen just the way you've described. There are several ways to transition into a hypothetical example. We'll list just a few here, but you can probably think of your own:

> *Imagine that someone moved into town and tried to annoy his neighbors...*
>
> *What would happen if a person moved into town and he immediately set out to annoy his neighbors, first by opening his windows and blasting his iTunes collection every midnight, and then moving on to...*
>
> *Suppose you discover that your new neighbor has posted on his Facebook page that he is hoping to drive everybody on his block crazy before the end of the week...*

You get the idea. Let readers know that your example is hypothetical. They'll probably respect you for the originality of the situation you've described, and maybe they'll become more convinced of the point you're trying to make.

How Long and Detailed Should a Story Be?

If you decide to include **narrative** (that is, a story) in your essay, how long should it be? A brief story—often called an **anecdote**—tends to be more effective in an essay than a long, rambling story. Stick to the point. Put only enough people in the story for it to make sense; don't bother to include the people who would be considered extras if the story were a movie. Leave out details that take up a lot of space but which do not contribute to the point you hope to make in the essay.

What if a detail is brief but makes the story more interesting or believable? Keep that detail in the paper. Let's say, for instance, that you want to tell a brief anecdote about all the things your kid brother made you buy him the last time you took him to the movies. Why not mention that he made you buy him Milk Duds and an extra-large order of goat-cheese nachos and a large bag of Skittles, even though he threw away all the green and yellow ones? Those details end up making the kid seem extremely picky (not to mention high on sugar), and maybe that's part of the point you're making.

Readers will be able to see details when you are specific. Well-chosen details can bring a story to life, especially when they don't take up much space.

When Should a Story Use Emotional Appeals?

Finally, before including a brief story in your essay, think very carefully about your reasons for doing so. Is it mostly designed to elicit pity from your readers? Many readers resist being manipulated by stories, and some even resent a writer's attempt to milk tears from them. If you have a sad, relevant story that deserves to be told and that is directly related to your main point, then, yes—share it. It could be a very important story, one that you should tell. Just don't fall into the trap of expecting your readers to all agree with your point simply because you've shown them something sad.

Suggestion Box: Using Dialogue in Your Narrative

Often, writers want to include **dialogue**—that is, conversation between two or more people—to help bring a narrative passage in an essay to life. Dialogue can be a helpful tool, as long as it's used carefully. Here are a few guidelines for making dialogue work in your essay.

- **Limit the amount of dialogue.** Avoid sharing pages and pages of back-and-forth conversation with your readers. A little bit of dialogue can go a long way. Excessive dialogue becomes tedious.
- **Choose the part of the conversation that really needs to be shared.** In any situation, much of what people say is disposable or not particularly quote-worthy. Small talk, routine greetings, and the types of things you would expect people to say typically do not need to be included. ("Good morning," for instance, does not have to end up in your essay, nor does "It's really nice to meet you.")
- **Share the bits of conversation that are likely to surprise readers or which reveal something important about the people about whom you are writing**.
- **Use quotation marks around the sentences that people speak.** "Did you have to work late," she asked, "or did you *want* to?"
- **Each time a different person speaks, begin a new paragraph.** This is how dialogue is typically formatted, even if it results in short paragraphs in that section of the essay.

Here's a brief example of how a writer might use dialogue within the narrative section of an essay that discusses applying for a job.

> My dad wasn't sure whether the store had any openings or not. "You're going

> to have to call them up," he said. "Or better yet, go there in person. That's part of being an adult."
>
> I glanced down at my jeans, which had holes in the knees. "I suppose I can't go in there like this," I said.
>
> "No, not if you want them to think about hiring you. Your brother did some laundry yesterday, didn't he? There should be some good slacks in there. It's worth the trouble, especially if you want the job."
>
> I leaned forward and stared out the window. I started to think it all through. Did I want to work at a store? Would I be any good at selling things to people? I mulled this over for a couple minutes. Finally I stood up and went downstairs, found some clothes, and started getting my mind in the right mood for asking for a job that I not only wanted but needed.

Comparing to Make Your Point

When you compare two things—that is, discuss what those things have in common—people will usually pause for a second and think about the similarities you've mentioned. Maybe they'll agree with you. Perhaps they won't. But at the very least, you'll cause them to stop and think.

Often you can shed some light on an unfamiliar idea or experience in your essay by comparing it to something with which your readers already have plenty of experience. The strategy of comparing is one more way to reach out to your readers where they are. Put what they already know and understand to good work on behalf of the idea you're trying to communicate.

In order for a comparison to work, you should keep a couple things in mind. First, your readers must already be familiar with whatever the new idea is being compared to. Let's say, for instance, that you want to compare the arteries and veins in the human body to an interstate highway system, or congestive heart failure to a traffic jam.

These comparisons will work only if readers already have some experience with interstate highways. Audience comes into play here. An Amish reader likely won't have a good frame of reference when it comes to interstates. People who drive semi-trucks, as well as many other drivers and passengers, know how an interstate works, and they'll likely understand what you mean when you suggest that arteries, just like interstates, can become clogged.

In addition, the two things that you're comparing should probably share more similarities than differences. If your readers consider your comparison and immediately think of differences rather than similarities, they'll be too preoccupied to keep an open mind about the point you're trying to make. To emphasize differences rather than similarities, draw a contrast: this can sometimes be a useful strategy, as long as it helps you to make some larger point. It's all about making or supporting your point. Readers may welcome a comparison that helps them to understand your idea. Most readers will not bother to pay attention if the writer ends up just showing similarities (or differences) for their own sake, without any connection to some larger point.

Arguing to Make Your Point

A strong argument can be a really effective way to develop your essay and convince your readers of your point. Of course, we're not thinking of the type of argument where people raise their voices, perhaps swear, and maybe storm out of the room in a huff. In this case, **argument** refers to an attempt to set out your ideas in a logical, persuasive manner. A good argument will allow readers to see the good sense in what you've proposed or what you are claiming.

Your first goal when presenting your ideas is to get readers to open their minds to your idea. Your second goal is to convince as many of your readers as possible. Both of these goals require that you treat your audience with respect—a habit that is important, actually, in any type of writing, but particularly in an argument, since your readers may feel that your claims challenge their own views.

These principles make more sense once we look at a sample argument you might make. Let's say your college currently charges thirty dollars a semester for the privilege of parking on campus. You would like to see that fee eliminated. Who has the power to do something about that policy, the power to get rid of the parking fee? Put another way: whom do you hope to reach with your argument? College administrators, probably. More specifically, you might need to get the attention of the college president, the board of trustees, and the director of public safety. You'll need to figure out a way to get those readers to take you seriously.

Ask yourself what types of arguments (what reasons, what claims) might make sense to that audience. Sure, you could use your entire essay to complain about how you'd like to spend that thirty dollars elsewhere. Yet you suspect that approach would not prove very successful with your target audience. Discussing the situation only from your own point of view is just too writer-based; that is, too focused on the writer's needs rather than the reader's. Instead, examine how your target audience thinks about the parking-fee situation.

Consider adapting the following exercise to prepare for just about any argument you're going to write.

>>> Exercise 9.2: Preparing for an Argument, Figuring Out Your Audience's Concerns

This exercise is designed to help you put into words some of the concerns and values that you will want to bring up in your paper as you construct a good argument. After you've completed the exercise, print out your answers (if you've been working on a computer). Set your answers out on a table or on the floor and sort through which ideas will play an important role in your argument. Then experiment with which of the ideas below might offer the best way of beginning your argument. Remember, as you do this, that one of your main goals in constructing an argument is to show respect for your readers and to earn their respect as well.

1. In one or two sentences, explain why you think some type of change is needed.
2. Using sentences, list what (if anything) your target audience likes about how the situation stands today.
3. Using sentences, list what your audience might be concerned would happen if a change were to occur. These are the readers' **objections**.
4. Do you think any of the concerns listed under #3 are reasonable? If so, which ones? Be sure to come up with a response to those objections. (In

> other words, try to answer those objections in a respectful way. Take the objection seriously; try to offer a solution or at least a partial solution that might take care of that objection.)
> 5. Do any of the objections from #3 seem less realistic, less likely to occur? Think of a logical way to explain why you think those things aren't likely to happen. Remember to be respectful of your audience.
> Do you notice any similarities in how you and the target audience are thinking about this situation? If so, explain what you and your audience have in common (for instance, what values or goals you both share). Be sure to emphasize this **common ground** when you build the argument in your essay.
>
> Keep in mind that answering these questions does not, in and of itself, give you a complete argument. You still need to turn your argument into one or more paragraphs. Most likely, that process will involve some revision; most people think through their argument and then rethink it some more as they write. But a little planning (such as you've done here) doesn't hurt.

Using Multiple Strategies in the Same Paper

Occasionally, instructors ask their students to write an essay that uses only one strategy for its development (for instance, a narrative essay or a comparison-contrast essay). More often, however, writers choose how they will develop an essay based on whichever approach they think will help them get their point across to readers. Practically speaking, that frequently means using multiple development strategies within a single essay. Such a "mix-and-match" approach is often very effective.

Plan, and Experiment with Strategies

Try to do two things as you decide how best to improve the development of your essay. First, reread your earlier draft and decide which idea is your main point, your thesis—that is, the one idea that you cannot afford to leave out of the essay. Second, spend ten to fifteen minutes experimenting with each of the development strategies discussed in this chapter. *Note:* That's a commitment of about an hour total. Yes, that is a significant chunk of your time. Keep in mind, though, that how you develop your ideas is one of the most important keys to an essay's success or failure. For most writers, this is time well spent.

In order to keep your mind fresh, you may want to spread this redrafting/redevelopment time out over a couple days. Spend this time figuring out which stories (if any) could help you support your point. Ask yourself how much convincing will be necessary, given your topic and the point you wish to make about it; consider also what types of arguments you might use. Think about what readers will need explained to them and how you can explain those things most clearly. Consider whether a good comparison could help you explain or support your ideas. Most of all, be sure to do at least some of this redrafting/redevelopment work in writing. Don't just play with your new ideas or examples in your head; get them on to the screen or the page. Writing out your ideas can help them take shape and grow stronger.

Organize the Essay

As you build up or rebuild the body of your essay, you may discover that some strategies will give you a few extra sentences. (For instance, you might need only a couple sentences to compare your messy yard to the bills that spring up like weeds in Congress.) Other times, you may need several paragraphs to use one of the development strategies to its full potential. That's fine. There's no rule that each section of your essay needs to be of equal length.

Of course, whenever you add new material to an essay, you'll want to rethink the essay's organization. What type of structure or arrangement will be best suited to your main point? In addition, what's the best order for discussing your ideas, presenting your examples or comparison, etc.? The only way we know for figuring this out is to try things one way, then another way. Move things around. Read the paper out loud and ask yourself which arrangement makes more sense. Seek the advice of people you trust, people who will be honest with you.

Suggestion Box: Using Transitions

As you work to organize your essay paragraphs, turn to Chapter 10, which provides coverage of and help with transitions. Transitions are useful no matter how you've developed your essay, but they're especially important when you use multiple strategies in a single essay.

When Complications Improve an Essay: Going Deeper

"Things got complicated." We've all said that at some point, and odds are we weren't happy about the situation. Most of us think of a complication as something that has gone wrong, an obstacle that got in the way of whatever we were trying to accomplish. In this section, however, we'd like you to think of **complications** as good things, at least when it comes to your writing.

Many people try to write very simple essays. They believe that in order to get a point across to their readers, they need to keep things simple. As a result, sometimes writers try to make things *too* simple. They leave out important details or ideas because they "just don't want to get into it" – *it* meaning, in this case, the sticky part of the situation they're writing about. Yet writers need to think about things from the reader's perspective. Isn't the sticky part of the situation (the "complicated" part) often the most interesting piece to read about?

We don't mean this just in a gossipy sort of way, either. Sure, when your eyes scan the headlines in supermarket tabloids, the complications in Brad Pitt and Angelina Jolie's relationship are pretty sticky and are also, therefore, interesting. But the same is probably true for the workplace picnic that turned into one big argument last summer. Think about it. What's more interesting – the list of who brought potato salad and who brought napkins and plates, or the way that the really good intentions behind the picnic turned into something downright ugly, all in the span of forty-five minutes?

When it comes to essays, a complication does not have to be something unpleasant. Really, the verb *complicate* is appropriate any time you want to take your readers deeper into an experience (take them beneath the surface, in other words) instead of just asking them to stay on the surface of the experience. Therefore, you could "complicate" your essay (in a good way) by adding in some discussion of how a flood in your basement, though stressful, led you to get to know your neighbors better and forced you to realize that you needed to de-clutter your living space. If you write that essay, you'll be getting into something that's more interesting to your readers than simply how many bags of trash you put out at the curb or how many bottles of bleach you went through while scrubbing the basement floor.

How to Complicate an Essay

The following section is designed to offer you some choices. Don't feel like you need to try to do all these things in each essay. Play around with one or two of these strategies and see whether they help you to make your essay better developed and more interesting.

> **Suggestion Box: What do Good Complications Look Like in an Essay?**
>
> - **At First...But Then...** Examine how you viewed the situation when you first encountered it, versus your later perspective. The contrast between these two stances will show a journey or progression that readers often find engaging.
> - **Tension** Identify and describe conflicting perspectives or information. Readers find tension interesting; having something at stake or up for debate will hook your audience.
> - **Paradox** Explore a situation in which two seemingly opposite things are both true at the same time; again, this is interesting to readers and will demand more careful exploration from you, the writer.
> - **Metaphor** Using figurative language or extended metaphors to move beyond literal descriptions can help give readers points of reference in understanding complex ideas; conversely, metaphors can also help complicate ideas that readers may have previously regarded as too simple.

At First...But Then...

This strategy is named after a sentence that seems to pop up (in slightly different forms) in many good, thoughtful essays. The idea is to examine how you viewed the situation you're writing about when you first encountered that situation, versus how you later ended up viewing the experience.

Here's an example of what we mean. Let's say you initially hated your job as a dishwasher in a busy, chaotic restaurant. After five or six weeks there, however, you began to thrive on the chaos. You and your fellow employees bonded well (and maybe decided to get together after work) because the craziness of the kitchen put you all in the same boat; each of you discovered you had something in common, and you ended up laughing at the same things as your coworkers. In your essay, you might begin to capture that "complication" with sentences such as these: *At first, I felt like I couldn't get out of that job quickly enough; that's how much the noise and fast pace got to me. A couple weeks later, though, I began to realize that I was enjoying this workplace because of its craziness and the way that craziness brought my coworkers and me together.*

You have a chance here to take your readers deeper, to show them what lies beneath your first impression of the place. In other words, you can complicate the piece in a good way.

Tension

Most people don't like it when a relationship turns tense. It's much more pleasant (isn't it?) when everybody gets along and people only do nice things. For better or worse, though, daily life has plenty of tension in it—times when conflicts pop up and people have to make choices, some of them very difficult.

The good news is that tension can really benefit your essay. If you have a choice between showing readers some tension and not showing tension, we think you should show the tension. Tension makes readers sit up and pay attention. Tension makes readers want to keep turning the pages to see how things turn out. Think about it this way: The fun part of watching (or participating in) a tug of war is that nobody knows exactly how things will turn out. No one knows for sure which side will prove stronger. There's tension in any tug of war. (You can picture the rope, which is as tight—as tense—as possible.) If readers see some type of tug of war going on in the experience you're writing about, they're more likely to want to see how things turn out.

When you are engaged in invention activities (e.g., freewriting, clustering, talking with a friend, etc.), keep watching for those parts of the experience that make you tense, either in the present or the past. Try not to skip over those parts. Instead, if at all possible, include them in the paper. Dig into the tough parts of the experience, the complex part of the idea that not everybody agrees about.

We recently read an essay in which the writer, a college student, was discussing her job at a pizza restaurant. She mentioned how her manager wanted her to be personable; he wanted her to use her best "people skills" to establish a warm relationship with customers. Yet the author reported that she quickly figured out that she had to keep things moving so that her customers would finish their meal in a timely manner and new customers could be seated at that table. There's real tension in that situation. (Tug of war: On one side, "Be friendly with the customers;" on the other side, "Make space for the next customers.") Any writer would be wise to exploit that tension to show readers that there's more to a server's job than they might imagine at first. Doing so makes for a more interesting, more compelling essay.

Paradox

The word **paradox** refers to a situation in which two seemingly opposite things are both true at the same time. An experience in which somebody is emotionally torn is one type of paradox, perhaps the most common type. Think, for instance, about a friend who wants with all her heart to break out of her home town and experience new things, yet she is at the same time sad about leaving behind people whom she loves and places with which she is comfortable. It's perfectly natural, of course, to experience both those feelings at the same time. We're all complicated, and so are our emotions and our ideas. Writing about a paradoxical situation will usually provide you with rich material. You'll be able to draw readers in because people like to read pieces that show the world in all its complexity, instead of essays that pretend that a situation is all good or all bad.

If you write about a situation or an idea that is full of paradox, it is not essential that you actually use the word *paradox*. But you probably will want to mention explicitly that the situation made you feel torn, or left you feeling conflicted, or proved to be a double-edge sword (that is, a situation that "cut both ways"). If you don't spell out that sense of conflict in some way, readers may just end up confused. They may conclude that you couldn't decide on a single direction for your essay and that you've accidentally ended up discussing two very different sides of your experience. Once you clue readers into the notion that the situation was complicated (not all bad, not all good), and you provide enough details to show what you mean, readers will understand that you're trying to avoid oversimplifying a complex experience. Most likely, readers will respect you for that.

Metaphor

Metaphors—extended comparisons—can be very useful in helping readers to understand a complex point you wish to make. Metaphors are useful because they help readers to think of a situation or idea in a fresh way, and they often make a paper much more vivid, more lively.

Before we go on, though, we probably should explain metaphors more fully. A **metaphor** involves comparing two things that at first glance are very different, yet which actually have something in common. Usually, metaphors involve extended comparisons; that is, they occur over the course of several sentences or even several paragraphs.

Strictly speaking, a metaphor occurs when a writer compares two things without using the words *like* or *as*. When the writer uses *like* or *as* in a comparison, we have a **simile**. Here's an example of a simile:

> I think of my friend Jim's life last year as a roller coaster–the rickety, clangy, wooden type of roller coaster that makes your bones shake. His January started slowly and calmly, just like the first twenty yards or so of the Big Rattle ride at Six Flags. If you close your eyes during that first part, you wouldn't imagine how bad things might get just a few yards into the future. By the time March was over, he was shaken to the core, just like the skinny kid riding in the front car of the Big Rattle. He was holding on as though the steel bar might give way at any second. He felt like his life was speeding along, fast enough to make him sick to his stomach.

A metaphor, by contrast, would make the same point without using the words *like* or *as*. In a sense, a metaphor is a more direct comparison. The writer and the readers alike imagine that one thing is standing in for the other in the comparison.

> My friend Jim's life last year was a roller coaster—the rickety, clangy, wooden type that made his bones shake. His January started slowly, just a slow crawl up the metal rails. By March, however, he was just the skinny kid in the front car, turning this way and that, searching for a familiar face that was never there, his fingers gripping the steel bar in front of him that he sensed might give way at any moment. His life was whipping along so fast his stomach felt sick. Neither Jim nor anyone around him knew how to throw the brake, bring the thing to a stop, get him back to the safety of the ground once more. Each day the ride continued—rattle, rattle, shake.

Now that we've shown examples of both metaphors and similes, we'll let you in on a secret. Metaphors and similes both count as **metaphorical thinking**. It's metaphorical thinking that we're trying to talk you into adopting. If you build a thoughtful, extended comparison into your essay, you can help readers understand things at a deeper level. It doesn't really matter if your comparison uses the words *like* and *as* or not. Metaphorical thinking is a trait, or habit, that can take your writing to a new level. It's often considered a sign of a mature writer, something that readers (teachers especially) tend to be impressed by.

Looking for a Challenge: Reaching Different Types of Readers

When writing a first draft, most of us probably have in mind readers who are similar to ourselves in many respects. We write, in other words, from our comfort zones. But a writer who learns how to appeal to different groups of readers can find it much easier to convince other people or to get a job when the people doing the hiring come from a different background.

As part of your revision work on your current paper, we're going to ask you to brainstorm (and perhaps freewrite) some supporting examples or explanations that could appeal to readers who are different from you in some important way: for instance, people of a different income group, different gender, different ethnicity, different sexual orientation; people who grew up in a different place than you; people who have a different disability status than you.

It's probably not realistic to address each of these differences in your audience in every paper. Doing so would overwhelm most writers. Just tackling geographical diversity in a really thorough way, for instance, might wear a writer out: Building in different examples that appeal to readers in Oregon, New Jersey, Kansas, and Florida could prove to be plenty of work—but most likely you *could* build in an example that appeals to city dwellers as well as an example that will reach people from more rural communities. (If you've never lived in a different type of area than where you live now, chances are someone you know has. Or perhaps a friend on Facebook grew up far from where you both live now, in a much larger or smaller community. We use our friends like this all the time, and so far they haven't complained about it!)

Come up with at least a few examples for your current essay that will expand the essay's reach and broaden its appeal to readers who are different from you. If you do this on a regular basis, you'll develop one of the most useful skills any writer can have—the ability to reach a wide variety of audiences, including people you might not imagine, at first glance, you can reach.

What Works for You?

Which types of support have you used the most in past papers? Which development strategies are brand new to you or seem most challenging? Which new strategies are you willing to try? Why?

Chapter 10: Localized Revision

At a Glance...

• Paragraphs help divide the paper into manageable pieces for the reader. • The introduction can be revised along with the body of the essay. • Transitions help signal a change for the reader. • Good conclusions often leave the reader with something to think about.	**For Writing or Discussion:** Consider your most recent visit to a large store—for instance, a grocery store, discount store, or a home improvement store. How did you manage to find what you needed without wandering around in utter confusion? How do store managers go about planning a store's layout? How do they make decisions about what merchandise will go where? What factors do they take into account about the potential shoppers' expectations? How can you apply similar strategies and thoughts to deciding how your paper should be arranged?

What Localized Revision Means and Why It's Important

This chapter deals with making changes to your writing after you've already rethought the truly basic issues (things like purpose, audience, tone—most of which were dealt with in the previous chapter). If you think of the previous chapter as dealing with the large "city" of your paper, this chapter will deal with local, neighborhood-by-neighborhood matters— matters like paragraphing, getting the reader's attention, and connecting the ideas in the paper for the reader's benefit.

Paragraphs

The most frequently voiced concern we hear about paragraphs has to do with how long they should be. A paragraph does not have a defined length. Someone may have given you a guideline for paragraph length at some time in your schooling, but that's all it was meant to be: a guideline.

>>> Exercise 10.1: What Makes a Paragraph?

Genre refers to different types (categories) of written documents. Readers have certain expectations when they approach a document that falls into one genre or another.
Find an example of writing from a couple different genres. Here's a quick list of writing genres you may want to choose from:

- textbook (other than this one)
- newspaper article
- magazine article
- novel

- blog entry
- print advertisement

This list is not all-inclusive. If you have other forms of writing nearby, use them!

Count how many sentences are in four consecutive paragraphs of each type of writing you find. Did the numbers change from one genre to another? Did each paragraph have the same number of sentences within a source type? Which types tended to have the most sentences in each paragraph? Were the paragraphs that had the most sentences always the longest paragraphs?

As the exercise above points out, paragraph length can fluctuate. Paragraphs are not defined by word count or number of sentences. Of course there are some guidelines about length. For instance, formal genres usually have longer paragraphs, and those paragraphs are usually more consistent than paragraphs in informal genres. Some styles of writing allow for a one sentence paragraph while other styles would strongly discourage it. However, regardless of writing genre, those paragraphs are not defined by sentence length. Writers don't stop writing a paragraph when they've reached a certain number of words or sentences; they stop writing when the paragraph feels finished.

The Purpose of Paragraphs

If word count and sentences don't define a paragraph, what does? Before we answer that question, let's ask a couple more: *What purpose does a paragraph serve? Why do we begin new paragraphs? Who are they for?*

Paragraphs help readers make sense of a writer's information. Imagine you're reading five pages of solid text, all of it broken into sentences, but none of it broken into paragraphs. Pretty soon into those five pages, all this information blurs together. Readers' minds grow bored with it.

A paragraph break gives readers a chance to breathe and alerts them that something is changing. It says, "Pay attention now. I'm going to do something slightly different and you'll want to notice it."

Many new paragraphs signal a change of topic. All of the sentences within a paragraph should relate to the same topic, so when a new topic is raised, it's mandatory that the writer start a new paragraph. If you think about it, though, any one paragraph is really on a subtopic, as all paragraphs in a paper relate to the topic of the whole paper. The paragraphs in a paper should connect to one another and yet also remain somewhat distinct.

Occasionally, you may find you're sticking with the same topic, rather than beginning a new topic, but the paragraph has grown so long that readers stand a good chance of losing their place. When a paragraph approaches the one-page (or even half-page) mark, it's tough for the reader to find a good place to pause. That's why writers will occasionally break a lengthy discussion of one point into multiple, medium-sized paragraphs. You could think of this as an optional paragraph break, one designed to make the reading experience easier for your audience.

Topic Sentences

When paragraphs are created to show the reader that a new topic has been started, you may want to begin the paragraph with a **topic sentence**. A topic sentence is a sentence that shows what the topic will be for the remainder of the paragraph. Some instructors require topic sentences in paragraphs, while others allow the topic to be explored without a specific sentence to alert the reader to the purpose of the paragraph. Whatever you do, make sure the reader is able to understand the flow of information. Transitions, or connecting words (see the next section), also help link paragraphs together.

In Chapter 6, we compared revision to remodeling a home. Walls can be torn out and others built. Redrafting at the paragraph level is closer to decorating the home. Rooms are painted to have their own look but also kept in a similar color palette so as not to be too jarring. Furniture may be moved from one spot to another (within the same room or even sometimes to a different room) until it feels like it is in the most useful and appropriate place. Maybe a personal touch is added to the room. Think of your paragraphs in the same way. They are rooms in the house of your paper. Each room/paragraph has its own purpose/topic, but they should all feel like they are part of the same house/paper.

Transitions

The experiences and ideas that run through your mind are not all separate, independent things. Many of them are connected to one another in some way. We understand those connections (at least much of the time) because the thoughts and experiences belong to us. What happens, though, when we set those thoughts out for a new audience? Typically, our readers will not grasp the connections that seem so obvious to us. That is, not without some help. Writers help readers understand connections when they craft effective **transitions**—the words, phrases, or sentences that show relationships among different events or ideas.

Types of Transitions

Transitions can be thought of in a couple different ways. Some transitions are a lot like turn signals; that is, they help readers notice when our writing is about to change directions. Major changes in directions require pretty obvious transitions. (Think about how you felt when you were trying to follow a friend somewhere and the friend used his turn signal so infrequently you thought it must be broken. No one likes to be left behind.)

We'll list a bunch of "turn signal" transitions here. Notice that some of these transitions work well for one purpose but not another. (In other words, they're not all interchangeable.)

To add or show sequence:

again, also, and, and then, besides, equally important, finally, further, furthermore, in addition, last, moreover, next, still, too

To compare:

also, in the same way, likewise, similarly

To contrast:

although, and yet, but, but at the same time, despite, even so, even though, however, in contrast, in spite of, nevertheless, notwithstanding, on the contrary, on the other hand, regardless, still, though, yet

To give examples or intensify:

after all, an illustration of, even, for example, for instance, indeed, in fact, in particular, it is true, of course, specifically, that is, to illustrate, truly

To indicate time:

after a while, afterward, as long as, as soon as, at last, at length, at that time, before, currently, earlier, formerly, immediately, in the meantime, in the past, lately, later, meanwhile, now, presently, shortly, simultaneously, since, so far, soon, subsequently, then, thereafter, until, until now, when

To repeat or tie up loose ends:

all in all, altogether, as has been said, in brief, in other words, in particular, in short, on the whole, that is, therefore, to put it differently

To show cause or effect:

accordingly, as a result, because, consequently, for this purpose, hence, otherwise, since, then, therefore, thereupon, thus, to this end, with this objective

To signal concession:

although it is true that, granted that, I admit that, it may appear that, naturally, of course, while it may seem that

Sentence Bridge Transitions

The transitions above are pretty simple and often quite effective. As you'll see throughout this book, we use them frequently. There are times, however, when a stronger, more original transition is called for. When it's crucial that your reader understand how two ideas (or an experience and an idea) are related to one another, you may want to create what we like to call **sentence-bridge transitions**.

In order to understand how sentence-bridge transitions work, it's helpful if you think for a moment about why and how people build bridges. Since your authors live near the Mississippi River, we end up using and thinking about bridges on a regular basis. Due to the congestion along the three major bridges in the downtown St. Louis area, a fourth bridge was recently built. The new bridge, like the other bridges, was custom-designed. After all, who would want to ride across a bridge that was not specifically engineered to meet the needs of that particular gap between the states of Missouri and Illinois? If there *were* such a thing as "off the shelf" bridges, they probably wouldn't work very well. The same thing is true when writing essays. Sometimes, you need an extra-strong, custom-designed bridge (transition) so that your readers won't fall into an enormous gap.

We'll show you three different types of sentence-bridge transitions so you can start to get a feel for them. Our guess, however, is that there are probably many different types of sentence-bridge transitions you'll create over the years. Custom-designing a good transition may take extra work, but it can result in strong connections—in the mind of the reader as well as the writer.

> **Repeated word transitions** echo an important word or phrase from the end of one paragraph in the opening sentence of the next paragraph. Here's an example, with italics added here only to highlight the key word:

End of old paragraph:

The poll reveals that the biggest problem reported with the words on the "Banished Words List" is *over-use*.

Start of new paragraph:

The word "amazing" is so *over-used* that everyone from Martha Stewart to Project Runway contestants declare everyday items as "amazing," often pronouncing it "ah-maz-ing."

> **Question and answer transitions** provide a natural reason for readers to read on—namely, to discover the answer to an important question asked at the end of the previous paragraph. An example:

End of paragraph:

Who determines gas prices, and why do they change so frequently?

Start of new paragraph:

While individual gas station owners can set the price within a penny or so, the real decision-makers are speculators, people who make a living by gathering information about the world and applying it to the price of gas.

> **Perspective seeking transitions** attempt to show readers the larger significance of events or issues discussed in the previous paragraph. In other words, they try to help readers develop some perspective about what has been discussed. (This is also what writers do when they craft an effective conclusion for an essay—they leave readers with the "big picture," a sense of perspective about the topic.) An example:

End of paragraph:

When parents want certain books banned, they tend to focus on all of these negative aspects [←The negative aspects were discussed earlier in the paragraph.]
Start of new paragraph:
But there is much more to those books than the witchcraft or cursing or rebellion. [← The paragraph goes on to talk about the positive elements in the banned books.]

Sentence-bridge transitions which introduce new ideas, or new angles on old ideas, are almost always much *more effective at the beginning of a new paragraph* than at the end of the old one. (Of course, with some transitions—the question and answer type, for instance—the two halves of the transition are split evenly between the new and old paragraphs. Generally, though, new ideas belong in new paragraphs.)

How Writers Answer the "So What?" Question

Reporting details will only get a paper so far. Readers almost always end up saying (either to themselves or to the writer) some variation of, "Okay...but so what?"

That might sound like a very sarcastic response. Most readers don't mean it in the most sarcastic way. Readers do, however, want writers to go beyond simple reporting of facts (a list of what the writer had to do once she got to her job, for instance) to explore why or how those details are significant, why they matter.

As shorthand, we think of this as the *"So what?"* question. It's an important question to consider as you revise your introduction, as well as your essay as a whole. In years to come, you will likely end up having to ask yourself—in most of the essays you'll write for college, as well as some of the things you may write on the job—a related question: **"What's the significance of this fact?"** The sooner you begin addressing that question in your writing, the better your readers will understand the point you're trying to make and the more impressed they will be by the quality of your thinking.

Why Introductions Matter

Introductions have two goals:

- to introduce the topic, and
- to obtain the reader's interest in reading further.

> **>>> Exercise 10.2: Thinking about the Goals of an Introduction**
>
> Which do you think is more important and why: to show what the topic of the paper is or to get the reader interested? Discuss your response with others.

Why do papers have introductions? There are many answers to this question, but all lead back to the reader. Introductions are needed because readers need a way to transition into a paper. Imagine your reader for a moment. Do you have any way of knowing for sure what that reader is thinking about in the moment before he or she picks up your paper? Not really. Maybe the reader has just watched something interesting on TV. Maybe the reader is really hungry because he skipped lunch. Maybe the reader is thinking about a dozen other things she needs to get finished right now. The point is that the reader could be thinking about any number of things. Your goal as the writer is to get him or her thinking about what you want readers to be thinking about: your paper topic. You have to provide the bridge for the reader from that person's thoughts to your topic.

Before we talk about how to do this, let's focus for a second on what happens if you *don't* do it. A paper without an introduction is like a conversation that begins in the middle without any sort of explanation at all. Perhaps you know people who are guilty of doing this. Maybe they were talking to you about an issue an hour ago, but conversation has drifted since then and maybe you've even walked in and out of the room a couple of times since that issue was last brought up. Then, all of a sudden, the speaker brings it up again without warning and uses pronouns like "she" and "they" without reminding you who "she" and "they" are. This is how a reader feels without an introduction. There's a moment of, "Hey, whoa, did I just miss something?" that is really uncomfortable. It does not make a good first impression.

Every so often, a writer will intentionally confuse the readers in order to make a point. This is tricky to do and only recommended if the writer chooses to make that point very clear very soon. Most readers prefer to be hooked into an essay. Think about it for a moment...don't you prefer that when you read?

>>> *Exercise 10.3: Introductions as Road Maps*

Writing a good paper can be a lot like giving clear directions to a place a friend has never been to before. You have to move the person from Point A to Point B without getting him or her lost along the way. What kinds of things do you think about as you give directions? What do you find most helpful when someone else gives you directions? How do these qualities apply to writing an introduction?

Types of Introductions

There are many ways to introduce a paper. One of the best things you can do as a writer is observe what you like as a reader. As you read, if you notice an effective introduction, make a note of it in a notebook or journal and then try that strategy in a future paper.

No matter which type of introduction you choose, make sure your introduction is free of errors. The introduction is the first part of your essay and the first time that your reader gets a real sense of what it will be about. Readers are more likely to notice errors in the very first paragraph when they are still determining whether or not they really want to read on.

➢ **Going from General to Specific:** This is probably the classic form of introduction. The first few sentences offer one or two general observations about the topic. The writer's goal, in this type of introduction, is to warm the reader up and get the reader interested in the topic, without shocking or confusing the reader. The introduction then transitions into more specific information about the topic, until it ends in a thesis statement that shows what the paper's main message will be.

Example: Mash-ups are a new style of music that blends (or mashes) multiple songs together to form a new song. The creator of the mash-up uses songs made by other people and rearranges them and manipulates them to create a new sound from old songs. Some people say that this style of music steals from the original artists. They say that mash-up artists aren't creative because they are not creating something brand new. Good mash-ups are creative because they make a brand new song even if they use old songs to do it.

Problems with general to specific: This type of introduction can sometimes be too generic. If the introduction is too broad, the reader may not be interested in the paper or may not have a clear idea of what the paper is really about. The opposite problem is sometimes also true of this type of introduction. A reader who is told *exactly* what the paper is going to cover may lose interest in reading the entire paper.

> **Suggestion Box: Revising General to Specific Introductions**
>
> Read over the introduction and ask yourself if the reader would know what this paper was really about or if the introduction could potentially introduce any paper on a similar topic. If the reader would be able to tell you precisely what is covered in the whole paper, then either the paper needs to be less superficial or the introduction needs to be more general. If the reader doesn't know what the paper is really about, then the introduction needs to be more closely related to the topic.

➢ **Starting with an Anecdote:** An anecdote is a short, interesting story. This can be a good way to begin because readers, in general, like stories. They like to be able to see a little bit of themselves or people they know in a paper. It helps them relate to the paper and may hook their interest. This method can also generate a little suspense if the writer chooses to wait to show what his or her point is until later in the paper.

Example (from an essay about bullying):

> Jessica ran into the girl's bathroom and slammed the stall door shut. She tried to slow down her breathing, but her heart still felt like it was up in her throat. Her eyes burned as tears gathered there. All she could think was, "Not again. Not again. At least this time, I won't cry." She tried desperately to stop from crying, knowing that she would need to return to class soon. She told herself that the girls in the hallway shouldn't be able to hurt her with words. Her breathing slowed. She wiped the tears from her eyes and blew her nose and returned to class, avoiding the hall she had just left. This wasn't the first time that Jessica had been bullied by a group of cruel classmates, and it wouldn't be the last.

Problems with the anecdote method: The anecdote has to be clearly related to the topic that follows. Readers will usually grant the writer some leniency initially, but their interest will fade if the story continues for a long time without revealing any clues about why the story is being told.

> **Suggestion Box: Writing Anecdote-based Introductions**
>
> - Keep the story brief and amusing or dramatic. Reveal only enough details to create curiosity and complete the story.
>
> - Make sure the story directly connects to your paper's topic or the reader will think, "That's nice, but what did it have to do with...?"
>
> - Try beginning the story in the introduction and then referring back to it during a later part of the paper. That tends to make the paper feel connected and united (as long as the story doesn't just restart and repeat what was already said in the introduction).

➢ **_Questioning:_** One way to get a reader interested in what you have to say is to ask a question. The beauty of asking a question is that it prompts the reader to search for an answer. The reader will be thinking about the topic before you've even given him the material that you want him to think about. If you ask the right question, then the reader may really want to discover the answers by reading further into your paper.

Example:
> Who are the people who create and upload YouTube videos? Many would assume they are teenagers or people who have too much time on their hands. It might surprise you to know that a great percentage of video uploads are from businesses that are trying to promote their product. YouTube has become an important tool in modern retailing.

Example of questioning combined with anecdote:
> What can you buy with $0.78? What is $0.78 worth to you? To little kids, $0.78 might be a big deal. They could buy some small prize or trinket with that amount. Someone else could find that amount buried in the crevices of a living room couch. Maybe it is the amount of change at the bottom of a purse or in a wallet. Imagine my surprise, then, when after waiting a guy's table for thirty minutes, I looked down to see that my tip was a measly $0.78!

Problems with questioning: Readers are unpredictable, so there is no way to guarantee exactly what the reader will be thinking. That makes it difficult to transition the reader's thoughts (which are unknown) into what you want her to think about (your message).

> **Suggestion Box: Questioning in an Introduction**
>
> - Use the questions sparingly. When writers ask multiple questions in a row without supplying any answers, the reader can begin to feel interrogated.
>
> - Make sure your question is a thought-provoking question. That is—do not ask a yes/no question. Ask one that gets the reader to wonder for a moment.
>
> - Don't ask too big of a question because the "wondering" will be too unpredictable. For instance, don't ask, "What is the best way to save the world?" for a paper about

recycling because your reader could mentally respond with: better medical advances, more (or less) technology, or even love.

- Make sure the sentence after the question moves smoothly from the question to the next part of the text.

Suggestion Box: Questions About Questions

How do you feel when you're reading a paper that asks a bunch of questions? Do the questions make you think about the paper topic? Or do they begin to make you feel like you are being interrogated? Does it make a difference if there is just one question or multiple questions? After a while, do you ever think, "Wow, I wish the writer would just tell me something instead of asking question after question"?

> ➤ **_An Interesting Quotation:_** Students often like to open their papers with a quotation from someone else. Doing this takes the pressure off trying to come up with a brilliant hook of their own. The idea is that the quote will create interest because the reader will recognize the speaker of the quote or even the quote itself. Maybe the quote is unusual enough that it prompts the reader to think about the topic from an unexpected perspective.

Example:

Maya Angelou said, "A bird doesn't sing because it has an answer, it sings because it has a song." I think it sings because it knows we need a song. I love music. I can't get enough of it. I've been singing since before I could talk. Music is an important part of my life.

Problems with quotations: This technique tends to be overused. When not chosen well or if not integrated adequately, the quote can feel unattached to the paper that follows.

Suggestion Box: Using Quotations in Introductions

- Make sure the entire quote is completely relevant to your paper topic. Do not build the reader's interest only to get their interest in a topic unrelated to your real message.

- Try to choose a quote by someone your audience should know. Otherwise, the impact of the quote could be reduced when your reader stops to think, "Should I know who this is?"

- Consider using a quote that is well-known...and then challenge its meaning or offer your readers a new perspective on it.

Why Conclusions Matter

Conclusions can be tough paragraphs to write. For one thing, sometimes it's difficult for a writer to decide whether the essay is really "over" or not. Reading the draft of your essay out loud can help you decide if you've finished discussing everything that is relevant to this paper. Reading the draft to someone else and asking that person what else needs to be addressed in the essay can also prove helpful.

Using Conclusions to Summarize Main Ideas

After you decide that you're ready to wrap up the essay, you're still stuck with the question of what do—what to discuss—in the conclusion. Often, writers will try to solve that problem by simply summing up (repeating) all of the major ideas or events that they've just finished sharing with the reader in the rest of the essay. That, however, is really more of a summary than a conclusion. When you sum up your main topics, the readers end up sitting through a rerun.

On occasion, a point-by-point rerun may be necessary. For instance, if the information you've just shared with the reader is incredibly technical and you're not sure whether the reader was able to keep up with you, then yes, a summary might be helpful. Summaries are also often necessary in very long papers.

Going Beyond Mere Summary in Conclusions

Most of the time, though, when readers see a summary up ahead, they do what you probably do when you realize Channel 30 is showing that *NCIS* episode you caught five or six days ago: they turn away from it, or they tune it out. In that case, the writer has missed a great opportunity to hit her point home one last time.

What can you do in the concluding paragraph or two, then? Probably you'll want to help your readers "draw a conclusion" from what you've already presented to them in the essay. That is, help them to think more deeply about what all those facts, ideas, and questions from pages one and two of your essay really add up to. Why are those details important? (You will *not* need to repeat them all in order to show readers what conclusion those details lead you to.)

> ➢ **Zooming Out** One good way to do this is with a conclusion that shows readers what the big picture is like. You've spent plenty of time showing them all sorts of details in the essay, but now it's your turn to do what movie directors often do at the end of films: Pull back your camera slowly (zoom out, that is) and let us see that what you've been discussing in the essay is really much bigger, much more significant, than a quick glance at those facts on page two would suggest. When you pull back your camera (so to speak) in the essay's conclusion, you can help readers see the big picture and how everything you've discussed in the essay is connected.

> **Looking for a Challenge: Endings**
>
> The next time you watch a movie, pay attention to the ending. Often the director will pull back the camera, and we discover that the film's final scene—which is set in, say, a small apartment—is actually part of a busy city block, and that block is part of Brooklyn. What happened inside that apartment is part of something larger; it's connected to the big scheme of things. The event in the apartment matters, even if people might sometimes forget that there is something happening in that apartment. Discuss the zooming out strategy in a movie you recently saw—or if you think another strategy is at work, describe that instead. How does this conclusion technique serve the movie? What impressions does it leave you with? Would a similar strategy work in your essay?

➢ **Raising Related Points or Questions** Another strong strategy for writing conclusions is to leave the readers with something to chew on, some food for thought. We don't mean that you should get all preachy in the conclusion (though if that happens in your first or second draft, it's something you can fix in the next draft). Instead, present your reader with the tough questions that are impossible to answer in a mere two or three pages—the questions that have grown out of what you discussed in the body of the essay. As long as you don't look like you're trying to evade a question that has a simple, obvious answer, readers will probably understand that you have a good point. There are questions that still need to be mulled over once the essay is finished. You can challenge your reader to continue to think about those questions, just as you plan to continue wrestling with them yourself. (A question that does not have a simple answer may stick with the reader. Writing teachers sometimes end up thinking about what their students wrote days or weeks earlier. Honest. Those tough questions, many of which were raised by students in the last paragraph of an essay, come back to us when we're busy washing the dishes or mowing the grass. The writer's essay, in other words, is still working on the reader.)

➢ **Calling for Action** If you hope for your readers to *do something* when they finish reading your essay, you can offer them a call to arms in your conclusion. Despite that label, nobody needs to use weapons. You could, however, convince some of your readers to write a letter, send out a tweet related to this issue, or join a protest in the parking lot at the corner of Fourth Street and Lemon.

When revising your conclusion, be sure to read your whole essay out loud, including the conclusion, to make sure there's not a drastic change of tone at the paper's end. It's easy to accidentally turn up the heat in a conclusion (or to go over the top in terms of humor), but that's something you'll want to catch before your final draft goes public.

>>> Exercise 10.4: Suspense Isn't Just for Horror Movies

Revision is about *rethinking our choices* as writers. One of those choices, of course, is the order in which we will present information to our readers. As a writer you have control over what your readers learn first (or last) in your essay. Sometimes, it's easy to see that one way of ordering the essay will make the essay easier to understand than some other way.

On occasion, however, you may want to play around with the essay's order. That is, you may decide to withhold some information until later in the essay—not just for the heck of it, but in order to give your readers a bit of a surprise, maybe even **suspense**. Not all surprises are welcomed by readers, of course. Suspense that only confuses readers should be avoided. Still, suspense can be a good thing—a most welcome thing—in an essay.

Read the scenarios below and imagine that you're the writer who is going to write and revise each of these essays. Think about how you could organize the material in your essay. Discuss the reasoning behind your choices. Pay special attention to the effect you think your choices would have on readers.

- Your aunt was diagnosed with breast cancer in 2011 and underwent multiple surgeries and radiation as part of her treatment. In the midst of her battle with cancer, she started the most successful landscaping business in her city. Consider starting the essay with the great success your aunt has achieved with her business, then reveal the serious health challenge she was facing as she simultaneously dealt with the stresses of starting a business. (How would arranging the essay this way affect your readers' impression of your aunt?)
- A month ago, you and your significant other both got violently ill after eating at a local restaurant, which we'll call Restaurant Z. The folks at the ER said that, yes, indeed, this was a likely case of food poisoning. You eventually recovered, but you vowed never to return to Restaurant Z. Last Friday, you spent an hour calling in to a radio station in an attempt to win a hundred dollar gift card to a mystery restaurant. Finally you were successful; you were told the gift card was yours. When you asked the station employee the name of the mystery restaurant, she said (with genuine excitement in her voice), "Restaurant Z!" (Consider how you should arrange this essay. Which part would you share with readers first? Which part last? How would that choice affect your readers' reaction to the material?)
- You're watching a reality show, maybe something along the lines of NBC's *Celebrity Apprentice*. One of the contestants is the former governor of a large state; he also served in congress for several years. You notice that this contestant is having trouble figuring out how to turn on a computer. As you watch the man fumble with the machine, you get the sense that this man has never actually used a computer before. (Which piece of information would you share with readers first—the contestant's background as governor, or his difficulty in using a computer? Which arrangement is most likely to give your readers a surprise? Put another way, which arrangement is more likely to cause readers to raise their eyebrows and say, "You're kidding!")

Now, examine the draft of your own essay. Is there any place in the essay where you might be able to withhold information for a short while and therefore *create more suspense* for your readers? Can you do this without making the essay confusing? Experiment a bit.

More Help: Quick Redrafting IV Checklist

After rereading either your own paper or your classmate's, answer these questions by using a scale of 1 to 10, with 1 meaning *weak* and 10 meaning *great*. Be as honest as possible.

- How well did the first paragraph or two introduce the topic?
- How interested were you in reading the paper?
- How effective was the conclusion?
- Was the paper long enough? Did it have enough support?
- How well did the paper flow from one topic to the next?
- How did the paper sound to you?
- To what extent did the paper feel like it was written by a real person who cared?

More Help: Quick Redrafting IV Peer Evaluation Activity

Rate the following items for effectiveness. Use a 1 to 4 scale with 1 meaning *needs to be a top revision priority*; 2 meaning *needs some attention*; 3 meaning *pretty good but could be changed a little*; and 1 meaning *excellent*.

- Paragraph length
- Paragraph focus
- Sentence variety
- Sentence correctness

Answer these questions as well:
- What do you think was the most important part of the paper?
- What was the strongest paragraph? The weakest?
- What grammar issue do you think the writer needs to work on the most?
- Tell the writer if the paper "jumped" at any point.
- Underline any sentences that were hard to read or understand quickly.

Beyond the Essay: Writers at Work

MIKE GUIDO,
President and principal architect of a firm in Rocky Point, New York

Successful architects do much more than draft blueprints. In addition to designing the plans that are the basis for new schools, business facilities, and homes, the firm of Michael J. Guido Jr Architect PC (located on Long Island) is responsible for writing the specifications that help ensure each building turns out the way it should. In fact, attention to detail in the firm's written materials is what gives it a shot at getting new projects.

Mike explains it this way: "When a school district or other public entity is looking to hire an Architect they issue requests for proposals [RFP]. The architects provide a written response to the proposal describing themselves, their firm's qualifications and insights into the contemplated projects. Without a well written response to the RFP, you have no chance of getting an interview and potentially the project."

It's important for a firm such as Mike's to be perceived as professional and capable. His skill as writer contributes to the firm's public image. "My goal for writing is to be as confident in what I write as I am in what I say." He adds, though, that this takes considerable effort and serious revision: "I've never written anything right the first time."

What role does writing play in your career? What types of documents do you write as part of your job?

All publicly bid projects require a set of detailed plans and specifications describing exactly how the building is to be built and the level of quality that is required in the workmanship and materials. For an average size project, this could mean 100 sheets of drawings (blueprints) and 400 pages of specifications. Poorly written specifications can destroy a project. For example, I had a project years ago where I called to "remove and replace a door". The contractor removed the door and then reinstalled the same door. After a lengthy discussion, he installed the *new* door. The most difficult part of my job is to make sure my plans and specifications cannot be misinterpreted either intentionally or unintentionally.

How much time do you spend on writing in one form or another?

In any given week I am spending approximately one-third of my time writing either proposals to get new work or specifications on work I already have.

What role does audience (a sense of who your readers/listeners are) play in your writing process? Do you ever have to write for a skeptical audience?

When responding to request for proposals or describing a potential project to voters, the entire success of the company rides on convincing the reader that your idea is the right one. Often when you propose a project to the public that could affect their taxes or their backyard, the audience starts out against you before they've read word one.

What would you say to a writer—especially a student writer, someone producing work for teachers as well as possibly a boss—who feels discouraged about his or her writing abilities?

Write what you mean to say and read it *over and over again* to make sure it says that.

For Writing or Discussion:

1. Mike mentions that "poorly written specifications can destroy a project." Think about another career field with which you're familiar. What problems could careless writing cause in that career?

2. Does reading your work over several times allow you to catch the errors that might occur in it? What can you do to make your "reading over" time more effective?

What Works for You

If you still have them, look through papers you've written for previous courses, or even from high school. Did you use any of the techniques for introductions or conclusions that are discussed in this chapter? Which one(s)? Which method or methods for writing an introduction appeal(s) to you most, and why? What about for writing a conclusion? Next time you write an introduction or conclusion, what is something you would like to specifically try or avoid?

Chapter 11: Editing for Correctness

At a Glance...

- Correctness is an important focus during the final stages of the writing process.
- When a writer edits effectively, readers are able to focus on the essay's ideas.
- Becoming aware of your error patterns will make editing easier and more effective.
- You can learn how to find and fix common editing errors.
- Proofreading involves a very slow, careful reading of the best version of your paper.

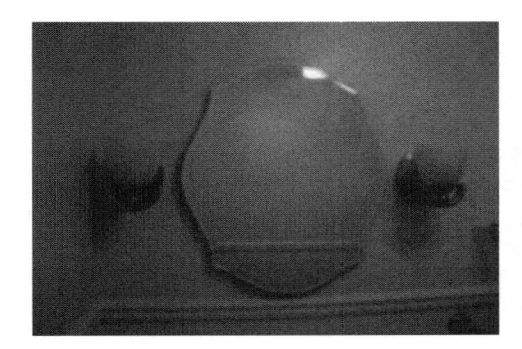

For Writing or Discussion: You might be in the habit of looking in the mirror before stepping out of the house in the morning or before leaving a restroom in the middle of the day. On other occasions, you might find yourself brushing crumbs off your shirt or using your hands to adjust your hair. What do these habits have to do with the editing stage? What do they have to do with editing for correctness?

What Correctness Is and Why It Matters

Cheering loudly, the table that my sisters carried through the door actually fit.

After reading this sentence, you may want to ask yourself: Shouldn't I be afraid of furniture that expresses emotion? Do I really want such an object in my home? Wouldn't I feel better about this whole situation if my *sisters* were the ones who were cheering, and not the table? (Let's try that out: *My sisters cheered loudly because the table they were carrying through the door actually fit.* Yes, much better.)

Correctness involves making sure your paper contains clear sentences and uses Standard English. Any essay you've bothered to redraft (revise) in a serious way also deserves to be edited with care. Doing so means your readers will be able to devote most of their attention to thinking about your ideas, rather than noticing errors. Effective editing means that you will gain greater control over how your readers react to the ideas and experiences in your paper. Good editing improves the odds that readers will take your work seriously—or, for that matter, get the joke you planted on page two.

Looking for Error Patterns in Your Writing

When you think about catching and correcting errors in your writing, you may initially feel overwhelmed. You might convince yourself that you'll never be able to do a good enough job cleaning your work up and making it error-free. Truthfully, though, many of your sentences probably communicate your ideas clearly and correctly. It's also likely that not all of the errors discussed in this chapter will pop up in your writing on a frequent basis. To put it another way: Not every error discussed in this chapter needs to make you sweat.

Writers who become good editors of their own work watch for **error patterns** in their almost-final drafts. They become more and more aware of the errors that tend to occur most frequently in their writing. They pay special attention to those errors in order to find them and fix them as they prepare the polished draft. As you might imagine, this involves an investment of time; it also may mean that you will need to get help—at least initially—from a teacher or tutor in identifying which error patterns are most common in your work. Once those error patterns are noticed and you become more skilled at catching those errors and fixing them, you stand a good chance of becoming more independent in your editing over the long haul.

Suggestion Box: Two Strategies for Identifying Your Most Frequent Error Patterns

1. Scan your teacher's markings. Often teachers will label errors that pop up in a student's draft, or the teacher might mark a paragraph or two of the draft in order to point out a typical range of errors that show up throughout the rest of the paper. If your teacher does this, make good use of this information by identifying what errors seem to pop up most frequently within a single essay or in just about every essay you write. Watch for the pattern. Make a list of the error types your teacher has pointed out. ***Ask your instructor if he or she has a list of error symbols you can refer to when looking over your own essay.***

2. Start an error log on your own. Ask your teacher to review a page or so of one of your drafts—preferably a draft in which you've already engaged in real revision. More specifically, you might ask your teacher to list the error types she notices in that section. The responsibility to do something with that list is yours. You'll want to start looking in this chapter for the errors your teacher named; you'll need to see what those errors look like in the examples provided here so that you can start to notice them on the page your teacher examined.

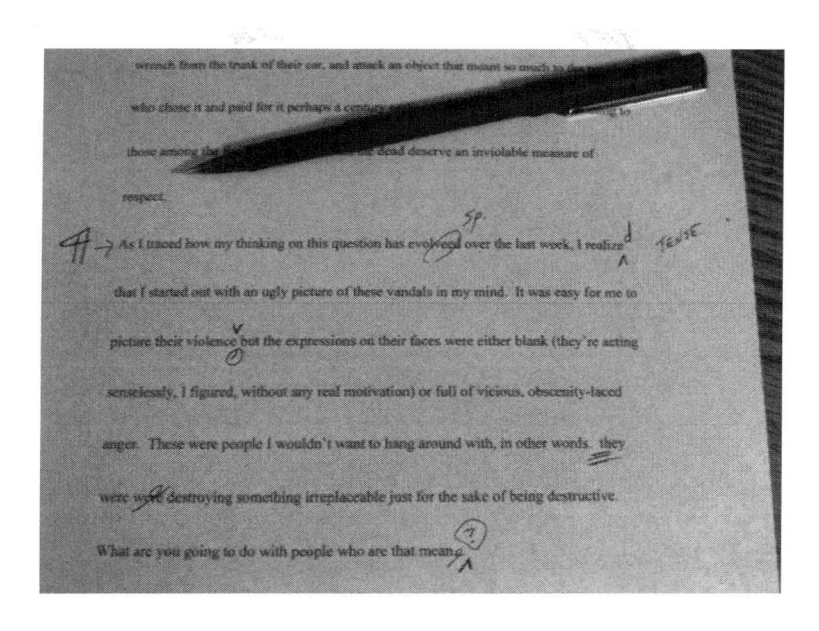

A sample paper with editing errors marked

Perhaps the process of detecting error patterns and tracking down and fixing actual errors doesn't sound very fun. Many students, though, are glad when they start to become effective and independent editors of their own work. Getting a handle on error patterns is a practical way to do that.

The rest of the Suggestion Boxes in this chapter are designed to help you once you notice a particular error pattern in your writing. Feel free to jump straight to the sections that discuss your most common error patterns.

What an Electronic Grammar Check Can and Can't Do for You

Many word-processing programs and electronic devices include something called a grammar checker. This feature will help you check your sentences for major structural flaws or punctuation errors. Grammar checkers are useful tools when you are in the editing stage; however, they do have their limitations. Grammar checkers do not, strictly speaking, understand the idea you're trying to get across to your reader. They do not understand the tone you're trying to employ, or the specialized vocabulary that may be part of the career you're discussing. In other words, there may be some things the grammar checker flags as "likely errors" which are not actual errors. A grammar checker—much like a spell checker feature—is actually a collection of complex rules that a human being has programmed into the software. But even the most complex grammar checker will give you poor advice on occasion.

What you can use the grammar checker for, however, is a heads-up. Think about a time when someone asked you, "Are you really going to go out like that?" That question alerted you to the possibility—just the *possibility*—that something was wrong with your appearance. (Did you have mustard on your sweater? Or did your friend not understand that your clothing was just fine for wherever it was you were headed?) You might want to use grammar checkers in a similar way. For instance, if the grammar checker tells you, "This may be a run-on sentence," be sure to pause for a good moment and reread the sentence a couple times—out loud, if possible. Is it really a run-on? Ask yourself what traits might cause it to be a run-on. Then turn to this chapter of *Use What Works* and look closely at the section on run-on sentences. After reviewing that material, does your sentence still look like a run-on? Or is it simply a good, correctly punctuated sentence that tripped up the grammar checker for who knows what reason?

You can take that approach for any potential error that the grammar checker flags in your writing. Do not make a change too quickly, without thinking through what that sentence is trying to get across and what type of punctuation the sentence really needs in order to be both correct and clear. As a human being—and the final editor of your own writing—it's your responsibility to second guess the grammar checker.

Fixing Problems with Sentence Boundaries

Sometimes writers have trouble deciding where one sentence ends and another sentence begins. In other words, they're confused about boundaries. Most sports involve boundaries. Lines that are marked on a basketball court or painted on a football field are important for both the players and those watching the game. If no boundary markings were visible, players wouldn't know when they were out of bounds. One player might think the other player ran off field or off court. Disagreements could occur. Similarly, confusion develops when writers don't mark sentence boundaries with care. A reader could begin reading a sentence only to find it definitely strays into another sentence. Or maybe a sentence was so incomplete that the reader felt it stopped before it had even started.

Read the following passage and notice what happens when writers do not mark sentence boundaries with care.

> It's very difficult to. Deal with rising prices when you go to the grocery store or. Need to fill up your gas tank on your way to work you may not have received a raise in a year or more (if ever) and sooner or later you notice that the prices are climbing again but

> you don't have any more money in your wallet to pay for all the things you have to buy you start to wonder why prices go up faster than your income. Sooner or later. You either need to find a better paying job or figure out a way to cut back. On some of your expenses.

We've been pretty dramatic in this example, chopping up some sentences into sentence fragments and combining other sentences into run-on sentences, mostly to help you see how easily readers can become confused. Fortunately, you can learn how to find and fix the two most common types of sentence boundary errors—fragments and run-ons.

Sentence Fragments

Simply put, a **sentence fragment** is an incomplete sentence. It's an imposter sentence—a "wanna-be" sentence.

In order to understand what we mean by "incomplete sentence," let's look at the traits a sentence must have in order to be a complete **sentence**.

- **A sentence must contain a subject and a verb.** A quick example would be: *George jumped*. The subject is *George*, and the verb is *jumped*. The sentence could contain lots of other words and phrases, of course, but at minimum it needs a subject and a verb.

    - What does **subject** mean? The grammatical subject is what the sentence is about: the person, place, thing, or idea that is the main focus of the sentence. The subject is often—but not always—near the beginning of the sentence.
    - What does **verb** mean? For the time being, we will say that a verb is a word that expresses an action. It might be an action that is easy to observe through your senses (for instance: *run, shout, kiss, drink, sniffle*), but it can also be something that occurs more or less invisibly within a person (for instance: *think, dream, guess, decide, regret, rejoice*).

- **A sentence must communicate at least one complete thought.** For instance: *The teacher opened a window*. That's a complete thought. We could, of course, add more information into that sentence in order to combine a couple thoughts or get more detailed about one main thought. The following sentences also qualify as complete sentences:

    - The teacher opened a window and a cool breeze blew in.
    - The students, who had been wilting in their seats, all seemed to come to life.

Look again at that last example above. It's a good sentence. But what if you presented only one chunk of it—an incomplete thought—to your readers? For instance, what if you gave them this chunk and asked them to make meaning of it?

> Who had been wilting in their seats.

Chances are your readers will be confused. They may try to puzzle it out for a moment. Perhaps they'll think you were trying to ask them a question (*Who had been wilting in their seats?*). Mostly, though, they will just be perplexed. Exactly who is this sentence supposed to be about? In other words, they will wonder what the grammatical subject of the sentence is supposed to be. They would be much more likely to understand your basic meaning if you gave them a complete thought—a complete sentence.

The students in Professor Hayden's class were wilting in their seats.

The length of a sentence is not what determines whether it is a complete sentence or a sentence fragment. Sentence fragments always have something important missing. They leave readers hanging in some important way; they leave readers confused.

Let's look at a few more fragments.

Example 1

Fragment: An addictive way to keep up with friends.

This is a fragment because the reader doesn't know *what* is an addictive way to keep up with friends or what this addictive way to keep up with friends will do.

Correct: Facebook can be an addictive way to keep up with friends.

An addictive way to keep up with friends can get in the way of actual friendship.

Example 2

Fragment: Because Reese was spending too much time on Facebook.

The problem with this sentence is that it needs to be connected to more information in order to be complete. The reader needs to know what Reese did about her Facebook problem.

Correct: Because she was spending too much time on Facebook, Reese decided to take a break from all social networking for a while.

This sentence would also be correct if the order of its parts were flipped:

Reese decided to take a break from all social networking for a while because she was spending too much time on Facebook.

Example 3

Fragment: Going to be difficult.

This is a problem because the sentence has a verb but no subject.

Correct: Quitting Facebook is going to be difficult.

Suggestion Box: How to Fix Fragments

There are several ways to fix sentence fragments. Each of these approaches can correct the sentence.

Decide which method to use after you've determined what caused the fragment and looked at the other types of sentences you already have in that same paragraph. Do not always choose the same method for fixing these errors. Aim for variety in your sentences so that your sentences do not all look like clones.

1. **Supply the missing information.** If the sentence fragment is missing a subject, then add the subject into the sentence. If it is missing a verb or even a linking (connecting) verb, then add that missing part.
2. **Connect the fragment to the sentence that comes right before or after the fragment.** This strategy should be used when the fragment is a phrase. In order for the phrase to fully make sense, it needs to be connected to an independent sentence. Ask yourself if the fragment would make better sense if it were connected to either the sentence before it or the sentence after it.
3. **Reword the sentence.** Sometimes, it is much simpler to state the idea in a new way. Think for a minute about what you want that sentence to accomplish and see if there is another way of saying the same thing clearly and completely.

Run-on Sentences and Comma Splices

When a writer smashes together two or more independent sentences, the writer creates a **run-on sentence**. Run-on sentences are confusing for readers because they lead the reader to read the sentence too quickly and to lose track of the thoughts the writer was trying to express.

A writer might create two different types of run-on sentences. A **fused sentence** (often just called a run-on) occurs when two sentences are slammed together without any attempt at showing a boundary. Here's an example of a fused sentence.

Her email account was hacked on Monday two days later her Twitter account was also hacked.

The reader has to stop and figure out where the first complete thought ends and where the second complete thought begins. In other words, the reader ends up having to supply the boundary himself.

Her email account was hacked on Monday. Two days later her Twitter account was also hacked.

Sometimes, a writer will have some sense of where a boundary *should* occur in a sentence, but she is not certain how to show that boundary. If she uses a comma where a period is called for, she creates a type of run-on known as a **comma splice**.

Her email account was hacked on Monday, two days later her Twitter account was also hacked.

Comma splices are usually easier for readers to understand than fused sentences, but both of these errors are run-ons. They're also both considered major errors in standard edited English.

Here are a few run-on sentences. Try reading each run-on out loud without pausing. Before you look at the corrected version, ask yourself what could be done to fix the run-on. What steps could be taken to help readers make better sense of the ideas in the run-on?

Example 1

Run-on:

The movie industry has been trying to crack down on people uploading pirated movies to the Internet in fact the film industry has sued people over this.

This is an example of a fused sentence. As you've probably noticed, the longer the run-on is, the more room there is for the reader to become confused.

Correct:

The movie industry has been trying to crack down on people uploading pirated movies to the Internet. In fact, the film industry has sued people over this.

The movie industry has been trying to crack down on people uploading pirated movies to the Internet; in fact, the film industry has sued people over this.

The first correction above uses terminal (end-point) punctuation, namely a period. The second correction uses a semicolon, a punctuation mark that will join together two sentences that are closely related in thought. (For instance, the sentences show a cause-and-effect relationship, or the sentences show the positive and negative sides of something.)

Example 2

Run-on:

People watch their favorite shows on a variety of devices, for instance, DeAndre watches *The Walking Dead* on his phone, his laptop, and even (on occasion) his television.

This run-on sentence happens to be a comma splice. The writer tried to avoid a run-on by inserting a comma after *devices*. Unfortunately, the comma is not a strong enough punctuation mark to prevent a run-on.

Correct:

People watch their favorite shows on a variety of devices. For instance, DeAndre watches *The Walking Dead* on his phone, his laptop, and even (on occasion) his television.

This correction uses strong, heavy duty punctuation—a period—to break the comma splice into two separate sentences.

Correct:

People watch their favorite shows on a variety of devices; for instance, DeAndre watches *The Walking Dead* on his phone, his laptop, and even (on occasion) his television.

In this correction, we've chosen to connect the two sentences using a semicolon, since the semicolon is another type of heavy-duty punctuation. Since the ideas of the two sentences are closely related, the semicolon works well here. We no longer have a comma splice or any other type of run-on sentence.

Example 3

Run-on:

Eddie and Carol have a unique looking house the outside of it is shaped like a boat for that matter, when you go inside the furniture and decorations are similar to the décor you might find on a boat.

This is an example of a run-on that is made up of three complete sentences that have been smashed together. What happens when you read it out loud slowly? Do the different chunks of it—the complete (yet closely related) thoughts—stand out?

Correct:

Eddie and Carol have a unique looking house. The outside of it is shaped like a boat; for that matter, when you go inside, the furniture and decorations are similar to the décor you might find on a boat.

We could have split the original run-on sentence into three separate sentences. However, we thought it would be nice to achieve some sentence variety as we fixed the run-on. Heavy duty punctuation is in place to help readers understand the different thoughts more easily.

Suggestion Box: How to Fix Run-on Sentences and Comma Splices

Even if you have many run-on sentences in your papers, you can get a handle on this error. Here are some steps that will help you.

1. **Read your paper out loud.** Eliminate distractions so that you will be able to focus on what you are reading.
2. **Pay attention to punctuation as you read.** When you come to a period, stop for three seconds. When you come to a semicolon, stop for two seconds. When you come to a comma, stop for one second. When there is no punctuation between words or phrases, do not pause.
3. **Listen for complete thoughts that get slammed into other complete thoughts.** In other words, pay attention to those moments when the meaning you're trying to convey in a sentence makes you want to pause for a good two or three seconds, but the punctuation does not allow you to pause. Mark those sentences in the margin (Possible R.O.?) for further investigation.
4. **Check whether the possible run-ons are actually correct sentences**. If the complete thoughts you're looking at are joined together with a **coordinating conjunction** (words such as *for, and, nor, but, or, yet, so*—also known as the FANBOYS words), chances are good that you have a complete sentence that simply has multiple parts. Here are a couple examples of sentences that are not run-ons:
    - *The search engine gave Antwone a thousand hits,* **and** *he knew he needed to limit his results.*
    - *His favorite search engine is Google,* **but** *he agreed to try the search engine his friend recommended.*
5. **Choose a solution for the actual run-ons you find.** Use one of the following strategies to repair run-on sentences. (These strategies work for both fused sentences and comma splices.)
    - Insert heavy-duty punctuation (either a period or a semicolon) between the two thoughts that were slammed together.
    - Join the thoughts correctly with a comma <u>and</u> a coordinating conjunction: *for, and, nor, but, or, yet, so.*

>>> Exercise 11.1: Getting a Handle on Sentence Boundaries

The following passage includes sentence fragments and run-on sentences (fused sentences as well as comma splices). Find the errors and figure out the best ways to fix them. Your goal is to improve the correctness of the passage and make it easier for readers to follow.

Technology is an often required part of a college education. For some students, this is a natural expectation, but for others, it comes as an unpleasant surprise.

Technology use is often a required part of a college education. Professors assume students will know how to use computers. And will have access to at least one computer outside of the classroom. Writing teachers, in particular, expect their students to type papers before turning them in.

Not everyone has access to computers or knows how to use them some students do not have reliable internet connection at home. Others not use them on a regular basis and have slow typing speeds. Some of the students who have computers at home sometimes have different word processing programs they do not know how to save their files in a way that can be accessed at school.

> Technology use is expected but it is not always taught. Who should be responsible for teaching it if it isn't learned already. Could go to a Writing Center or a tutor. Maybe the professor can take some class time to go over some technology basics in the beginning of the semester. Technology should be a tool to help students instead it sometimes gets in the way and holds some students back. In the end, though, it is something that all students will need to know how to use.

Fixing Problems with Verbs

Verbs play important roles in sentences. They are essential to how a sentence works. Sometimes, though, they need to be adjusted because they are out of whack with the rest of the sentence, just as a car's alignment needs to be adjusted on occasion or the strings on a guitar need to be tightened.

Subject/Verb Agreement Error

In the section on sentence fragments, we said the grammatical subject in a sentence is what the sentence is about. The subject is often—but not always—near the beginning of the sentence. The subject will be either a **noun** (that is, a word that refers to a person, place, thing, or idea) or a **pronoun**, a word that takes the place of a noun (for instance, *she, he, it, that, who*).

A verb, meanwhile, is a word that either expresses action or mentions a state of being.
- Action verbs probably leap to your mind readily—words such as *laugh, chew, wrestle, sing, score, break, burp,* and *tumble.*
- State of being verbs, on the other hand, are the almost-invisible words that we use every day but which we sometimes forget are verbs—words such as *is, are, was, were, have, had, seems,* and *does.*

Verbs can take different forms depending on how they are used in a sentence. One main factor that determines what form a verb will take is the sentence's subject. If the subject is singular, the writer needs to make sure the verb matches it.

Rob eats lunch down the street.

Shawn's phone is broken, just as it was last year.

If the sentence's subject is plural—either because a plural noun or pronoun is used or because the sentence has a compound subject (consisting of two or more subjects)—the writer will want to ensure that the verb matches the subject.

They plan their weekends out as though there's a science to it.

Rob and Shawn are exhausted beyond belief.

When the subject and verb are placed close together in the sentence, chances are you'll have the correct subject/verb agreement. Other times, though, the verb will end up further away from the subject; you may have five or even fifteen words between the subject and the verb. In those instances, it's more likely that a subject/verb agreement error will occur.

Example 1

Subject/verb agreement error:

The computer desk, littered with dog-eared romance novels and burger wrappers, are the last place I would like to work.

What is the subject? Which word is the verb that needs to be brought into agreement with the subject?

Correct:

The computer desk, littered with dog-eared romance novels and burger wrappers, is the last place I would like to work.

Example 2

Subject/verb agreement error:

He know he need to be back before the concert.

This sentence contains not one but two subject/verb agreement errors. Did you catch both of them? In this sentence, both errors resulted from what is sometimes called a "dropped *s*." This occurs when one's spoken English frequently includes the dropping of word endings, including the *s* that appears at the end of many verbs.

Correct:

He knows he needs to be back before the concert.

Suggestion Box: How to Fix Subject/Verb Agreement Errors

Most of the time, reading your paper out loud—slowly—is one of the best methods for finding subject/verb agreement errors. Often, your ears will help you notice that something doesn't sound quite right. If, however, you believe your spoken English is not standard, asking someone else to read your paper out loud can be another way to get at the same problem.

Here are a couple other methods that should help.
1. **Find your subject and circle it.** Hint: The subject will never be part of a

prepositional phrase. Prepositions include words such as *around*, *out*, *in*, *up*, *down*, *behind*, *to*, *alongside*. An easy way to remember this: Prepositions are anyplace a mouse can run (into a cabinet, beneath the car, across the driveway, etc.), plus the word *of*, the stray preposition that has nothing to do with mice running around.

2. **Identify and underline all the verbs (action verbs and linking verbs) in the sentence.** You will want to underline *all* verbs because the verb that actually belongs to your subject may be hidden away in a distant part of the sentence.
3. **Read the subject out loud along with its possible verb partners.** Do this test for each possible combination of subject and verb. Which verb makes the most sense with the subject?

Once you've located the verb partner for the subject, check the verb's form. Make sure the verb's form (especially its ending) matches the subject. Change the verb form if necessary so it will agree with the subject.

Verb Tense Errors

Writers use a variety of **verb tenses** in sentences. Which verb tense is used depends on several things, the most important of which is when the events in the sentence take place. Here are the most common verb tenses.

- **Present tense** is used when the situation is happening now or is ongoing.

  - The phone is fully charged.
  - She works in the testing center at Lincoln University.

- **Past tense** is used when the situation happened in the past.

  - Rachel hated playing Monopoly as a kid.
  - The game always took three or four hours, and she found herself falling asleep before it was over.

- **Future tense** is used when the writer is projecting into the future—even two minutes in the future.

  - The library will close in five minutes.
  - Fifteen years from now, I may live in Colorado or New Mexico.

Writers sometimes also combine the verbs *have* or *be* with another verb to create a few other verb tenses, usually known as "perfect" tenses.

  - You will have grown tired of Halloween candy long before the supply runs out.
  - Ten years from now, he will be well into his career.

When writing your first draft, you probably didn't stop to think carefully about the verb tenses you were using. That's as it should be, of course. During the editing stage, however, verb tenses do deserve your attention. What you will want to keep an eye out for are shifts in verb tense that occur for no good reason—shifts that make the writing sound inconsistent or confusing. Here are some examples of such shifts.

Example 1

Verb tense error:

The varsity basketball team had enthusiastic players last year. My cousin Kristopher, who worked a part-time job and maintained a good grade point, managed to never miss a practice. At the start of every game, there he is, bounding out on to the court, smiling his smile, ready for the game. He grabs the ball when it's passed to him, and before you know it, he's sunk another basket, his fiftieth of the season.

What verb tense is used for the first part of this passage? Where does the writer shift into a different tense? What advice would you offer this writer?

Correct:

The varsity basketball team had enthusiastic players last year. My cousin Kristopher, who worked a part-time job and maintained a good grade point, managed to never miss a practice. At the start of every game, there he was, bounding out on to the court, smiling his smile, ready for the game. He grabbed the ball when it was passed to him, and before you knew it, he had sunk another basket, his fiftieth of the season.

Example 2

Verb tense error:

Working as a paramedic is challenging work. The paramedic constantly needs to be ready to spring into action; she needs to be ready to make good judgments. Perhaps the patient was in poor shape when the paramedic arrived on the scene. The paramedic had to figure out how to stabilize the patient and get him ready for transport to the hospital.

Correct:

Working as a paramedic is challenging work. The paramedic constantly needs to be ready to spring into action; she needs to be ready to make good judgments. Perhaps the patient is in poor shape when the paramedic arrives on the scene. The paramedic has to figure out how to stabilize the patient and get him ready for transport to the hospital.

Most verbs follow a fairly predictable pattern when you are trying to figure out the right verb tense in a sentence. For instance, the verb *cry* takes these forms: *cry* (present); *cried* (past); and *will cry* (future). Verbs that follow a predictable pattern are called **regular verbs**.

Some verbs, however, change much more dramatically from one tense to another. For instance, the verb *drink* ends up evolving: *drink* (present); *drank* (past); *will drink* (future). There are too many irregular verbs to list here, but you can find a good list of them by typing *irregular verbs English* into any search engine. If in doubt about whether you have the correct form of a verb, look it up in a dictionary or online to see if it's an irregular verb.

Suggestion Box: How to Fix Verb Tense Errors

This is another time when the secret to good editing involves looking for patterns. The steps below will help you begin to notice how you are using verbs in your paper; these steps will also give you a start on fixing verb tense errors.

1. **Circle each verb in your sentences.** Do so for linking verbs as well as action verbs. Every verb gets circled.
2. **Draw a line from each verb to the margin, then mark the tense of each verb you see**: present, past, or future.
3. **Figure out which tense pops up most frequently in that passage.** Decide whether or not that tense is most appropriate for the situation you're discussing in the passage.
4. **Notice which verbs in that passage are exceptions**—that is, which verbs use a different tense. Look extra closely at those verbs. Ask yourself whether there's a good reason (a reason you can name) why those verbs use a different tense. If you're satisfied with the reason, you'll probably want to leave the verb alone. If there seems to be no good reason for the shift in tense, you will likely need to fix the verb.

Fixing Problems with Pronouns

We mentioned in the subject/verb agreement section that **pronouns** are words that stand in for nouns. A few examples of pronouns: *he, she, it, one, someone, anything, everyone*. Pronouns come in handy because our sentences would sound clunky and boring if we had to repeat the same noun over and over, such as in this passage:

> My lawnmower sounds like my lawnmower is about to explode. I vaguely recall hitting a rock with my lawnmower last October, and now my lawnmower might be beyond repair. I think I'll have to get a new lawnmower before summer.

This next version sounds better, thanks to the pronouns we've used. We'll italicize the pronouns so you'll notice them better. (Of course, there are many other fine pronouns out there that we don't have space for here.)

> My lawnmower sounds like *it's* about to explode. I vaguely recall hitting a rock with *it* last October, and now *it* might be beyond repair. I think I'll have to get a new *one* before summer.

Vague Pronoun Reference

Sometimes, writers accidentally use pronouns in a vague, unclear way. When you're standing next to a friend and you say, "There's no way I'd want to buy that one," chances are good your friend will be able to figure which shirt (or car, or dryer) you're referring to. Maybe you've nodded toward a particular model, or pointed; or perhaps there's only one shirt on the counter.

Your readers, however, are much more at your mercy as they try to figure out what it is (or who it is) you are referring to in your paper. They need for you to be clearer, more specific, in pinpointing what or whom you mean.

Example 1

Vague use of a pronoun:

When I went shopping with my friend the other day, we ran into the most annoying sales clerk. She could not believe the way she followed us, constantly asking us if we needed help.

Try reading this sentence out loud. What might cause readers to become confused?

Correct:

When I went shopping with my friend the other day, we ran into the most annoying sales clerk. My friend could not believe the way the clerk followed us, constantly asking us if we needed help.

In this version, the reader no longer has to figure out whom *she* refers to in each instance. Readers will probably understand the intended meaning without reading the passage a second time.

Pronoun/Antecedent Error (Pronoun Mismatches)

An **antecedent** is something that comes before something else. In sentences, an antecedent is the word that a pronoun refers back to.

For instance, in the sentence below, the pronoun is *his* and its antecedent is *Bart Simpson*.

Bart Simpson has been a challenge for *his* parents for twenty-some years.

In this next example, *they* is the pronoun and *car stereos* is the antecedent.

Car stereos are one of those things drivers often like to replace, and *they* are also one of the things a thief is most likely to steal.

When antecedents and pronouns are matched correctly in number—that is, they both seem to refer to the three stereos, or they both refer to just one stereo—the sentence will make sense and seem clear. However, when there's a mismatch between the pronoun and its antecedent, readers are likely to become confused.

Example 1

Pronoun/antecedent error:

> A customer walks into an electronics store, and they are immediately drawn to the car stereo display.

What or whom does *they* refer to? At the beginning of the sentence, we only had one customer. Assuming the customer did not clone himself as he walked through the store, how did we end up with the plural pronoun, *they*?

Correct:

> A customer walks into an electronics store, and she is immediately drawn to the car stereo display.

You'll notice that when we changed the pronoun from plural to singular, we also needed to change the verb that went with that pronoun.

Fixing Problems with Modifiers

A **modifier** is a word or phrase that describes or clarifies another word in the sentence. Once you start to look for them, you'll notice modifiers in many sentences. In the following examples, the modifier is underlined and the word it modifies is in bold print.

> The **Ford Focus**, <u>newly washed</u>, looks better than the day you bought it.
>
> **Friends** <u>who are loyal</u> are the best.
>
> She'll be here in a moment; I just got a **text message** <u>explaining her delay</u>.

Modifiers are typically **adjectives** (words that describe nouns or pronouns) or **adverbs** (words that describe verbs). A modifier can also be a word or string of words that functions as an adjective or adverb, even though the word is not technically an adjective or adverb.

   Adjective examples: *green; cold; delicious; crazy; valuable; exhausted; messy*

   Adverb examples: *carefully; thoughtfully; quickly; angrily; enthusiastically; softly*

Misplaced Modifiers

Normally, you'll want modifiers to appear as close as possible to the word(s) they modify. Doing so will generally make the sentence clearer. Sometimes, however, you'll end up with a few words in between the modifier and the word it modifies. Usually this is not a problem, as long as the sentence's meaning is still clear.

That laptop includes a webcam, is blue, and weighs less than all the other laptops.

Most readers will recognize that the modifier *blue* describes the laptop itself (not the webcam that's built into the laptop). This sentence is reasonably clear, so the placement of the modifier is not a problem. (Of course, the sentence might flow better if we were to reword it slightly: *That laptop, which includes a webcam, is blue and weighs less than all the other laptops.*)

Sometimes (by accident) a writer makes a sentence unclear by placing a modifier far away from the word it is meant to describe. We call this error a **misplaced modifier**. Here are a few examples. We've underlined the modifiers in these sentences.

Example 1

Misplaced modifier:

I downloaded my music collection to my laptop, <u>which includes everything from 50 Cent to Mozart</u>.

The reader may be confused—at least briefly—by this sentence. It's the *music collection* which includes all that different music, but the placement of the modifier right after *laptop* makes things slightly confusing.

Correct:

I downloaded my music collection, <u>which includes everything from 50 Cent to Mozart</u>, to my laptop.

Example 2

Misplaced modifier:

He owes me seventy dollars from the last time he needed a loan <u>(a lot of money, as far as I'm concerned)</u>.

Correct:

He owes me seventy dollars (a lot of money, as far as I'm concerned) from the last time he needed a loan.

Example 3

Misplaced modifier:

Let's plan on working on our project on online dating at the library.

What's wrong with this sentence? (What does it suggest is happening at the library?)

Correct:

Let's plan on going to the library to work on our project on online dating.

Slowly reading your writing out loud usually will help you notice sentences that are unclear due to a misplaced modifier. If you come across such a sentence, circle the word that is being described, then underline the word or phrase that is supposed to describe it. Rework the sentence so that the modifier ends up closer to the word it modifies and the sentence sounds clearer. Test the new sentence out by reading it to a few other people.

Dangling Modifiers

Another problem that sometimes occurs with modifiers is the **dangling modifier**. A dangling modifier is a word or phrase that really has no word in the sentence that it can modify. The word that the dangling modifier seems to "point" toward is actually missing from the sentence, and the dangling modifier is left to just...well, dangle there in the sentence.

Here's an example. We've underlined the dangling modifier.

Bench-pressing one hundred pounds, sweat started rolling down his forehead.

The reader is left to wonder: *who* was bench-pressing one hundred pounds? Certainly not the beads of sweat. Let's fix this sentence so that the modifier has a noun (in this case the name of a person) that it can "point" toward.

Bench-pressing one hundred pounds, Larry had sweat rolling down his forehead.

We could also fix the sentence this way:

As Larry bench-pressed one hundred pounds, sweat started rolling down his forehead.

Here's another example:

Smoking cigarettes while pregnant, the fetus often does not gain enough weight.

This sentence makes it sound like the fetus is smoking a cigarette. This is clearly not what the writer intended. The following solution changes the modifier into a phrase:

When a woman smokes cigarettes while pregnant, her fetus often does not gain enough weight.

The second solution adds the missing mom and her modifier to the end of the sentence:

> The fetus often does not gain enough weight when a mother smokes cigarettes while pregnant.

If you suspect that a sentence contains a dangling modifier (or if your teacher has told you your draft contains one or more), underline any and all phrases that are supposed to describe some other word in the sentence. Then go looking for the word that the modifier is supposed to describe. If that word is not in the sentence, rewrite the sentence so that your readers will know which word each modifier is supposed to point to.

Fixing Common Punctuation Errors

Writers use punctuation marks in order to make their readers' work easier. Readers appreciate that effort. Punctuation plays a big role in fixing sentence fragments and run-on sentences (see the earlier sections in this chapter). A few other useful punctuation marks are also worth discussing here.

Apostrophes

Apostrophes (') are sometimes under-used (the writer doesn't put one in when it is needed) and other times over-used (the writer puts one in even though there is no ownership or contraction). You can learn how to use apostrophes correctly if you remember that they have two uses: showing ownership and indicating where a contraction has been used.

Apostrophes and Ownership: Another word for ownership is **possession**. An apostrophe helps show that someone owns or possesses something else. A simple example would be: *Tristan's cat*. The apostrophe allows the writer to create a short-cut. Instead of writing *The cat is owned by Tristan*, we can simply say, *This is Tristan's cat.*

This gets a little more complicated when the person who owns the item has a name that ends in an *s*. Let's just say that Tristan gave his cat to Charles. Now the cat belongs to Charles. It is Charles' cat.

Where did the *s* after the apostrophe go? Well, there is a rule that when the name ends in *s*, the *s* after the apostrophe is only needed if it is pronounced. In the case with Charles, we don't say, "Charleses," so no *s* is needed. This would be different if Charles' friend Carlos owned the cat. Most people would pronounce the extra syllable at the end of Carlos, so it becomes Carlos's cat. (Whoever ends up with the cat, we sure hope it goes to a good home.)

When the person or thing that possesses something is one of the following **possessive pronouns**, do not insert an apostrophe or change the word in any other way. These pronouns already have possession built in:

your/yours   our/ours   their/theirs   my/mine his   hers   its

> *****NOTE:***** No apostrophe is added to *its* as long as the word is actually possessive. However, if the word is simply a contraction for *it is* (for instance: *It's about time you got an award!*), you will need an apostrophe.

Apostrophes and Contractions: Contractions are words that have been created by combining two separate words and leaving out one or more letters, which results in a shorter word. Apostrophes are used in these words to represent the missing letter. For instance:

She couldn't focus on her work. He tried to help, but he wasn't able.

In this case, *couldn't* is the contraction for *could not*, and *wasn't* is the contraction for *was not*.

Contractions happen frequently in our speech. In very formal occasions, speakers strive to rid their speech of contractions. Most of us use contractions on a regular basis in our speech. We even use some that are informal and unacceptable in standard English (for instance, the nonstandard *ain't* for *is not*).

Some teachers prefer for their students not to use any contractions in their writing. You will need to get a sense of which of your professors have strong opinions about contractions. You'll notice that we have used contractions fairly freely in this book. In the preceding sentence, for instance, we chose to have one contraction (*you'll*) while leaving one out (*we have* could have been *we've*). The choice to use a contraction or not is most often perceived as a stylistic choice the writer must make. When a writer does use a contraction, of course, the apostrophe has to be there.

That said, there are certain shortenings that should be avoided in professional settings. Take a look at these three sentences.
- He woulda avoided commenting if he'd known what would happen.
- He would of avoided commenting if he'd known what would happen.
- He would have avoided commenting if he'd known what would happen.

Only the last sentence is correct. The others are representations of what it often sounds like we say. In reality, though, the sentence is supposed to include *would have* or *would've*. The first two sentences would be considered nonstandard English.

Quotation Marks

When you want to include spoken conversation in your essay—or when you wish to refer to the exact words that another writer has used in his or her piece—you will need to use quotation marks. "Quotation marks usually look like this," your authors announced.

Quotation marks serve two purposes. First, they show that you are trying to give credit to your source for the phrases or sentences you've borrowed. Second, quotation marks make it easier for readers to figure out who is speaking at what point in your essay. It's still a good idea, however, to mention the speaker or writer by name. For instance:

Professor Hussain announced, "Next week's exam is the most important part of the course so far. Please be sure to study harder than you've ever studied in your life."

As you'll notice from the quotation above, we usually use double quotation marks (") at both the beginning and end of a quote. If, however, you find yourself with a quote within a quote (that is, one source whom you are quoting happens to be quoting another source), you will need to use a set of single quotation marks (') at the beginning and end of the quote within a quote. For instance:

Dr. Wreford once observed, "I used to abide by that old saying, 'Never trust anyone over thirty.' One day, though, I realized I hadn't been thirty in quite a few years; nevertheless, most days I trust myself a good deal."

Remember that quotation marks usually only work when they are used in pairs—that is, at the beginning and end of a quotation. Don't forget the ones at the end.

Commas

Commas serve a number of purposes. They come in handy when a writer needs to:
- separate items in a list
- make a reader pause after a long introductory phrase
- set off extra (non-essential) information from the rest of the sentence
- set off a word or brief phrase that interrupts the flow of the sentence
- join two separate, complete thoughts into a single sentence with a coordinating conjunction

Commas and Lists: If you need to list three or more items within a sentence, commas can help your readers keep track of everything. Here are a few examples of commas used as part of a list.

Jerry stopped by the store and bought a carton of eggs, a pound of goat cheese, and a bag of pork rinds.

Chantay organized her desk, checked her calendar, and packed her briefcase.

I'm trying this month to lose weight, quit smoking, and take my dog for more walks.

Lizzie sent text messages to Alicia, Denise, Dianna, and Chad before her phone decided to die.

Commas and Introductory Phrases: Usually, a long introductory phrase needs to be set off with a comma. Without the pause that a comma creates, the reader is likely to jumble the introductory phrase in with the sentence's main idea.

After the end of the space shuttle program in 2011, experts spent a few years debating whether the country should have invested more heavily in the next generation of space vehicles.

Without the comma that follows 2011, readers could easily run together the last part of the introductory phrase and the beginning of the sentence's main idea, ending up with a very confusing string of words: "in 2011 experts spent a few years..."

> During the five months I've owned my printer, the manufacturer has sent me twenty emails encouraging me to buy a more expensive model.

The comma after the introductory phrase (*During the five months I've owned my printer*) prevents any confusion that might result from the reader speeding through the sentence and accidentally stringing together phrases that are meant to be processed separately.

How long does an introductory phrase need to be before it requires a comma? Some teachers tell students to include the comma if the introductory element is more than five or six words long. That's not a bad rule of thumb. However, you may want to insert the comma after any introductory phrase that seems likely to trip readers up—even if the phrase is fairly short.

> On the roof, I find it impossible to not stare at the beautiful night sky.

Commas and Extra (Non-essential) Information: There are a few other instances where a comma can be used strategically to help readers process information in more meaningful chunks. That's the case when the writer decides to include extra information in the middle of a sentence—information that is not essential to the sentence's basic meaning.

Even though such information might prove helpful to readers, you can think of it as extra information. Extra information can be set off by two commas, one on either side of the information. For instance:

> Cable television, which has been around for decades, can cost more than a thousand dollars a year.

Sometimes a sentence will seem, at first glance, to make sense regardless of whether or not you set a chunk of information off with commas. At times, though, having those commas around the information changes the sentence's meaning in an important way. Consider the difference between these two sentences:

> My sister who is a doctor speaks Spanish fluently.

> My sister, who is a doctor, speaks Spanish fluently.

In the first sentence, the writer is specifying which of his sisters he is referring to. In the second sentence, the writer is including the phrase *who is a doctor* because he seems to be implying that it's a good thing for doctors to be able to speak Spanish. The two sentences carry different meanings, owing mostly to the two commas that set off the extra information.

Commas and Phrases That Interrupt Sentences: If you need to insert a word or brief phrase into the middle of a sentence, do so in a place where the interruption will not cause the reader to lose track of the sentence's meaning. Set the word or phrase off with commas on either side.

Are you willing, *Ms. Teele*, to accept a late paper just this once?

You should not, *however*, make a habit of turning your work in late.

Commas and Combined Sentences: Earlier in this chapter, one of the Suggestion Boxes showed you techniques for fixing run-on sentences and comma splices. One of those techniques involved coordinating conjunctions—that is, words that join together two things that are grammatically equal (for instance, two words or two sentences). Once again, here are the coordinating conjunctions you might use: *for, and, nor, but, or, yet, so* (the FANBOYS words).

When you join two complete sentences (two complete thoughts) with a coordinating conjunction, you will usually need to insert a comma right before the conjunction. Here are a few examples:

The library is on the south end of campus, but the career center is near the north end.

I need to complete my project before Monday, so I will be using the library's computers all day Saturday.

Notice that the sentence below does *not* need a comma inserted before its coordinating conjunction.

Svetlana is proud of both her Russian heritage and her taste in American music.

This sentence discusses what is essentially one thought—namely, what makes Sventlana feel proud. The two chunks of information that are connected with the coordinating conjunction (*and*) in this sentence are not presented as separate, independent ideas. For that reason, no comma is needed before the coordinating conjunction.

> **NOTE:** Many writers overuse commas. Frequently, writers misuse commas when they are trying to repair a run-on sentence. Remember that a comma alone cannot take the place of a period or a semicolon in a run-on sentence. Commas are light-weight punctuation; run-ons demand heavy-duty solutions.

Finding and Fixing Spelling Errors

We have good news: spelling has little to do with intelligence. Many smart people misspell words on a regular basis. But there's a catch: most of the people who do that come up with a plan for catching and fixing their misspellings. Taking the following steps will help you reduce the chance of a misspelling slipping into your polished draft.

Remember that every word deserves attention. When drafts are not reviewed at the word level, some misspellings slip in that are really **typographical errors**, or typos—meaning the error was more in the writer's fingertips than in her mind. During the final stage of the writing process, pay attention to each word in the essay. Watch out for those spots where *car* might accidentally take the place of *care*, or *gory* is standing in for *glory*.

Suggestion Box: How to Eliminate Spelling Errors

You've probably heard about the "i before e except after c" rule many times. We won't bother asking you to memorize dozens of spelling rules (though it won't hurt you if you do learn a few of them). Most of those rules are actually guidelines, meaning that there are times when the "rule" does not apply.

The strategies shown here are designed to help you notice—and fix—spelling errors that keep popping up in your writing.

1. **Use a cover sheet to slow your eyes down.** Slowing down is vital if you want to catch mistakes, especially misspellings. One of the best ways to force yourself to read slowly (instead of speeding up, which is what most of us do after we've been reading something for a while) is to grab a blank sheet of paper and use it to reveal only one line of type at a time. Start at the top of the essay's first page and work your way down the page. Reveal only one line of type at a time. Notice each word as you go. (Yes—using a printed-out copy in itself will probably help you catch more errors. Most people's eyes frequently miss errors on a computer screen.)

2. **Use spell-check, but don't rely on it for what it won't help you with.** Before submitting a final draft of a paper, you should always check for spelling errors. The simplest way to do this is to run spell-check. Spell-check is a feature on most word processing programs and is often symbolized by an icon that has an "ABC" and a checkmark near it. It may also be found under "tools" if you have that toolbar on your screen. When you run spell-check, a program on the computer will check to see if there are any misspelled words. For instance, if the word *misspelled* had just been spelled *mispelled*, spellcheck would have caught that and suggested the properly spelled version. Spell-check will help you catch many misspellings and typos. But it won't help you realize you've used *wind* instead of *window*. In addition, it may flag your last name as a possible error even though you spelled it correctly.

3. **Create your own list of problem words.** Most people who misspell on a regular basis discover that certain words give them problems. Maybe *tomorrow* is one such word for you, or perhaps *necessary* is your problem, or maybe you get confused over *which* and *witch*. In any case, start keeping a list of the words that frequently cause you problems. Then, after you've run spell-check, follow up by using the "Find" feature in your word processing program. Do a "find" search for each word on your problem word list. If that word pops up in your paper, be sure to stop and look it up, making certain you have the right word—and the right spelling.

Beyond the Essay: Writers at Work

KATRINA SINIFT,
Accounts payable for a feed and grain company in Tulare, California

Katrina's work as an accountant generally involves working with numbers. She processes invoices and sends out checks. This work involves monitoring accounts for an agricultural company. A vital part of the job is communicating with the other companies that her company does business with.

Most of her communication takes place via email. On a daily basis, she emails co-workers in her company as well as the companies they buy from. This communication takes place throughout the day via email, fax and memos. We asked her a few questions about her experiences writing on the job.

What role does audience play in your writing?
Audience plays a big role in my writing process. Am I writing a quick email to a co-worker to ask a question or get information? Then my writing would be more casual and something I would spend less time on. Am I writing to someone in management in the company? Then I definitely take time to compose a professional sounding email. Or am I writing to a company we buy from? In this case, it's most important that I'm sure to include all the necessary information and explanations to help them know what I am referring to. I should not assume they know what I'm talking about or how my company does things.

What tricks or strategies do you use that others should try?
I think the most important strategy is to find the strategy that works best for you. Not everybody writes in the same way. As you take writing classes, you'll be taught about different strategies. Try them all out and see what helps you write best. Here is one of the strategies that works for me: I find it helpful to just start writing, getting all my thoughts and information on the page without worrying about how well it sounds at first. Once I have everything down, I go back and structure the writing in the way it sounds best."

Any other advice?
Writing is everywhere; more than people realize. And when people are not working on a major piece of writing like a book or essay, they may not see it as "writing" and therefore don't take what they put down very seriously. I get invoices and emails all the time that have no regard for clarity or correct spelling and grammar. First of all, it makes the person or company look very unprofessional. It can also be time consuming if the errors affect the clarity of the communication. So good writing is a very important skill to learn, no matter how simple or basic the writing is that you will be doing.

For Writing or Discussion:

1. "Katrina explains that different people she communicates with throughout the day require different amounts of information or professionalism. Think about the job you do or plan to do. What varying levels of professionalism might be required in that work?

2. Katrina says that "writing is everywhere, more than people realize." What smaller

types of writing do on a regular basis without thinking of it as real writing? What, if anything, would change if you started to regard it as writing? Why or why not?

3. In her advice to writers, Katrina shows that unprofessional writing can hinder communication in the office. How does that make the company as a whole look less professional and what impact can that have?

Proofreading: The Final Soundcheck

Have you been in a club or bar as a band was setting up—that is, before they started playing their first song? You probably couldn't help but notice that the musicians checked their instruments (any loose strings on the guitars? did someone remember to bring in the cymbals from the van?) as well as adjusted their amps and microphones. Proofreading is the writer's version of a good soundcheck. Before the show (essay) goes live, before the audience starts paying attention to the public performance (the polished draft), there are some things that deserve one more check. Now is the time to check—before the show goes live.

Suggestion Box: Becoming a Better Proofreader of Your Own Work

- Remember that proofreading involves reading your work slowly and carefully. This is not the time to skim. Proofreading is the opposite of a quick last glance at your paper.

- Use a cover sheet to slow your eyes so you will notice errors. Any blank sheet of paper will do. Move the cover sheet down the page slowly, revealing one line of text at a time.

- Read your writing out loud and read it accurately. That is, if your sentence is missing a word that should be there, read it that way—and circle the problem so you can go back and fix it.

- Ask a friend or classmate to listen carefully as you read your paper out loud. Before you begin, ask your friend to stop you when something does not sound right. Put a question mark next to any phrasing or word choices your friend mentions. Return to those parts later so you can give them extra attention.

- Take a break from proofreading if you notice that you're getting sloppy or going too fast. Mark where you're leaving off, then come back to the paper when you are

> fresh.
- Review the paper's heading and title. Make sure they are formatted the way your instructor expects.
- If submitting a hard copy (print-out), check to make sure your pages are stapled in the correct order.
- If submitting an electronic copy, double check that you are attaching or uploading the correct version—your latest, best version that includes your final changes.

>>> Exercise 11.2: Finding and Fixing Editing Errors

The following passage includes a variety of editing errors, including sentence fragments, run-on sentences (fused sentences as well as comma splices), subject/verb agreement errors, misspellings, pronoun errors, apostrophe errors, and so on. Virtually any error discussed in this chapter might appear in this passage. Use your best editing and proofreading strategies to find the errors and decide how you will go about correcting them. Your goal is to improve the correctness of the passage and make it easier for readers to follow.

Sometimes people shy away from using the technology that everyone else around them was already using. Its my belief that there are many reasons. Why people put off learning knew technology. One reason is that they were afraid that the new technology will be to difficult to learn. It often take courage for people to try something new especially if they feel they may embarrass himself while he's learning how to use it. On the other hand they may be hoping that the new technology is just a fad, if they give it a little time the new devices or software will just go away.

My neighbor is one such person. Tony is about sixty yrs old and does not think this Facebook thing is going be around for much longger. He says he's seen many popular trends come and go he even remembers when people bought these things called pet rocks back in the nineteen-seventies no one. Has one of those things around anymore. Still, something tells me Facebook is going be around for several more years. Or even decades.

Tony is also afraid that he will loose some of his privacy if he go online. Hes heard about websites collect information about the people who visit them. They wont even know that their informaiton is being collected. The companies that run those websites might be sneaky and they somehow manage to find out what town they (the customers) live in. Before too long they start seeing ads online that are for businesses located near them. There is some truth here, Tonys fear of his privacy being invaded is not completely unreasonable.

All the same, the Internet contains just as many benefits as pitfalls people who are not online yet may not realize this of course. That's why why I intend to ask Tony again if he wouldnt like my help in figuring out how to get online and use the Internet in a safe and enjoyible way. In the end though the choice to go online or not is his.

>>> Exercise 11.3: Starting Small—Pick a Paragraph

It's easy to feel overwhelmed when you know you need to edit your paper. Why not start small? Pick one paragraph from a paper that you have already revised thoroughly. Use the strategies and examples from this chapter to help you examine that paragraph and zero in on any errors that may occur in the paragraph. Focus especially on error patterns that have popped up in your writing in the past. Be on the look-out also for typos, those errors that sneak in even though you know how to punctuate or spell effectively. Make this paragraph as clean and clear as you can, and take your time.

>>>
Quick Editing for Correctness Checklist

Answer the questions below for your essay. Be as honest as possible.

- Have you checked your paper for sentence fragments? Have you fixed any that you found?
- Have you checked for run-on sentences? Did you repair each one you found?
- Did you search out and fix subject/verb agreement errors?
- Are your verb tenses consistent (except for those places where you have a specific reason for using a different tense)?
- Will readers easily know what each pronoun refers to?
- Have you watched for tangled sentences? Have you taken time to untangle any sentences that needed help?
- Have you reviewed the essay for basic punctuation such as apostrophes, commas, and quotation marks?
- Did you run spellcheck and follow up on any frequently misspelled words?

What Works For You?

What strategies from your past have you found helpful during the editing stage? What habits have you developed that allow you to find more errors? What new editing habits do you plan to develop?

Chapter 12: Editing for Style

At a Glance...

- Style is the *flavor* that readers get from your writing.
- As writers, you make choices; these choices can help you achieve different styles.
- Making your writing clear takes priority over other stylistic choices.
- Reading widely will help prepare you to experiment with your writing style.

For Writing or Discussion: *Think about a major project you (or a friend) undertook at some point. Make a list of the important steps that had to be tended to during the project, the parts of the project that could not be left undone. Then make another list—this time of the special touches, the optional elements that became a source of pride in the project or made that project different from how another person would have tackled that project. What were the special touches? Were they worth the trouble? Why or why?*

What Editing for Style is and Why it Matters

When you have revised your paper and edited it for correctness (see Chapter 10), you are able to turn your attention to style. Style has to do with how writing sounds and the "flavor" that readers experience in your writing.

Style involves things such as variety in the sentence types and sentence length; the types of words you use; and the tone you create in the paper. Some stylistic choices are made (often on the spur of the moment) during the drafting stage. Giving yourself a chance to reconsider those choices—and perhaps change the paper's style—means that you have even more influence over how your readers react to the paper.

No single style or approach will fit every essay you write. Different rhetorical situations call for simpler or more complex sentences, different word choices, and different tones. This is true for workplace writing as well as essay writing; for instance, a business's formal bid to take on a major project will look and sound different than the friendly newsletter or blog through which that same business maintains a connection with its most loyal customers. You'll know you are a strong writer when you are ready and willing to adjust your style to the writing situation.

One final point needs to be made before we go any farther: *Being clear is more important than having any particular style in your writing.* Nothing you do to improve the style of your writing should get in the way of the message you hope to get across to your readers. If you try a strategy from this chapter and find that it makes your writing more confusing, you should either smooth out that wrinkle or save that strategy for a different paper, one where it might be better suited.

Finding the Right Tone

Tone is how a piece of writing sounds; that's the easiest way to think of it. We all have some experience with tone. Most people recognize changes in tone when they listen to or watch someone speaking. Think about encounters you've had recently with friends, parents, siblings, bosses, teachers, or your significant other. Most of those individuals change their tone from time to time, from message to message, because they know that how a message sounds—how it comes across—is often just as important (if not more important) than the precise content of the message.

>>> *Exercise 12.1: What's the Tone? Where's It Coming From?*

Bring as many greeting cards as you can to class. (Used cards are fine; just be sure to black out any messages that might be too personal to share with others. You can also find printable e-greeting cards online for free.) In a small group, examine the assortment of cards. Pick a half dozen cards that are different from each other in important ways. Decide how you would describe the tone in each of these cards. Then (again, as a group) figure out where that tone comes from—what specific elements of the card helped create that tone. (Some examples of things that might influence a card's tone: the image on the front; word choices; the joke or sentimental message printed on the inside of the card; the color of the card; the fonts chosen for the card; three-dimensional features such as lacy ribbons, sound effects, etc.) Choose the two cards that are most different from each other and present your findings to the class. (You may also want to mention whom in your life each of those cards would or would not be appropriate for.)

When is Tone Important?

Some types of writing—for instance, the instructions for setting up an Xbox 360 console, or reports that explain scientific studies—are deliberately written in a toneless, neutral manner. (The person producing that writing, of course, may be excited about the topic, but she realizes that her audience is expecting a very factual, uninvolved tone.) However, in other writing situations, you will have a wider variety of choices available to you when it comes to creating a tone that works for your audience and for the goal you're trying to achieve in that particular piece of writing. It's a good idea to think about tone during the redrafting and editing stages.

Where does Tone Come From?

Tone is based largely on a writer's choice of words as well as the supporting examples and details used. Some words, as well as some types of examples, are more effective in giving readers a sense of how enthusiastic (or serious, or angry, or frustrated) the writer feels. Often, a writer who pays careful attention to tone can influence how the reader ends up feeling about the topic.

How do Writers Use Tone?

We're not suggesting, however, that you should try to play mind games with your readers. It's easy, though, for writers to accidentally create a tone that readers feel is disrespectful, even manipulative. For instance, writers sometimes choose to use words and phrases that are "loaded." Loaded phrases contain the type of words that are likely to trigger a predictable response, either in a positive or negative sense.

If, for example, a speaker refers to another's political position as "anti-woman" "or "anti-gay," it's a safe bet that the person whose position has been described that way is likely to take offense. Similarly, when a speaker/writer describes someone as a "courageous, hardworking, patriotic defender of America's liberty, someone who is fighting for this land's freedom," the reader or listener may feel boxed in regarding how he or she is expected to respond. (We don't know anyone who proudly proclaims, "I'm totally against freedom!")

Sometimes word choices are more subtle—for instance, when someone refers to another person as *shrewd* instead of *intelligent*. *Shrewd* means intelligent, yes, but with the ability to scheme or get things done in a sneaky way. Those two words have slightly different connotations.

A word's **connotation** is the "baggage" or special shade of meaning that the word carries, beyond the definition—also known as the denotation—that appears in the dictionary. For instance, *full-figured* has a positive connotation, while *heavy* often carries more of a negative connotation.

Even within this range of tones, there's a continuum, or a sliding scale of sorts. For example, anger can come with different "volume levels." Quiet, controlled anger *occasionally* can be an effective tool in an essay. (When a writer discusses a recent injustice that has occurred and wants to encourage readers to take some action to fix the problem, a bit of anger may be called for—along with a very logical explanation of what exactly the problem is.) Anger can also come out, however, as full-blown, out-of-control rage, which may frighten readers rather than persuade them.

Suggestion Box: Strong Feelings that Arise in Your Writing

Most of us have had at least a few experiences, at one time or another, that enraged us. Writing—especially freewriting that is intended for the writer's eyes alone—can be a useful tool for venting during moments of extreme anger or when you are feeling sad or depressed. If you notice, however, that your writing frequently seems to be full of anger or pain, you should know that most college campuses have professionally trained counselors who can help you learn to deal with difficult emotions, especially if those feelings seem to be taking over your life. Most of the time, a conversation with a professional counselor remains completely confidential. If you are interested in meeting with a counselor to discuss personal matters, look for contact information and available hours on your college's website or ask your instructor for help in tracking down that information.

How Writers Control Tone

Tone is a product, at least in part, of how a writer feels about the subject she is writing about. Yet tone isn't just a matter of whim. Tone can be controlled. A first draft may end up with a tone that the writer never intended.

Sometimes, upon rereading that draft, the writer may decide she likes how the essay sounds, even though she was not aiming for that tone when she started out. Other times, however, the writer will discover her early draft contains a tone that accidentally crept into the essay and which she doesn't think works especially well. (Perhaps she let her logical argument turn into a sarcastic mocking of the other side's views. Or maybe she intended to write in a very thoughtful, academic way about the history of romantic love in literature, but the first draft ended up sounding more sappy than academic.) Sometimes, the tone of an essay will shift dramatically—and unintentionally—from one paragraph to the next. Essays are usually most effective when writers manage to maintain a fairly consistent tone.

>>> Exercise 12.2: Your Essay's Tone

Return to your own essay. Read your draft out loud and listen to the tone that seems to come through. Pay special attention to the introduction, but look at the rest of the essay as well. What tone comes across in your current draft? Are you satisfied with that tone or not? (How effective is that tone for the message you're trying to communicate, as well as the audience who will be reading the essay?)

If you are not pleased with the essay's tone, find the specific details, examples, or word choices that helped to create that tone and change or eliminate those elements in your next draft. Do the same thing if you find that your tone keeps changing from one section to the next.

Examining and Rethinking Your Draft's Tone

1. Read your title out loud. How does it sound? Serious? Joking? Full of boredom? Excited? Suspenseful? Make a note about the impression this title is likely to leave readers with—specifically, what readers will expect the rest of the essay to sound like or deal with after they have seen this title.

2. Read your first paragraph out loud. What tone of voice and what facial expressions do you think your intended readers will most likely use when *they* read that material out loud? Do your best to picture them (even if you don't know your readers personally) and to hear how they sound. Make a note about how readers are likely to react to this section.

3. In the body of the essay, pay special attention two things that might affect the essay's tone:
    a. Locate and examine any questions you ask your readers. Do your questions sound serious, as though you really want readers to consider what you're asking? Or do your questions obviously have only one appropriate answer? (For instance, "Are you in favor of children being severely beaten?") Is your question likely to be read in a sarcastic way? Or interpreted as a joke? (If so,

is the humor appropriate to the essay's purpose? Sometimes humor is useful in an essay. Other times, however, a joke can take a paper far off course.)

   b. Look at the examples and details you've used to support your ideas. Do they all contribute to the tone you were hoping the essay would have? If not, what changes will you need to your examples and details to achieve the tone you want the essay to have?

4. Read your conclusion out loud. Is the tone here consistent with the rest of the essay? Do you still sound interested in your topic, or will readers think you've grown bored with your paper, as though you're just going through the motions at the end of the paper? (See Chapter 9 for tips on writing effective conclusions.)

You can also ask others for help. Give copies of your draft to at least two (perhaps as many as three or four) readers, preferably people who do not know you well. This is one time when you will *not* want to read the essay out loud to them. Let your readers concentrate only on what they are picking up from the written page. When your readers are finished, ask them to respond to these questions:
- How would you describe my attitude toward this topic? (Not what my main idea is, but my attitude.)
- Was there any part of the essay where you wondered why the essay was starting to sound different? Where in the essay did you notice that shift?

Suggestion Box: What to Do if Your Tone is Too Informal

If your instructor or another reader suggests that your essay is too informal, changes such as these can make the paper feel more businesslike or academic:
- **Change second-person sentences to the third-person point of view.** The second-person point of view puts the reader into the sentence: *You should always charge your phone before going on a long trip.* Such sentences can usually be recast in the third person: *People going on long trips should recharge their phones before leaving.* Third-person sentences make an essay feel less casual.
- **Eliminate conversational words and slang.** A well-placed *Well...* at the beginning of a sentence can be a friendly, casual transition word; it doesn't work so well, however, when you're aiming for a more formal tone. The same would apply to words you might use with a friend but not with a boss who dresses very formally and speaks very seriously: words such as *yeah* (instead of *yes*), *grown-up* (instead of *adult*), or *rug rat* (instead of *toddler*). Also watch out for words that do not convey much meaning but only act as filler: for instance, the word *like* (as in *He was, like, going to call me*) and the phrase *sort of* (as in *I thought she sort of did not care one way or the other*).
- **Avoid using too many questions.** Asking a question of your readers can prove very effective, but it does give an essay more of a back-and-forth, conversational feel.
- **Eliminate contractions.** While there is frequently nothing wrong with using contractions (*they're* for *they are*, etc.), contractions do make a paper feel less formal.

Suggestion Box: What to Do If Your Tone is Too Formal

If you feel that your essay's tone is too formal, or if your instructor says that the essay is too stilted or full of something called "**Engfish**" (fancy-sounding phrases that really don't convey much meaning), you may want to consider trying some of the strategies below:

- **Aim for shorter sentences and/or shorter paragraphs.** There's no magic length for a good paragraph, but informal types of writing frequently employ short paragraphs, as well as a greater percentage of short sentences.
- **Consider using more humor.** Obviously, if you are writing about funeral directors' efforts at providing comfort to grieving families, humor is out of place. In a great many other situations, however, humor might just have a place in the next draft of your essay, as long as it works with your purpose for writing the essay.
- **Allow yourself an occasional (very brief) digression.** Digressions are also known as rants. As you might imagine, in a formal, business-like report or a very serious essay, there's not much room for rants. If you're trying to create a less formal feeling, though, you could always insert (perhaps in parentheses) a brief side-track that somehow—sooner or later—connects back to your main point. A good, brief rant is a chance to allow a bit of your personality to come through. Even in an informal essay, however, be careful not to go overboard in a huge way, and be ready to pull back in your next draft if you've gotten too far off track.

Editing for Word Choice

Writing almost always centers around ideas and experiences. Most writers don't set out to write principally because they want to create interesting sentences, or choose interesting words. Eventually, though, a writer's individual word choices do matter. Some words are more powerful than others; some words are more vivid. Some words are more precise.

As writers, we usually don't think of words as wrong or right. We think of words that are appropriate or less appropriate—effective or less effective—for a given audience or a particular occasion. The writer's purpose and audience (the rhetorical situation, in other words) play an important role in deciding which words might be useful and which words are best avoided.

Think about the list of words/phrases below. Some of these are more vivid, more precise, than the others.

> *airplane*
> *jumbo jet*
> *Boeing 747*
> *American Airlines Flight 1224*

The last three are certainly more specific than *airplane*. Even if you aren't sure whether Flight 1224 is a plane that holds 40 people or 400, you might still end up with an image of a real plane, with real passengers hauling real luggage, hoping to get to a real place before dinner time.

You can ask yourself other types of questions about word choices. For instance, imagine that a writer is thinking about using any or all of the terms below to refer to a twenty-seven year-old woman who is second-in-charge of the accounting department at a large company.

> *businesswoman*
> *girl*
> *lady accountant*
> *young professional woman*

Two of those terms (*business woman* and *young professional woman*) seem factual and fairly neutral. The other two terms will seem like a problem for a good many people in your audience. The word *girl* is fine for describing a child, but it hardly seems accurate for a woman who is in her late twenties. What's wrong, though, with *lady accountant*? Well, you don't hear people referring very often to a *gentleman accountant*. The term *lady accountant* seems to suggest that accountants are normally male, with this one exception. If you're thinking, "Hey, this is all just a bunch of political correctness," think again. We're actually talking about audience. No writer can afford to offend or turn off an audience when doing so is not absolutely necessary.

Using a Thesaurus with Care

Writers sometimes try to improve their vocabulary and amplify their text by consulting a thesaurus. The motivation behind this is great, but too often writers stop short of distinguishing the differences between words that have similar meanings—or how and when to use a synonym.

You obviously recognize the differences between a *shack*, a *skyscraper*, and a *garden shed*, but all those terms could appear under the heading *building* in a thesaurus. When you understand the terms listed in the thesaurus, you're on solid ground. However, when unfamiliar words appear, you owe it to yourself to look them up in a dictionary. You may even want to type an unfamiliar word into a search engine to see the contexts in which that term is frequently used.

Here's an example of what is often referred to as **inflated writing**. It uses language that is too formal or pompous for the situation. This example also misuses a word.

> On particularly **interminable** road trips with my family, I liked to **fantasize**, **scrutinizing** out the window. While my **progenitors** were in the front seat, I would be thinking about my possible **prospects** and dreaming of my **suitor**.

Note that this language does not seem natural. Some of the words are too formal for the situation. Others are not too formal but give the wrong impression entirely.

>>> Exercise 12.3: Rewording

How would you reword the previous example (the one that begins, "On particularly interminable road trips...")? Make your version clearer and more natural sounding than the original passage.

Good style includes thinking carefully about your word choices, especially the ones that might create confusion or hard feelings. And remember, this is something that can wait for the later stages of the revision and editing process. Word choices are not nearly as important in your first draft.

You'll find some more help with effective word choices by looking at the Glossary of Usage (Using the Right Word) in this book's appendix.

Suggestion Box: When Repeated Words Matter and When They Don't

During the editing process, writers often become self-conscious when they notice that certain words pop up repeatedly in their essays. You've probably learned that you should watch for repetition in your essay and eliminate it when possible. Generally, that's good advice, but there are times when you will need to use a few key words or phrases frequently in an essay.

If, for instance, you are writing a paper about *teenage parents*, it's likely—even natural—that you will use those two words frequently. (Other words that may pop up frequently in an essay on that topic include *adolescents*, *teenagers*, *teen mothers*, and *teen fathers*. Some variety is possible, obviously, but even those alternate phrases will likely be used more than once in your essay.) Readers don't mind writers using their main subject terms throughout an essay.

What readers do tend to notice, and frown upon, is when a writer uses the same descriptive words (adjectives and adverbs) over and over. For instance, take a look at these two sentences, both of which appear in the same essay:
- Caring for infants and toddlers can be a demanding and physically draining experience which leaves a parent fatigued for days at a time.
- Childcare responsibilities may have a fatiguing effect on even the most energetic person; the demands of infant care may drain the mother or father's physical or emotional resources.

When writers have lots of choices about the words they use to describe the parenting experience, they should not re-use the same words repeatedly. That's different, however, from a writer referring to *teen parents* nine times in an essay on teen parenthood.

Editing for Conciseness

Just possibly, you have at some point felt intimated by the length requirement in one of your essay assignments. Maybe you even thought about how you could "pad" the paper. Who knows—maybe you actually *did* pad your essay. (We won't tell.)

When you first start to write a draft, anything that makes your essay longer might seem welcome. For instance, the phrase *at this point in time* takes up more space than the word *now*. Similarly, *due to the fact that* eats up more space than *because*. Unfortunately, the more empty phrases you throw at your readers, the less attention they pay to your message. There are even a few different labels for those empty phrases: *wordiness . . . clutter . . . fat*. All these terms mean the same thing—too many words used.

Get into the habit of cutting clutter out of your writing. Go through your draft and mark words and phrases such as the ones you see below. Decide if these words are truly necessary or if your writing will be crisper and clearer once they are cut. (Count how many words a sentence has before and after you've deleted the clutter. You might have fun taking a sentence from 20 words to 14.)

> ***Do I Need These Words?***
> *awfully, extremely* (occasionally useful; often not)
> *very* (sometimes necessary; often not; be sure to avoid *very unique*—things are either unique or they are not)
> *in this day and age* (go with *today* or *currently* instead)
> *in the year 2013* (*in 2013* is shorter)
> *for the purpose of* (usually *for* works well)
> *in my personal opinion* (why not *I think* or *I believe*? or just skip the phrase altogether)
> *leads me to the conclusion that* (go with *I think*)
> *on account of the fact that* (try *because*)
> *for all intents and purposes* (probably just skip the phrase)

Editing for Clarity

You will write many fine, clear sentences in your life. And, like the rest of us, you will occasionally write a sentence that seems to trip all over itself, a sentence that gets more confusing the longer it goes on. (If you write enough sentences, a few of them are bound to be clunkers.)

One of our colleagues refers to such sentences as **tangled sentences**. Tangled sentences come in many different shapes. Frequently, they are very long sentences—though not every long sentence is a tangled sentence. A sentence can be long, complex, and very clear. Tangled sentences, by contrast, are just very confusing. Readers get tripped up in tangled sentences; in fact, the writer often gets tripped up, too.

Here are two examples of tangled sentences from students' essays:

> A child today often wants his or her first cell phone before facing the first pimple or the first shave, because all of the child's peers seem to have phones and if technology is a part of being a tween or a teenager today, the child's parents are reminded that every kid just has to have a first phone even though the child is not sure why the phone is needed right now.
>
> We cannot eliminate traffic jams completely because there are jams that are caused by many different causes, including construction and bad drivers, so we should at least come up with a good system for warning you if there is a traffic jam a few miles up ahead of you on the road.

The best thing you can do when you come across a tangled sentence is to read it out loud, rather slowly, and ask yourself what parts of the sentence create the confusion. Draw a wavy line under those parts. Then, ask yourself what part of the sentence is most vital to the message you're trying to get across. Now, try rebuilding the sentence without looking at the original version. In fact, look away from it. As you build a new (replacement) sentence, be sure that the vital idea from the original sentence is at the heart of the new sentence. Be ready to add in a few more details as necessary, but try putting those details in a different spot in the new sentence. Delete words and phrases that convey nothing of real value—phrases that only tripped up the reader in the original version.

Editing for Sentence Variety

Have you ever felt that an essay didn't flow well? Or thought that a passage felt particularly choppy or clunky? Sometimes this problem involves organization; that is, you may be presenting your ideas in an order that makes them seem disconnected. Frequently, though, the reason a passage feels choppy is due to a lack of sentence variety. Your sentences may all sound very similar. This is something you can work on while editing the paper for style.

Reading your draft out loud may be enough to help you notice that most of your sentences are too similar to one another. But we have two other strategies you can apply in order to figure out whether a lack of sentence variety is a problem.
1. Choose a page or two of your essay and count out how many words are in each sentence. Write the number of words just above the last word of each sentence. Afterwards, use the margin to list the different word counts you came up with. If most of the numbers in your list are pretty similar, that would suggest a lack of variety in your sentence lengths and sentence styles.

> hing -- which led them to do damage.   *16*
>
> What led these adolescents (which is
> genuine (if blood-free) aggression?   *18*
>
> plenty of studies showing how people   16
>
> when surrounded by a group of their   18
>
> mmon during adolescence, when a   15
>
> m and dad and define himself as an   17
>   15

2. Look for patterns in the phrases that you use to begin or end sentences. When you notice that a similar string of words (or a string of words of a similar length) appears in multiple sentences, make a point of underlining that pattern each time it appears in your draft. (If you happen to notice two different patterns popping up, mark the second pattern in some other way—for instance, with a big X.) Here's an example of a word-string pattern that a writer used frequently at the start of sentences:

> If people want to stop smoking, they...
> If this is ever going to change, teens...
> If society does not want to pay large health care costs, laws...

The more frequently your essay uses that particular type of sentence pattern, the bigger the problem with lack of sentence variety.

Having a number of sentences that are set up in similar ways or are approximately the same length is not an error, but a paper can start to develop a monotonous *bump-bump-bump* rhythm after a while, similar to how a car with a flat tire sounds as it moves down the road.

Improving Sentences That Sound Too Similar

What can you do if many of your sentences sound alike? We'll offer several suggestions here; in all likelihood, you will want to use not one but several of them to remedy the problem. (If you used only one of these suggestions over and over, guess what? You'd end up with lots more sentences that all sound very similar.)

Turn some very long sentences into two or more short sentences. If you do this, you will want to be sure that you are not creating sentence fragments.

Combine a couple very short or medium-length sentences into a longer, more ambitious sentence. Only do this, however, if you are confident that you know how to avoid run-on (fused) sentences and comma splices. Semicolons can help you in this task.

Add an occasional transition word or phrase to the beginning of a sentence. For instance, the sentence you are now reading contains a brief transition phrase in the sentence's opening slot.

Move a transition word or phrase from the beginning of a sentence to the middle of the sentence. You should do this, however, only if doing so will not disrupt the sentence's meaning.

Notice the use of the transition *however* in the middle of that last sentence. Here's another example: we could say, *In the unlikely event of a storm, we will hold the Fourth of July picnic inside; let's just hope everyone remembers to bring enough food.* Or we could say, *We will hold the Fourth of July picnic inside, in the unlikely event of a storm; but let's just hope everyone remembers to bring enough food.*

Make a conscious effort to offer readers a mixture of long, medium, and short sentences (not necessarily in that order) over the course of a paragraph. Of course, you don't want to move sentences around randomly. The paragraph still has to make sense.

Play around with loose sentences and periodic sentences. There's no need for you to memorize those terms, but the concept can come in handy. A **loose sentence** has the most important idea or fact near the beginning of the sentence. In a **periodic sentence**, by contrast, the main idea is located near the end of the sentence. Can you see how you might end up with a more interesting rhythm if you gave your reader two loose sentences, then a periodic sentence, then a loose sentence, then... ? There's no perfect pattern, of course; the idea here is variety. Obviously, it's even more important that your writing makes sense. Be sure not to place so much emphasis on the types of sentences you're using that your point gets lost.

>>> Exercise 12.4: Add Variety—But Make It Clear

Choose one paragraph (ideally, a well-developed paragraph) from the paper you are working on right now. Decide whether you want to focus on varying sentence lengths or sentence patterns.

Use the appropriate methods from this section of *Use What Works* to add more variety to your sentences in this paragraph. Be sure, above all, that your writing is clear. (Being clear is even more important than being interesting!) When you are finished, repeat the process with another paragraph.

Suggestion Box: R U txting 2 much?

Between text-messaging, Twitter, and Facebook, today's students make a regular habit of using electronic short hand. It comes as no surprise that when this habit is second-nature, it slips into other forms of written communication as well.

If u find urself using shortcuts n ur writing, then u'll need 2 b more vigilant about checking 4 it when editing. One way to do this is to use the search feature in your word processor to look for the most commonly used terms. As there are so many, a thorough reading of the paper for just this issue is probably a good idea.

Getting Active Voice into Your Writing

Audiences love action. Many readers enjoy writing that causes them to question their beliefs. People want a sense of completion at the end of an essay.

All those things are true, most likely. But what if we expressed them this way?

> Action is loved by audiences.
> Writing that makes them question their beliefs is enjoyed by many readers.
> A sense of completion at the end of an essay is wanted by people.

The sentences above convey the same basics thoughts as the original versions, but something is missing: the sense of people doing things, the sense of people really enjoying things. The sentences above are in the **passive voice**—meaning that the people in the sentences are shown in a fairly passive role. Passive voice is not an error; it is, however, a stylistic feature that tends to drain the energy out of sentences. This is especially true when multiple passive voice sentences appear in a row or when several appear in a paragraph.

When writers use the **active voice** in their sentences, we get the sense that the people in those sentences have some life in them. With the active voice, we have someone performing an action or someone experiencing a thought or feeling. On the other hand, when the passive voice is used, the sentence is constructed in such a way that the person performing the action receives less attention.

Active Voice	**Passive Voice**
Michael scored a touchdown.	A touchdown was scored by Michael.
Kevin provided great computer advice.	Great computer advice was provided by Kevin.
The doctor remembered her ID at the last moment.	Her ID was remembered by the doctor at the last moment.
The photographer snapped eighty pictures.	Eighty pictures were snapped by the photographer.

Most of the time, the active voice results in more energetic writing. As you'll notice from the examples above, active voice sentences are usually briefer and more direct. Your writing will "pop" more when you find opportunities to edit out passive voice and replace it with the active voice.

Sometimes you'll notice the passive voice creeping into a sentence as soon as the sentence begins. Whenever you see a sentence that begins with one of the following constructions, you have a passive voice sentence:

> *There is...*   *There are...*
> *There was...*   *There were...*

Again, passive voice is not a matter of a sentence being incorrect, and sometimes a sentence does sound better—or conveys its meaning more effectively—in the passive voice. (In fact, we've used some passive voice on this page, and we're not about to beat ourselves up over that.) Look at the following passive voice sentence, for example, where we might actually want the emphasis to be on the gift rather than the unknown driver who delivered it.

> The battered hockey stick—signed on the blade by Wayne Gretzky—was delivered to my front door by a UPS driver the night before my birthday.

It's also true that most of us have occasionally chosen to use the passive voice (even if we didn't know that term) because we weren't eager to take responsibility for our actions.

> Mom, your vase of flowers got knocked over a few hours ago.
> Exactly *who* knocked it over? Hmm...

> The fee was increased from five dollars to fifteen dollars.
> No human beings were involved in making this decision? Really?

> Mistakes were made.
> Indeed, plenty of mistakes were probably made. However, readers are bound to ask themselves who made those mistakes, and why hasn't that individual admitted responsibility? This is a use of passive voice that may irritate readers because it borders on dishonesty.

When you see an opportunity to put more action into your sentences—or when you wish to put more emphasis on people doing things and/or taking responsibilities for their actions—look for passive voice sentences that can be improved by switching them to the active voice. You'll end up with writing that is more energetic and full of life.

>>> Exercise 12.5: Add More Active Voice

> Find a passage in your current draft that seems to contain several passive voice sentences. Examine each of the suspect sentences. Is the sentence really in the passive voice? If so, should it stay in the passive voice (as in the case of the sentence about the Wayne Gretzky hockey stick above)? Or would the essay seem more lively, more interesting, if you changed this sentence to active voice? Experiment with how a new version of the sentence might sound. Is the new version clearer? More direct? Shorter? Be sure to save your new draft of the essay under a slightly different name in case you wish to return to the earlier version.
>
> Write a brief paragraph in which you explain why you did or did not make changes to the passage you examined. Choose a few sentences to discuss in more detail. Paste those sentences into this paragraph, then reflect on how effective your prose is in those sentences. Be prepared to turn this writing in as a journal entry or share it with your classmates.

Noticing Other Writers' Styles

Reading widely will help you become more aware of all the choices that are available to you in terms of how you go about writing something. That notion applies to writing in general, but it's especially true when it comes to style. A writer reads lots of different things for the same reason an aspiring chef samples lots of different foods: they both want to have a sense of the possibilities that exist—and the sampling itself can be fun.

There's no need to put yourself on a rigid schedule when it comes to sampling different types of writing. Keep your choices open and let your curiosity and instincts be your guide. But just for a moment, let's imagine how many different writing styles you would encounter in a week if you had the following texts on your plate:

- Sunday: the first chapter of a book on an exciting scientific breakthrough (a book written for laypeople, i.e., non-scientists)

- Monday: a blog entry in which the writer turns his miserable apartment-hunting experience into something so funny that your sides hurt

- Tuesday: a 500-word article from a news website about changes in financial aid laws that affect college students

- Wednesday: the greatest-hits collection (in book form) of your favorite newspaper comic strip

- Thursday: a one-page excerpt from your Philosophy 101 textbook in which a modern philosopher discusses the role that ancient myth plays in romantic relationships in the twenty-first century

- Friday: five or six different reviews of last summer's big movie on a site such as Amazon.com

- Saturday: a profile of your favorite (or least favorite?) celebrity in *People* magazine or on the *E! Online* website

Obviously, you wouldn't be able to put all those styles to work immediately in your writing—certainly not in a single paper, anyway! But all your reading experiences should give you a sense that, at least most of the time, there's more than one way to write any document. When you've seen a particular style in action, you end up with a better sense of where and when that approach will work (and when it won't work, too).

>>> *Exercise 12.6: Start Small—Try One Technique*

As a writer, you have many choices to make about the style you wish to employ in your work. Sometimes, you will have a wide range of options available; at other times, your range of choices will be narrower due to the expectations of your audience.

In any case, you're wise to start small. Look over your introduction and apply a few of the techniques from this chapter to improve how your writing sounds and the flavor your reader gets from it. Once you're satisfied with your introduction, move on to the body of the essay. Edit for style over the course of a day or two if possible. Don't try to do everything at once. Start small and work from there.

Breaking the Rules on Purpose

Chapter 11, which deals with editing for correctness, encourages you to make your writing conform to standard edited English—that is, to free your sentences of errors and distractions that might cause most readers to say, "Oh, I guess the writer didn't bother to edit carefully."

However, there may be times when you have a very good reason to break a rule. Perhaps you're trying to create a special effect in your paper, and using an intentional sentence fragment (one that you included even though you knew it was a fragment) will help you achieve that effect. Consider the example below.

> *Sirens blaring. Trees leaning toward the west. Trash cans rolling down the street at a fast clip.* I didn't have the radio on, and no one had called me to warn me, but I knew well enough that this was tornado weather and I needed to get to the basement before one more minute went by.

The first three items in this paragraph are sentence fragments. The writer placed them there in order to help set the scene and create a sense of someone taking in these details quickly. Most likely, the writer is aware that he has fragments; he used them purposefully rather than accidentally. (NOTE: If your teacher points out a fragment which you wrote accidentally, we encourage you to be honest about it and try to fix it! Don't claim it was an intentional fragment if it really wasn't.)

On a rare occasion, a writer might even write an intentional run-on sentence because she's trying to show readers how nerve-wracking and endless and intense an experience seemed. Every once in a while, that approach may work and readers may cut the writer some slack. More often, though, such an experiment ends up seeming more distracting than effective. In that case, the writer can always edit the sentence in order to eliminate the distraction. She may still want, however, to play around with that passage and see if she can come up with another way to convey the feeling she was trying to create in the reader. Sometimes it does pay to experiment—a little, anyway—once you know the rules of standard edited English.

>>> ### *Quick Editing for Style Checklist*

Answer the questions below for your essay.

- Is the tone of your essay appropriate to your audience and purpose? Is the tone consistent?

- Do your word choices help you get your point across without unnecessarily distracting your readers?
- Are your sentences clear? Have you fixed any tangled sentences?
- Is there enough sentence variety in your essay to make it interesting and allow readers to avoid a sense of monotony?
- Do most of your sentences use active voice when possible?
- Have you eliminated clutter from sentences?

What Works For You?

Think about a paper you've written in the past or are currently working on. What techniques not discussed in this chapter would you like to experiment with in order to give that paper a personal touch or achieve some special effect? What strategies from this chapter might you also try?

Student Essay Walk-Throughs: A Collection of Multiple Drafts by Student Writers

This section of the book is the part we find most exciting. Many of our students have given us permission to share their essays with you. Even more exciting, though, is the fact that they are willing to share not just their finished essays, but some of their invention material and multiple early drafts.

Our goal in this section is for you to see how writing can improve over the course of several drafts. That's one of the most important truths you can learn in any writing class: Writing gets better the more you work at it. When you revise your essays in a serious way, your writing is more likely to achieve its aims with your audience and in your own eyes.

We also hope that this section of the book will provide you with an opportunity to see various writing strategies at work. There's no single way to write a good essay, as the examples in these pages show.

Questions for Discussing Student Drafts

The questions below are designed to help you as you read, discuss, and evaluate the student drafts included in this section of the book. The first few questions deal with essays in general. The remaining questions could be discussed with regard to any of the student drafts. Your instructor might ask you to focus on one particular draft (for instance, the second draft of Karlos Martin's essay, "The Helping Hand").

These questions are numbered simply for ease of reference. You or your instructor, however, may have good reason for discussing them in a different order.

1. How, in your view, should we go about defining what an essay is? What does an essay need to include? What's the difference between an effective essay and a great paragraph?

2. What qualities (traits) do you need to see in an essay if it is to stand a chance of drawing you in as a reader?

3. How important is it, in your eyes, for a writer to take a risk in an essay? What's the "down side" of risk-taking? Do you see the author of the essay taking any risks? How well did that decision turn out, in your view?

4. If you were asked to assign a grade to the essay, what grade would you give it? Why?

5. What aspects of the essay did you most focus on while reading it? How big a role did those things play in the grade you decided to give it?

6. What would you say is this essay's greatest strength? In other words, what is the writer doing well?

7. What advice would you give the author if he or she wished to improve the essay but only had one day in which to do so?

8. Let's assume that not all people read for, or value, the same things in a piece of writing. Look again at the essay you've just read. Invent a new audience for the essay. (For instance, if the author has written the essay for people who work part-time at fast-food restaurants, you might change the audience to owners of fast-food establishments.) What changes would the author need to make in order to appeal to the new audience? How could the author get the new audience to take the essay seriously, read it with an open mind, etc.?

9. If you knew that the draft you've just read was a discovery draft (that is, a first draft where the author was just "test-driving" an idea to see where it took her), how would that affect your response to the draft?

10. This question is the flip side of Question 9. If you knew that the author intended the draft you've read to be her "final final" draft (one she will not revise any further), how would that affect your response to the essay?

Alaine Loehr, "What 'We Are the World' Means to Me"

About Alaine's paper:

The assignment was to write about a song that was meaningful to the student [see sample assignment on page 261]. As part of her coursework in this unit, Alaine responded to three different questions about the song as an invention activity. She also participated in in-class discussion about the assignment prior to writing her first draft.

Alaine grew up in the Philippines and her first language was Tagalog. Because English was not her first language, she tended to make some mistakes with spelling and verb endings. Her ideas and details were very strong, as you'll see in the following example.

In a journal entry about this essay, Alaine said that it was more difficult than other papers she had written for the class because this time she needed to write about someone else's ideas instead of her own. She felt that working with someone else's ideas (the song) and combining those ideas with her own experiences made the paper more complicated than other assignments. She was very proud of the end result.

> Do you find it easier to write about your own experiences or to write about someone else's ideas? Why?

For more information about this song, look up the full lyrics online or view the video online. Make sure you choose the version of the song from 1985.

Invention: Journal entry

Title of Song: We are the World

What is the song about?

This song is basically about the humanity in this world that go through some suffering, or been involved of tragedy that had happen. We try to make it better, I know we can't replace all the lost they been through but that love, support and the caring will do as good. This will help them realized that they are not alone in this world. Its always good helping one another, because you wont know when you will need others help. Be opened mind and bring this world back to where it started, meaning: no more fights, stealing, violence, crime, kidnapping, pick-up after yourself, recycle, make this world a better place for us.

> Is the writing in Alaine's journal different from the writing in the final draft of her paper? How so?

After all, we the one that would suffer for all our carelessness in our surrounding.

Choose one meaningful line from the song to write about:

"As God has shown us by turning stones to bread. So we all must lend a helping hand."

I pick this line because it tells you right here, that if god itself who created us and this world, have a good hearth to turn the most impossible object into something that will benefits everyone, then I say we should have too. I know we don't have that power to turn anything into something, but a small change such as helping, caring, respect and love, I think we all be alright. We must lend a helping hand and don't expect nothing in return, this how you give and trust me, it feels good when you know in your hearth that you have done a wonderful thing to someone. God always watch, and he will bless you for every good deeds you made.

> **Invention:** Notice this part of Alaine's essay is planned during invention, but she does not work it into the paper until a much later draft.

What is the sound of the song and how does that help you to understand it better?

The sound of the song I picked " We are the World" is the sounds of the healing, needy, love and caring melodies. It brought out the words on the lyrics to come alive, it became more powerful message that it want's to bring. It will make you feel that your part of this song and even the one whose in need, its so strong and yet so gently soft, its mad and yet its a happy notes. The sounds itself will speak to your hearth, but with the words that supported it, it was a magic. Listen to it yourself, you will feel how I feel and to be honest, everytime I listen to this song I cried, call me silly but that how this song got to me, it touched me everytime. lol!

Invention: Informal Outline

Intro idea: Should everyone listen to this song?
How the song came about.
    Michael Jackson and Lionel Richie
    Lots of stars
    To raise money
    USA for Africa
Why I like it
    What happened: Mount Pinatubo
How the song inspired me and can inspire others

First draft

> When you read this draft, notice what you think the student does well. Which parts (be specific) make you think that the paper has "good bones" [see Chapter 5]

1   We are the world, is it the song for everyone? From my opinion yes it is. But is it the song everyone want's to hear? Then I would say no. I think for those who don't seem to like this song, or someone even haven't heard it before should at least give it a chance, so why not? If you give this song a try you might just like it, maybe its not the best song you have heard before, or maybe don't even want to hear it anymore after trying.

2   This song is written by Michael Jackson and Lionel Richie, it was sung with the biggest rock stars, pop, rhythm and blues, and country singers back in old time. They come together not for their fame but for the sake of others. We are the world is a charity song that was made for the super group USA for Africa in 1985. It was the biggest hit back then with over ten-million sold worldwide, also it became a team song for every tragedy that had happen ever since. This song still lives in my hearth; I know what it meant and the purpose of it.

3   I was in fifth grade when the Mount Pinatubo Volcano erupted in my country called Philippines. Everyone was devastated and tried to evacuate, people everywhere fighting and stealing food from abandon store. There where no lights, electrical wires are down and broken; the thick clouds blocking the sun, it was pouring rain and so as the ashes with it, then the rocks that about big as a penny. We all looking for a safe place to hide and rest but it was too hard to look for one, roof's are collapsing from that rain and ashes that turned into mud, it wasn't safe nowhere and everywhere you go there's danger. Light poles and trees are falling to the ground and people are getting hit by it, there were no lights and darkness was everywhere. I remember when we can't even tell the time, and what day it is anymore because there is no day time and it was like that for almost two months. People everywhere are missing and dying, some got covered with mud and some got collapse on by the sealing of their own home. When it was all over with, everyone finally step outside from their own little shelters or cars that we have turn into our own safe hideouts, and was just thankful for seeing and feeling the sun beaming on our faces again. Afterwards I couldn't believe my eyes, my hearth felt like it had drop on the ground and I couldn't breath. People are pulling their kids and siblings out from the ground, they would dig and shoveled the thick ashes that cover their family, and they were all died. All I can hear was screams from everywhere, moaning and crying. From that moment on I learned how to be strong, it's like I know how it felt to lose someone even without loosing anyone, I learned how to start caring and helping others even if I don't have to. By being so young and hopeless I became aware, it thought me not to take advantage of life nor take anything for granted.

4   I started cooperating in school donation activities and help those in need. I gave clothes, shoes, toys and foods to school and to help others that lost more than I did. This is what this song all about, if you can just feel how I felt, and for those people now that go through this, you will understand the purpose of it. I am not asking for a donation, it will not cost you to listen to the song either, but if you know the message it's bringing, you will appreciate it more. Let's be one, let's be more open minded about this, let's help one another and just give it a try.

Second Draft: We are the World

1   We are the world, is it the song for everyone? From my opinion yes it is. But is it the song everyone want's to hear? Then I would say no. I think for those who don't seem to like this song, or someone even haven't heard it before should at least give it a chance, so why not? If you give this song a try you might just like it, maybe its not the best song you have heard before, or maybe don't even want to hear it anymore after trying. My point is, I just want this song to be heard for its overall message even if the sound and lyrics do not appeal to you.

2   This song is written by Michael Jackson and Lionel Richie, it was sung with the biggest rock stars, pop, rhythm and blues, and country singers back in old time. This people not only known for their great voice and talent, but they gathered as one with no fancy clothing, make-up or bling, and not being able to shine like if they where in their own show. They come together not for their fame but for the sake of others. Each one of them had sung a line and you will see that they meant these words like of they were actually saying it to someone.

3   We are the world is a charity song that was made for the super group USA for Africa in 1985. It was the biggest hit back then with over ten-million sold worldwide, also it became a team song for every tragedy that had happen ever since. This song still lives in my hearth; I know what it meant and the purpose of it. Let me be more clear about what I mean by this, this is from my own experience and hopefully it will help people to appreciate and understand why I wanted this song to be heard.

4   I was in fifth grade when the Mount Pinatubo Volcano erupted in my country called Philippines. Everyone was devastated and tried to evacuate, people everywhere fighting and stealing food from abandon store. There where no lights, electrical wires are down and broken; the thick clouds blocking the sun, it was pouring rain and so as the ashes with it, then the rocks that about big as a penny. We all looking for a safe place to hide and rest but it was too hard to look for one, roof's are collapsing

---

Did Alaine add to the paper in ways that you expected? What would YOU have changed in between draft one and draft two?

Central Point, or Thesis: Alaine added a thesis statement.

Support: Added details about the group of people who participated. Divided one paragraph into two and expanded on each.

Purpose: Emphasized the importance of the song.

Details: When Alaine wrote this paragraph, she felt she said everything she wanted to say in great detail and in a good order. She waited to edit it until she was pleased with the rest of her paper.

from that rain and ashes that turned into mud, it wasn't safe nowhere and everywhere you go there's danger. Light poles and trees are falling to the ground and people are getting hit by it, there were no lights and darkness was everywhere. I remember when we can't even tell the time, and what day it is anymore because there is no day time and it was like that for almost two months. People everywhere are missing and dying, some got covered with mud and some got collapse on by the sealing of their own home. When it was all over with, everyone finally step outside from their own little shelters or cars that we have turn into our own safe hideouts, and was just thankful for seeing and feeling the sun beaming on our faces again. Afterwards I couldn't believe my eyes, my hearth felt like it had drop on the ground and I couldn't breath. People are pulling their kids and siblings out from the ground, they would dig and shoveled the thick ashes that cover their family, and they were all died. All I can hear was screams from everywhere, moaning and crying. From that moment on I learned how to be strong, it's like I know how it felt to lose someone even without loosing anyone, I learned how to start caring and helping others even if I don't have to. By being so young and hopeless I became aware, it thought me not to take advantage of life nor take anything for granted.

5   I started cooperating in school donation activities and help those in need. I gave clothes, shoes, toys and foods to school and to help others that lost more than I did. This is what this song all about, if you can just feel how I felt, and for those people now that go through this, you will understand the purpose of it. I am not asking for a donation, it will not cost you to listen to the song either, but if you know the message it's bringing, you will appreciate it more. Let's be one, let's be more open minded about this, let's help one another and just give it a try.

> **Unity:** Added information that connected the Mount Pinatubo experience back to the song.

Third Draft

> **Formatting:** Added a title

My Meaning of "We are the World"

1   Helping one another and giving that respect is always welcome and good for our environment, especially for people who's in need and had lost someone in life or going through hard times. We all go through life obstacles everyday, and its nice to know that someone out there are willing to help and support you in anytime and this facts are based on the song "We are the World". It was written by Michael Jackson and Lionel Richie. And it was sung by the biggest rock stars, pop, rhythm and blues, and country singers back in old time. This people not only known for their great voice and talent, but they gathered as one with no fancy clothing, make-up or bling, and not being able to shine like if they where in their

> **Organization:** Created a new introduction from material that was in the first two paragraphs.

own show. They come together not for their fame but for the sake of others. Each one of them had sung a line and you will see that they meant these words like of they were actually saying it to someone.

2   "We are the World" is a charity song that was made for the super group USA for Africa in 1985. It was the biggest hit back then with over ten-million sold worldwide, also it became a team song for every tragedy that had happen ever since. This song still lives in my hearth; I know what it meant and the purpose of it. I hope that people can learn from my experience and appreciate why I want this song to be heard.

> **Formatting:** Put song title in quotation marks.
>
> **Wordiness and Tense Shifts:** Eliminated both types of errors from this sentence.

3   I have a life experience that will support and relate to this song that I wanted to share to everyone. When I was twelve years old, I was in fifth grade when the Mount Pinatubo Volcano erupted in my country called Philippines. Everyone was devastated and tried to evacuate, people everywhere fighting and stealing food from abandon store. We all looking for a safe place to hide and rest but it was too hard to look for one, roof's are collapsing from that rain and ashes that turned into mud, it wasn't safe nowhere and everywhere you go there's danger. There where no lights, electrical wires are down and broken; the thick clouds blocking the sun, it was pouring rain and so as the ashes with it, then the rocks that about big as a penny. Light poles and trees are falling to the ground and people are getting hit by it, there were no lights and darkness was everywhere. I remember when no one could not tell time, and what day it was because there is no "day time" and it was like that for almost two months. People everywhere are missing and dying, some got covered with mud and some got collapse on by the sealing of their own home. When it was all over with, everyone finally step outside from their own little shelters or cars that we have turn into our own safe hideouts, and was just thankful for seeing and feeling the sun beaming on our faces again. Afterwards I couldn't believe my eyes, my hearth felt like it had drop on the ground and I couldn't breath. People are pulling their kids and siblings out from the ground, they would dig and shoveled the thick ashes that cover their family, and they were all died. All I can hear was screams from everywhere, moaning and crying. From that moment on I learned how to be strong, it's like I know how it felt to lose someone even without loosing anyone, I learned how to start caring and helping others even if I don't have to. By being so young and hopeless I became aware, it thought me not to take advantage of life nor take anything for granted.

4   I started cooperating in school donation activities and help those in need. I gave clothes, shoes, toys and foods to school and to help others that lost more than I did. This is what this song all about, if you can just feel how I felt, and for those people now that go through this, you will understand the purpose of it. I am not asking for a donation, it will not cost you to listen to the song either, but if you know the message it's bringing,

you will appreciate it more. Let's be one, let's be more open minded about this, let's help one another and just give it a try. This song became a part of me ever since that tragedy, and every time I hear this song that memories comes flashing back like if I was there.

5   If we ask ourselves, is this the song for everyone? From my opinion yes it is. But is it the song everyone wants to hear? Then I would say no. I think for those who don't seem to like this song, or someone even haven't heard it before should at least give it a chance, so why not? If you give this song a try you might just like it, maybe it's not the best song you have heard before, or maybe don't even want to hear it anymore after trying. My point is, I just want this song to be heard for its overall message even if the sound and lyrics do not appeal to you. From my perfective, I think you will learned and appreciate this song more if you become part of it. How about just dedicated it to those who going through rough times.

Support: Added this sentence to the paragraph to sum up the paragraph and show the reader what to think about the information.

Conclusions: Alaine added a conclusion that connects the experience and song to the reader more. (It gets deleted in the next draft)

Fourth Draft

What "We are the World" Means to Me

1   Helping one another and giving that respect is always welcome and good for our environment, especially for people who's in need and had lost someone in life or going through hard times. We all go through life obstacles everyday, and its nice to know that someone out there are willing to help and support you in anytime and this facts are based on the song "We are the World". It was written by Michael Jackson and Lionel Richie. And it was sung by the biggest rock stars, pop, rhythm and blues, and country singers back in old time. This people not only known for their great voice and talent, but they gathered as one with no fancy clothing, make-up or bling, and not being able to shine like if they where in their own show. They come together not for their fame but for the sake of others. Each one of them had sung a line and they meant these words like if they were actually saying it to someone.

2   "We are the World" is a charity song that was made for the super group USA for Africa in 1985. It was the biggest hit back then with over ten-million sold worldwide, also it became a team song for every tragedy that had happen ever since. This song still lives in my hearth; I know what it meant and the purpose of it. I hope that people can learn from my experience and appreciate why I want this song to be heard.

3   My point is, I just want this song to be heard for its overall message even if the sound and lyrics do not appeal to you. The lines that mean the

Titles: Changed the paper's title

Point of View: Eliminated "you will see that"

Invention: Created this paragraph from material found in her journal

187

most to me are: "Send them your heart so they'll know that someone cares. And their lives will be stronger and free. As God has shown us by turning stones to bread. So we all must lend a helping hand." This certain part of the song really got to me, because it was there when I needed someone to care for me, and I can only imagine how other people feel that go through these tragedies. Like it says, if God can turn the hardest thing on this earth and make it into something that everyone needed to survive, then I think we can do even the smallest thing to help others. I know we don't have the power to turn anything into something, but whatever we do that will open a heart of a child will make the biggest difference in the world.

4   When something happened when I was young, people were there for me. When I was twelve years old, I was in fifth grade when the Mount Pinatubo Volcano erupted in my country called Philippines. Everyone was devastated and tried to evacuate, people everywhere fighting and stealing food from abandon store. We all looking for a safe place to hide and rest but it was too hard to look for one, roof's are collapsing from that rain and ashes that turned into mud, it wasn't safe nowhere and everywhere you go there's danger. There where no lights, electrical wires are down and broken; the thick clouds blocking the sun, it was pouring rain and so as the ashes with it, then the rocks that about big as a penny. Light poles and trees are falling to the ground and people are getting hit by it, there were no lights and darkness was everywhere. I remember when no one c ould not tell time, and what day it was because there is no "day time" and it was like that for almost two months. People everywhere are missing and dying, some got covered with mud and some got collapse on by the sealing of their own home. When it was all over with, everyone finally step outside from their own little shelters or cars that they have turn into safe hideouts, and was just thankful for seeing and feeling the sun beaming on their faces again. Afterwards I couldn't believe my eyes, my hearth felt like it had drop on the ground and I couldn't breath. People are pulling their kids and siblings out from the ground, they would dig and shoveled the thick ashes that cover their family, and they were all died. All I can hear was screams from everywhere, moaning and crying. From that moment on I learned how to be strong, it's like I know how it felt to lose someone even without loosing anyone, I learned how to start caring and helping others even if I don't have to. By being so young and hopeless I became aware, it thought me not to take advantage of life nor take anything for granted.

5   I started cooperating in school donation activities and help those in need. I gave clothes, shoes, toys and foods to school and to help others that lost more than I did. This is what this song all about, if you can just feel how I felt, and for those people now that go through this, you will understand the purpose of it. I am not asking for a donation, it will not cost you to listen to the song either, but if you know the message it's bringing, you will appreciate it more. Let's come together, let's be more open minded about this, let's help one another and just give it a try. This song

---

Unity and Coherence: Changed the topic sentence/transition to make it less of an announcement

Point of View: Eliminated "we" and "our" to keep this sentence in the same point of view throughout.

These sentences get deleted in the next draft. Should they have been kept or was it wise to delete them?

became a part of me ever since that tragedy, and every time I hear this song that memories comes flashing back like if I was there. From my perfective, I think you will learned and appreciate this song more if you become part of it. How about just dedicated it to those who going through rough times.

Fifth and final draft

What "We are the World" Means to Me

1   Helping one another and giving that respect is always welcome and good for our environment, especially for people who are in need and have lost someone in life or going through hard times. We all go through life obstacles every day, and it's nice to know that someone out there are willing to help and support you in anytime and this is what I have based on the song "We are the World". It was written by Michael Jackson and Lionel Richie, and it was sung by the biggest rock stars, pop, rhythm and blues, and country singers back in old time. These people are not only known for their great voice and talent, but they gathered as one with no fancy clothing, make-up or bling, and not being able to shine like if they were in their own show. They came together not for their fame but for the sake of others. Each one of them had sung a line and you will see that they meant these words like if they were actually saying it to someone.

2   "We are the World" is a charity song that was made for the super group USA for Africa in 1985. It was the biggest hit back then with over ten-million sold worldwide-- also it became a team song for every tragedy that had happen ever since. This song still lives in my heart; I know what it meant and the purpose of it. I hope that people can learn from m y experience and appreciate why I wanted this song to be heard.

3   When something happened when I was young, people were there for me. When I was twelve years old, I was in fifth grade when the Mount Pinatubo Volcano erupted in my country called Philippines. Everyone was devastated and tried to evacuate. People everywhere were fighting and stealing food from abandoned stores. We were all looking for a safe place to hide and rest but it was too hard to look for one, roofs were collapsing from that rain and ashes that turned into mud. It wasn't safe anywhere and everywhere we went there's danger. There were no lights, electrical wires are down and broken; the thick clouds blocking the sun, it was pouring rain and also raining ashes from the thick cloud when the volcano erupted, then the rocks that were about as big as a penny. Light poles and trees were falling to the ground and people were getting hit by it, there were no

---

Fixed run-on sentence by adding a comma.

Tense Shifts: Corrected the verb tense: "come" changed to "came."

Spelling and word use: Changed "hearth" to "heart." Similar types of corrections were made in the following paragraph too.

lights and darkness was everywhere. I remember when no one could tell time or what day it was because there was no "day time" and it was like that for almost two months. People everywhere were missing and dying, some got covered with mud and some got collapsed on by the ceiling of their own home. When it was all over with, everyone finally stepped outside from their own little shelters or cars that they had turned into safe hideouts, and was just thankful for seeing and feeling the sun beaming on their faces again. Afterwards I couldn't believe my eyes, my heart felt like it had dropped on the ground and I couldn't breathe. People were pulling their kids and siblings out from the ground, they would dig and shovel the thick ashes that covered their family, but they were all dead. All I could hear was screams from everywhere, moaning and crying. From that moment on I learned how to be strong; it's like I knew how it felt to lose someone even without losing anyone, I learned how to start caring and helping others even if I didn't have to. And like the song said, "When you're down and out, there seems no hope at all. But if you just believe there's no way we can fall. Let us realize that a change can only come when we stand together as one." So from being young and hopeless I learned not to take advantage of life nor take anything for granted.

4   My point is, I just want this song to be heard for its overall message even if the sound and lyrics do not appeal to you. The lines that mean the most to me are: "Send them your heart so they'll know that someone cares. And their lives will be stronger and free. As God has shown us by turning stones to bread. So we all must lend a helping hand." This certain part of the song really got to me because it was there when I needed someone to care for me, and I can only imagine how other people feel that go through these tragedies. Like it says, if God can take the hardest thing on this earth and make it into something that everyone needs to survive, then I think we can do even the smallest thing to help others. I know we don't have the power to create something out of nothing, but whatever we do to open the heart of a child, then it will make the biggest difference in the world.

5   Because of what I went through, I started cooperating in school donation activities and helping those in need. I gave clothes, shoes, toys and food to schools and to help others that lost more than I did. This is what this song is all about-- if you can just feel how I felt, and for those people now that go through this, then you will understand the purpose of it. I am not asking for a donation, it will not cost you to listen to the song either, but if you know the message it's bringing, you will appreciate it more. Let's come together. Let's be more open minded about this. Let's help one another and just give it a try.

Many surface changes were made within this paragraph. Which changes do you think made the message clearer?

Compare the last sentence in Paragraph 4 to the same sentence in the previous draft. What kinds of changes were made here?

Organization and Coherence: Added a transition.

Parallelism: Added "ing" to the second verb to make it the same type of verb and keep it parallel.

Terrence Westbrooke, "Does Mark McGwire Belong in the Hall of Fame?"

About Terrence's paper:

Terrence was a writer who struggled with multiple issues. He was not a strong typist. This contributed to some of his mistakes and missing words. His sentences tended to run together, and his work always started out as one large paragraph. He also needed help with spelling and capitalization. This is all in addition to needing help with expanding and organizing his ideas. Terrence persevered all semester to make improvements in all of these areas.

First draft

Did Marc McGwire Confess To Get In The Hall, And Did Help The Other Major Stars In That Era

The question of the day is did Marc McGwire confess to his steroid use because of he knew that he had no chance of getting into the Hall Of fame, my answer would have to be no I think he he knew that this would be to much of a distraction to the St.Louis Cardinals as their hitting coach.I think Marc McGwire is a stand up guy and the interview was real contrite about his apology,I also think whether he confessed to doing it or not that he wasn't going to get in the HOF anyway.The voters pretty much has made their decision about McGwire and that decision is to not put him in with their vote.Now the argument that many would say that McGwire did confess to steroids because of his poor Hall voting percentage, and that he might come closer to the percentage points that he need to get in.Another argument that I have is why do they keep him on the Hall Of Fame ballot if he is never gonna get in the.I feel Like that keeping him on the ballot is showing that baseball itself don't care about the game as I think he deserves to be in the Hall with the numbers he put up in his career,as he is the only player in Baseball history to have at 500 home runs and not get in the hall and I think it is a shame the he isn't in the HOF.the basball commentators argument is that his numbers was tainted and that he might not have reached them numbers without ever taking steroid of HGH.I can see the argument from both prospective but what if he played the full seasons when he was hurt maybe he would've crushed the all-time home run record or maybe he wouldn't have hit as many home runs,I look at it like this his rookie year he hit 49 homers and that's was before he he had ever used steroids.Another argument that I have is did McGwire hurt the chances of the other stars in the Steroid Era ever getting

> Terrence did not know how to use spellcheck or grammarcheck on his computer. He was shown how to do so after this draft. This draft has many typing errors in it.

> This draft is an extension and revision of some of Terrence's freewriting.

in the HOF.My argument is that he didn't,remember McGwire didn't get in front of congress and lie about his usage,he just didn't answer the question.I think like McGwire,Bonds and clemons had a good career before they was accussed before steroids and think they deserve to get in the Hall Of Fame,but many argue that since bonds trainer was arrested for illegal steroids and have HGH,and the same year Bonds hit 72 home runs.Many say that Bonds career have been tarnished and that like McGwire they wouldn't vote for him to get in the Hall,but I say that Bonds is a Hall Of Famer,and that his career was legendary before the aquisations and that he will eventually get in the hall.Now Clemmons was the most dominant pitcher of era,and yes unlike Bonds his trainer was squealing that he used steroids and HGH at the end of his career when he played with the Yankees and his former best friend Andy Pettite also testified against Clemmons in front of Congress that Clemmons was lieing.My argument is just like the other two is that Clemmons was a dominant pitcher before the media was acussing him of his doping and that what I think might get him in.Now the media argument is how long was Clemmons on steroids before his trainer and Ady Petitte actually confessed that he and Clemmons was gettint the dope from the trainer.I also think that if you not gonna put people in the Hallthen strip all the records,awards and ect. from that era,I think all the major stars in that era deserve to be in the Hall,but with an asterisk aside their name because of the era they played in even is they weren't accused of doping,even if they will never get the votes to get in the HOF,and the voters got their reasons for not putting them in,but my argument is,was steroids going on in baseball before the actual ere ever thought of.Was doping going on the 1950's,60's,and 70's,when when they called baseball the glorified years,what if somebody say that Hank Aarron,Micky Mantle,or Willie Mays or any of the other HOF members was on steroids to keep their glorified career going what would the hall do then,or just put a separate wing of the hall up for the steroid era just get over the fact that they played in that particular era and say it's nothing we can do about it.

> **Paragraphing:** Notice the need for paragraph division and sentence division.

Second draft

Why Did Marc McGwire Confess:

1 Many have questions to why did Marc McGwire confess to his steroid use and did he totally screw it up for the other legends of the famous steroid era of baseball. He could've admitted to his steroid us five years earlier at the Congressional hearing, in which he told the congress that he wasn't there talk baseball's past.
2 Many people feel that Marc McGwire confessed because if he wouldn't have admitted to his doping he probably wouldn't have made into the hall. My argument is that he admitted b/c he didn't want this to be a distraction

> Terrence truly redrafted his paper by not only adding indentation but also adding new text, deleting text, and rearranging material.

to the St. Louis Cardinals now that he is the hitting instructor, and I feel that he pretty much know he will probably know he will never get in the hall, as the voters and writers pretty much have made up their mind not to vote Marc McGwire into the Hall Of Fam.

3   Another argument I have is that Marc McGwire does deserve to be in the HOF, his numbers speak for itself. His rookie year he hit 49 home runs, it take a lot more than steroids to hit home runs, you got to have great hand/eye coordination to even hit the ball. Just because you take steroids, don't mean you can hit a curve, fast, or change up pitch or everybody will be doing it. I also feel like that if the voters and writers not going to vote him in the hall then take McGwire off of the ballot, why keep putting on the ballot if you not going to vote him in the Hall Of Fame and I think is a shame to kill of his name like the way the voters and writers keep trying to do.

4   If not going to vote McGwire into the HOF then what do they do to the other great players who have admitted, caught or accused of their steroid use like Bods, Sosa, Clemmens, Palmeiro, Alex Rodriguez, and Manny Ramirez. Well if I had a vote I will vote all of the great players from that era into the Hall Of Fame even if many disagree, I feel either put an asterisk on next to their name or get a separate wing in the Hall for the steroid era.

5   Well the voters say numbers supposed to get you in the Hall, well is that is true McGwire have over 550 HR's, Sosa have 600 HR's, Clemmens might be the greatest pitcher of all-time, A-Rod have over 550 HR's, Manny have over 500 HR's, and Bonds is the game's all-time home run king so if numbers is what get you into the hall than all of the steroid era should get in the hall easily. I get tired of the voters saying that they won't vote any of that era in is b/c of the integrity of the game, well how do they know if any of the hall members didn't take performance enhancers, they didn't test for drugs back in those days.

6   For many who might argue against McGwire remember that McGwire did admit to his usage and didn't back down from it even if it was five years later and in my book that makes him a Hall of Famer.

> **Paragraphs and formatting:** Paragraphs have been created, but the indentation needs to be a full tab over.

Third draft

Why I think that Mark McGwire and the other superstars belong in the Hall

Of Fame:

1   Many have questioned why it took so long for Mark McGwire to confess to his steroid use, and many fell that McGwire could have screwed it up for the other legends of the most famous era of baseball (the steroid era). He could've confessed to the steroid use 5 years earlier at

> In each draft, Terrence deletes material, adds new material, and rewords what he keeps. Added material has been highlighted in this draft.

the Congressional hearing; but instead he chose to tell Congress that he wasn't there to talk about baseball's past, but only the present and. That's when many people thought his legacy took a hit; but not me I really thought he was trying to protect the game, he didn't try to tell on any other players, or he didn't write a book on all the players that he knew was using performance-enhancers.

2   I will start with, many people think that Mark McGwire only confessed for all the wrong reasons, like he did it selfishly to gain some votes to get in the Hall Of Fame and to stop people from talking about his steroid usage. My argument is that I think that Mark McGwire confessed to his doping usage for all the right reasons, he knew that if he didn't confess that the story would have not benefited the Cardinals, as in October he became the Card's new hitting instructor. I also feel that he confessed so that he wouldn't be a distraction by all the media, and he didn't want the players and hitters on the Cardinals to say why should we take instructions from a cheater and a fake, and he did the best thing he could've ever done by confessing and trying to earn back the respect of the guys he is instructing. Mark McGwire pretty much know that he's not getting into the Hall Of Fame, because I think it was too late for the confess, but even though I think he is a Hal Of Famer (which I would later explain) it's no way the voters would vote for if he confessed or not.

3   Another argument I have is I think that Marc McGwire deserves to be in the HOF, his numbers speak for itself. McGwire was a home run hitter before all the accusations about doping, in his rookie season he hit 49 home runs, which shows you it take a lot more than steroids to hit a baseball you got to have hand/eye coordination to even make contact with a baseball. Just because you take steroids or HGH doesn't mean you can hit a curve ball, fastball, or change up pitch or everybody will be doing it. I also remember after the 1994 player strike that Major League Baseball being surpassed by the National Football League and nobody was interested in baseball as they once was. Then came the 1998 season, all the hypocrites who is saying now that McGwire doesn't deserve to be in the hall was the same people praising him and Sammy Sosa in summer of 1998 as the two single handily saved baseball, you didn't hear all the criticism even though they knew both players was on baseball. The chase of Roger Maris was the only thing on the writers mind they didn't care if McGwire of Sosa was on steroids, bodybuilders or anything else they was caught up in the hype, every newspaper in the country was talking about the chase and not about the two being on steroids and HGH. So why when the players retire to be so hypocritical remember all the praise that they received about the two saving baseball, if they bats and the balls that they hit when both of the men broke Roger Maris record remains in the hall please tell me why the men that hit them ball don't deserve to be in the hall, that to me is some hypocritical thinking.

4   If you not going to vote McGwire in the hall then why would they keep putting his name on the ballot, I guess it to keep mocking his name

> **Punctuation:** Terrence added new material to this paragraph and experimented with new punctuation marks. Unfortunately, he made new mistakes, but he continued to revise.

knowing that it is a slim to none chance for him to get enshrined into the hall. What do they do with the other players from that era who admitted to doping such as Alex Rodriguez, or the players who was caught red handed as Palmiero, and Ramirez, and the players who was put in the same position as Mark McGwire was put in being accused before they were ever caught for doping usage such as Sosa, Clemmons, and most of Barry Bonds. Well if I had a vote I would vote all the in because they have HOF numbers, even if many disagree with my statement of putting an asterisk on this era that was accused, caught or admitted to using steroids their own separate hall away from the other members. Many feel the asterisk would put a black eye on the hall, and that if you give the steroid era players their own spate hall then that would be disrespect the game, well it's the voters who said that it's numbers get you in the hall well if the voters don't remember McGwire got 583 HR's, Sosa over 600 HR's, Bonds the all-time home run man single season and career of all-time, A-Rod 584 home runs, Palmiero over 500 HR's, Manny Ramirez over 500 HR's, well I guess their argument would be that those numbers was due to the fact that they took performance enhancers and I would say that is BS. How do we know that the players before them ever took steroids so that they could have great careers it was no testing for steroids we would never know, but if the numbers is what get you in than all the players I mentioned deserve to be in the hall of fame.

5   For many who might argue against McGwire and the rest of the illustrious steroid era, remember the 1998 season, when all you hypocrites didn't care if he used steroids to break the record and remember he said he used the juice in 1998 not 1999 when he hit 66 HR's even if he didn't break the record in 1998 he would have broken the record in 1999. I feel even if it was years later he admitted it, he could have token this to the grave, and to the voter remember what McGwire did for baseball in the 98 & 99 seasons so don't let your feelings get in the way and vote the man in. McGwire is the only player in MLB history to hit 500 HR's and not get into the hall, and that's a shame in itself.

> **Spelling**: The spelling has improved but is not perfect. There are words like this (token instead of taken) that spellcheck did not catch.

Polished draft

Why I think that Mark McGwire and the Rest of the Superstars from the Steroid Era of Baseball Belong in the Hall Of Fame

1   Many have questioned why did it take so long for Mark McGwire to confess to his steroid involvement, and many feel that McGwire might have screwed it up for all the other legends who either where accused or either admitted to their steroid involvement in the most famous era of

> This draft is the last draft that Terrence wrote of this paper for class. The draft is not perfect, but it is a vast improvement over his initial work. As you read this paper, try to focus on Terrence's accomplishments.

baseball (the steroid era). Many feel he could've and probably should've confessed to his steroid usage 5 years earlier at the Congressional hearing, but instead he chose to tell Congress that he wasn't there to talk about the past of baseball, only the present and future. That's when his legacy really took a hit as many started to believe that he was on performance enhancers, but not me I thought he was trying to protect the game, remember McGwire didn't tell on other players. He also didn't write a book about all the players he knew who were taking performance-enhancers.

2   The media think that Mark McGwire confessed for all the wrong reasons, like he selfishly confessed to gain support of the voters voting him into the Hall of Fame. My argument with them is that I think Mark McGwire confessed for all the right reasons. I believe that McGwire knew that his chances of being inducted in the Hall Of Fame are slim to none whether he ever confessed or not. In October 2009, McGwire was hired as the Cardinals hitting instructor and he knew if he didn't confess to his steroid usage he wouldn't have benefited the Cardinals or himself as a hitting instructor. I also believe he confessed so that he wouldn't be a distraction to the team with all the negative media if he wouldn't have confessed, and he also didn't want the Cardinals batters saying things like, "Why would we take instructions from a fake and cheater?" Mark McGwire pretty much knew his Hall Of Fame dream was never going to come true, as I think he confessed too late.

3   For those who argue about McGwire's steroid usage, remember the 1994 players strike when nobody wanted to go to a baseball game after the strike and baseball was being passed over as America's favorite sport by football? Then came the summer of 1998 when McGwire of the St. Louis Cardinals and Sammy Sosa of the Chicago Cubs both made a chase of the famous home run record of 61. Everyone knows that the Cubs and Card are the second biggest rivalry in baseball and this only added fuel to the rivalry. Nobody was even thinking about McGwire's or

Sosa's steroid usage, as the two single handedly brought baseball back to the forefront and also made the Cards/Cubs rivalry more intense. During the chase McGwire would not talk to the media while Sosa had as much fun with the chase as possible and the two became good friends. When the season ended McGwire would finish with 71, and Sosa would finish with 66.The next season McGwire would finish with 65 home runs and Sosa would finish with 63.Everybody was crazy about baseball again and it was all due to McGwire hitting the long ball.

4   The media says that the steroid use helped McGwire's numbers, but I can believe that he used the dope for his injuries as steroids help you recover faster from injuries and workouts. I also say that steroids do not give you the skill to hit a baseball. It takes skill and hand/eye coordination to hit a breaking pitch, a curve, or even a fastball. If that was the case everyone would be a baseball player.

5   Another argument is that not only does McGwire deserve to be in the Hall but the other players that have great numbers from that era also belong in the Hall, just based on their accomplishments and numbers alone. McGwire was a home run hitter before all the steroid speculation. His rookie season he hit 49 home runs and he followed that season up with 32 homers the next season. Barry Bonds numbers were Hall Of Fame worthy before his speculation, Roger Clemens was the most dominant pitcher before the claims. A-Rod, Manny Ramirez, Palmeira all had the numbers, but Sosa was the only shaky one as he had never hit more than 35 home runs before the 1998 season. If the voters are not going to vote these particular players into the hall then don't mock their careers. My solution is for everyone to vote them in the hall and either open up a hall for just the steroid era or put an asterisk next to their name, and state that these players were either accused, admitted to, or were caught using performance-enhancers but they deserve to be in the HOF as they say they all have the measuring stick numbers. I would also say that back in

the old days we don't know for sure what those players did or took to get their number to where they got them.

6   In closing, the steroid era was the best era of baseball, as the 1998 and 1999 season brought baseball back from the grave. All of these players would probably never get in the Hall because of the media speculation and claims. Bonds, Sosa, A-Rod, Palmeiro, Ramirez, and McGwire will probably be the only players in history to hit 500 or more home runs and never sniff the Hall, and Clemens will get in but not after he suffers like McGwire. McGwire will be the poster boy for the steroid era, but I feel it is a shame that the media has disgraced his career and kept him out of the Hall of Fame.

Questions about Terrence's writing:
1. Terrence was a big baseball fan during the steroid era, so he was able to create the support for the paper by relying on his memories of that time. Locate a place in the paper that could be stronger if Terrence had quoted an expert. What kind of research might be helpful in that spot and why?
2. Who was Terrence's audience? How much did his audience need to know about baseball in order to understand his argument? Which parts of his argument are most convincing?
3. Skim through the first draft of Terrence's paper and then skim through the final draft. What kind of work happened in between? Would it have been possible for Terrence to write the polished draft without writing any of the earlier drafts? Explain.

Evelyn Minick, "How Families at Home Cope with Military Deployments"

About Evelyn's paper:

When her instructor asked her to choose a topic that she had first-hand experience with [see sample assignment on page 255], Evelyn (whose husband had been in the military for a couple decades) knew she wanted to wanted to write about the military life. She began by brainstorming the following potential topics.

Topics related to military life:
--military housing (or on-base housing vs. off-base)
--military base = self-contained town
--stereotypes around military life/military families (how TV/movies get it wrong)
--having a family budget and living within it
--how families cope when loved one is deployed
--kids' adjustment to new schools (etc.) when military family is transferred
--the military tradition (multiple generations of your family in the military)

Invention: Freewriting and Brainstorming

Evelyn used freewriting to explore several of these topics in more depth. Her first two rounds of freewriting are shown below.

> How does alternating between freewriting and brainstorming help Evelyn find and narrow her topic? How does Evelyn's freewriting compare to your own?

First round of freewriting: Military base as self-contained town
A military base usually feels like a town in itself. The base is right next to another, regular town (usually—unless it's way out in the middle of nowhere), but it's almost like a separate town, a town that has gas stations and its own huge store (the BX). Also has its own fast food restaurants (example—Burger King). Its own movie theatre. Even has its own education center where you can take college classes (at least the bases I've lived on usually have that). What else does it have? Skating rink (roller skating). Recreation center/gym. Hill for

sledding in the winter. Chapel for religious services. Its own library (don't have to go into a separate town to check out a book—plus the base library can get just about any book for you). But it's not exactly the same as any other town. Security. Security like you wouldn't believe—for a good reason! Gates where they check your I.D., secure fences that they monitor around the entire base. People who have never been on base before are nervous about that, but it's normal for any family that's lived on base, any type of military base. I guess I've mostly been thinking about Air Force bases. Wonder if army bases are that much different. Are they laid out the same? (My cousin has been in the Army for nine or ten years. Should send him a Facebook message and find out how similar or different an Army base is from an AF base.) You can get what you need right on base. That's my experience. But would you want to always stay on base?? Me, I like to get out and explore—not just the base, but the town, the whole region if I have enough time and a car to explore with. Think I've wandered off my topic. Wasn't I going to write about how a base is like a town? But I'm wondering if I might want to talk about getting out and exploring the area...Maybe that idea will work.

Second round of freewriting—How families cope when a loved one is deployed:
Well, this is a complicated topic. It's not easy to cope when your husband is deployed for months at a time—or your wife, or your mom or dad I guess. (I could write about this from my perspective as a spouse who is not in the military but who is part of a military family. Or I guess I could look at it from my son's eyes. Maybe it's different for him. But how is it different? I should ask him I guess, rather than just assume I know how he felt when his dad went overseas...) Okay, so it's not easy. But I need to explore—I guess I need to write down some things that make it tough. For one thing—that person (your loved one, the person who is deployed) is not there to talk to. The simple conversations but the ones you have to have! Conversations about practical things...which bill we should try to pay extra on this month, or whether the car is worth repairing or not. But then there are the other conversations you need to have with that person. Telling them you love them. You can write that in a letter (email), but saying it to his face—that's different. And there's other stuff that makes a deployment hard for those left at home. The missed birthdays, or school plays, the excitement of a teenager getting her first job and coming home and wanting to tell Dad (or Mom) about it. It doesn't even matter how far away your loved one is deployed. (Well, maybe. Maybe not. If they're in a war zone, you'll worry more. But even if they're not—let's say they're in Florida and you're in Maryland—you're going to miss them and yeah, you'll probably worry too. How could you not worry!) On the practical side—having to do everything for yourself, going from being a two parent family in our case to single parent all of a sudden, at least temporarily—the parent who is not deployed ends up becoming the go-to parent every day of the week, it's all on you. But military families are

good at toughing it out. They support each other. They are there for each other. A neighbor will come over sometimes and help out the family by cutting the grass (when we were living off base, and the block was mostly military people), or babysit a couple hours. Military families all sort of understand what a deployment does to a family. It doesn't have to be an awful situation, even though it's not fun to be away from your loved one. Not easy for the person who is deployed, either!

She followed up this second freewrite with more specific brainstorming on military deployments.

Things the deployed person will miss:
Birthdays, anniversaries, maybe even the birth of a child, child's first words, loss of child's first tooth, parent-teacher conferences, some achievement (promotion at work?) of the non-military spouse, Thanksgiving dinner and the chance to argue about football afterward with brother-in-law

Struggles or rough times the family goes through on its own:
Illness (e.g., flu, energy-draining case of mono), disappointments (daughter or son with broken heart), death of a pet, getting bills paid when money is tight, balancing the schedule as a single parent, loneliness, maybe a sense of isolation if you don't know many people on base

Ways families can cope:
Letters (old-fashioned kind...handwritten!) and cards; emails and text messages; social networking (if the deployed person has access to those sites); cell phone; family blog; Skype or other video-conferencing tools; care packages in which the kids include something they've made

> **Organization**: Notice how Evelyn created categories for her brainstorming. Categories such as these can help writers create paragraphs in a first draft.

The invention activities Evelyn engaged in convinced her she had something worthwhile to say on this topic, and the topic meant a good deal to her. Before starting the first draft of her essay, however, she wrote a couple of brief notes to herself.

Message I want to get across to my readers:
It's sad when your loved one is deployed. But you can make the situation better for you and your family. That's what military families do.

Question I keep asking myself about my readers:
Will my readers even know what a deployment is? Not everyone has been in a military family like me.

Drafting: First Draft

> What do you think are the best moments of this first draft? Which parts were less interesting?

Military Deployments

1   As you can imagine, military deployments affect all the people involved, both the person who is deployed and the loved ones at home. A deployment can last from 6 months to 15 months (or even longer). Whether the person deployed is headed to Afghanistan or will be stationed six states away, there's a big adjustment ahead for everyone.

2   The person who is being deployed, for starters, will face plenty of packing and preparation. However, once they arrive at their destination, there's a good chance they may have a hard time dealing with the birthdays, anniversaries, and other milestones that occur while they're gone. (I know two men whose children were born while they were overseas; also, I know someone who became an aunt while deployed and the niece was walking by the time she first met her.) The military does a pretty good job of feeding its troops, but it's not the same as home-cooked meals eaten with spouses, children, and long-time neighbors. The deployed person faces challenges.

3   If you are one of the people staying home during the deployment, those long and lonely days without your loved one will probably be the longest 6 months of your life. Every day, week, and month goes by at a snail's pace and all you can do is wait, and wait, and wait some more. You might find it easier if you do not focusing merely on the end of the deployment and try to live your life normally by doing the same things you would normally do like running the same errands, going to school, eating out, and having fun with friends. But still, you will find yourself missing the person who is deployed, and you will wish they were present for all the occasions when families normally want to be together. This time is a major challenge for the entire family; you need to be honest with yourself about that.

4   Sometimes, there are sicknesses and even deaths in the extended family and you don't have a shoulder to cry on because your spouse or parent isn't there to help you get through it. Then, there's the stress of having to do everything by yourself like paying the bills, getting the car fixed, cooking, cleaning, driving the kids to/from sporting/school events, and getting the kids ready for school. Your kids will miss the family member who is deployed; they want dad or mom to be there.

5   Living without your loved one temporarily isn't all bad, especially when you work through it as a family. Sometimes families pull together more when they face difficulty, and a military deployment does count as a difficult time. Other military families, people who know what this experience is like, often manage to help out. Families survive deployments. It can be done. But the experience is not an easy one, and every family has to find ways to cope.

Redrafting: Outlining

A couple days after writing that first draft, Evelyn wanted to get a better handle on the ideas that had popped up in her essay. Consequently, she created a quick, informal outline of that draft's contents.

> At what other points in the writing process are outlines useful to writers?

"Military Deployments" – quick outline of what is in my first draft:

Paragraph one:
--how long a deployment can last
--deployments are a big adjustment (my main idea)

Paragraph two:
--person who is deployed has to pack, get ready
--they'll miss a lot while gone (special days, family meals)

Paragraph three:
--for ones at home, time drags
--still have to carry on with life (errands, spending time with friends, etc.)

Paragraph four:
--stressful situation for parent at home AND the kids

Paragraph five:
--not all bad…can work through it as family
--sometimes military families help each out during deployments

Redrafting: Reflections

After looking over this "what's in the draft" outline, she wrote a brief reflection in which she discussed what was actually happening in that first draft and what she was thinking about doing differently in her next draft.

I started off with just this general idea—deployments lead to a big adjustment. And that's true, they do require everyone to adjust. But even though I originally set out to cover all the people in the family (that is, how a deployment would affect the member of the military, then the spouse/partner, then any kids they might have), I notice that I spent a lot more time on how the family AT HOME adjusts. I guess I have more to say about that. I've been the spouse at home. Haven't been the one in the combat zone. I know from talking with my husband some of what he has experienced while deployed, but still...I think I really want to focus on the people at home. Also, when I reread this draft it kind of seemed like I was just putting three main categories of information in the essay (deployed spouse, spouse at home, kids) and it almost felt like three mini-essays instead of one essay where everything is pulling in the same direction. So maybe that's one more reason I should narrow my focus—so that I can go into more detail on the people who are left at home.

Redrafting: Peer Editing and Draft #2

Evelyn's peer group ended up pointing out many of the same issues. Consequently, in her second draft, Evelyn decided to narrow her focus. She also developed her main ideas in much greater depth. Her new draft is a few pages longer than her first.

> In Evelyn's first draft, her introduction refers to the people involved in deployment without defining those people at all. How is this introduction different? What is the impact of that change on you as a reader?

How Deployments Affect Military Families

1   Being a part of a military family definitely has its pros, but like all things, it also has its cons. Having a family member in the military also means that there's a 100% chance that they're going to deploy to an overseas location, likely in a combat zone. As you can probably imagine, deployments in general have a tremendous impact on families everywhere. When a loved one is deployed, it forces the families to live without that person for at least 6 months (in some cases 15 months), go through life without them by their side during special occasions (i.e., birthdays, anniversaries, holidays, etc.), and it leaves each family member hoping and praying that wherever their loved one is, that they're safe and out of danger. It doesn't matter if your loved one is being deployed to Florida, Iraq, or Afghanistan, deployments still give us (the families) a sense of loneliness when they're not around. Many of us with a military spouse or parent have

unfortunately experienced firsthand what life is like while a loved one is deployed for 6+ months.

2   At first, 6 months don't sound like much. In reality though for those affected, it seems like an eternity. Those long and lonely days without your loved one will probably be the longest 6 months of your life. Every day, week, and month goes by at a snail's pace and all you can do is wait, and wait, and wait some more. During those 6 months without them, days seem to take forever to finish and then when you wake up in the morning, you realize that it's only been a mere 24 hours that have passed. All you can do is count down the days, one by one, until they finally come home. I found deployments much easier to cope with by not focusing merely on the end of the deployment and trying to live my life normally by doing the same things I would normally do like running the same errands, going to school, eating out, and having fun with my friends. It's not healthy for you or the deployed member to believe your world would come to a screeching halt just because they're gone even though living life is much more difficult without them there with you.

3   Having to go through life without your deployed member by your side is the hardest part. Along with missing significant events like mentioned previously, sometimes, there are sicknesses and even deaths in the extended family and you don't have a shoulder to cry on because your spouse or parent isn't there to help you get through it. Then, there's the stress of having to do everything by yourself like paying the bills, getting the car fixed, cooking, cleaning, driving the kids to/from sporting/school events, and getting the kids ready for school. Speaking of kids, even they have a hard time coping with their parent being gone, especially teens. Teens don't have the other half of their support system when they are going through their hormonal changes and dealing with every day high school or even middle school drama. These are some of the most life changing, influential, and important years of their young lives and their mom or dad isn't there to help or just be with them when they need them the most.

4   And of course, it's hard for the spouse. They're missing their other half, the one they love the most. Their side of the bed is left un-touched, cold, and lonely and there's no one to come home after work and ask, like always, "how was your day honey?" But, like stated before, your world does not stop when your loved one is deployed. Sure, they may not be there, but you can still live a somewhat normal life or do some enjoyable things to fill the void during their absence. Some of these enjoyable things include allowing your kids into your room to sleep with you for a couple of nights, hanging out with friends a little more often than usual, having your kids come home and say "Hey Mom/Dad, I'm home! How was your day?" Although to some, these things may sound trivial, but for those missing their loved one, it really does help out a lot and makes things easier for all concerned. So, living without them temporarily isn't all bad, especially when you work through it as a family.

5   When you can't see them and talk to them every day, all you can do is hope and pray that they are alright wherever they are. Praying for their safety gives you confidence that God will be watching over them for you and keeping them safe, sound, and strong while they are away. Knowing they're safe gives you a

sense of security and a peace of mind. Because of the significant advancements in Information Technology, on days when you can video chat or talk on the phone are especially valuable, because you can actually see them, hear them, and talk to them in near real-time instead of just typing or writing letters. This way, you know for sure that they're okay and how they're doing. A simple "Hey, how are you doing?" gets everything started and you just act naturally from there by telling your loved one what you've been doing regarding work, school, sports, and other outside activities. You could go on and on talking about the simplest things and once you see them online and have their ear and undivided attention, you never want to stop talking and turn off that webcam. Doing so means you'll have to wait another week or two until they can get back online. It may sound simple, but those talks with a loved one deployed will likely leave you in happy spirits and feeling reassured which allow the rest of the day to go by so fast (as you reminisce). You know for sure that they're okay and that's enough to keep you happy. All we can do though is hope, pray, and tell them we love them as much as we possibly can. With the deployed member gone, military families must bond together. United as one, families can and usually do endure the 6-15 long months without their loved one with them. Although united, those months seem like the longest months that you will ever have to go through because life just goes by so slowly when you know that your loved one isn't there with you.

6   Hopefully this essay identified how deployments affect military families. As the above dialogue reflects, deployments don't always have to be doom and gloom. Of course it is sad to have someone missing in your life, but you can do a lot of things to take your mind off of the negatives and make the bad situation better for you and your family. You don't have to sit and constantly worry for them or isolate yourself from the rest of the world just because they're gone. You can do a lot of things to make the situation better, and that's what many families do. Overall, deployment has many effects on families around the world, whether they are positive or negative. Deployments are definitely something that neither the military member nor their families look forward to, but it is necessary for the safety of our families, country, and our freedom.

Redrafting: Instructor Conference

> Evelyn narrowed the focus of her paper. How did that help her to add more material?

At her writing conference, Evelyn's instructor told her he was impressed with all the details she had added to the essay. He also agreed with her decision to narrow her focus, since doing so had allowed her to give more attention to the people who are at home during a deployment. Later in the conference, he told Evelyn that her second draft seemed to jump around a bit. He also challenged her to try working more with third-person explanations (e.g., *Military spouses must learn to adapt...*) instead of using the second-person (*You must learn to adapt...*) so heavily. (Third-person language usually makes an essay seem more formal or academic.) Since this was something she had not worked on much in previous essays, she agreed that this challenge could help her strengthen her writing skills.

Yet Evelyn also wanted to keep some of her own experiences in the essay, since this was a subject where her expertise was strong. Her instructor encouraged her to use the first-person (*I, me, mine*) where appropriate, while using third-person language in other parts of the essay.

Redrafting: Third Draft

> Describe the cuts that Evelyn made between her second and third draft. Are they effective, and why or why not?

Here is Evelyn's third draft of her military deployment essay. This draft ended up slightly shorter than her second draft, but still much longer than her first draft.

How Families at Home Cope with Military Deployments

1 Having a spouse or partner in the military means there's a hundred percent chance your loved one will deploy to an overseas location, likely in a combat zone. As you can imagine, deployments have a tremendous impact on families. When a loved one is deployed, families are forced to live without that person for at least six months (in some cases, fifteen months); go through life without them by their side during special occasions (i.e., birthdays, anniversaries, holidays, etc.); and worry about whether or not they are safe. It doesn't matter if a loved one is deployed in Florida, Iraq, or Afghanistan; the deployment will prove challenging not only for the person who is deployed but for the family at home. As a military spouse, I have first-hand experience with this situation.

2 At first, six months may not sound like much. In reality, though, it seems like an eternity for those who are waiting at home. Those long and lonely days without the loved one will probably be the longest six months of a spouse's life. Each day, week, and month goes by at a snail's pace and all the spouse can do is wait, and wait, and wait some more. Days take forever to finish. At first, I thought all I could do was count down the days until my husband's deployment ended. I've found this is very common in military families.

3 Sometimes, there are sicknesses and even deaths in the extended family and the spouse at home doesn't have a shoulder to cry on. Loneliness is tough to cope with. This is only natural for people who are missing their other half, someone who is dearly loved. The other person's side of the bed is left un-touched, cold, and lonely. There's no one to come home after work and ask, "How was your day?" In addition to loneliness, the spouse who is at home has to do everything himself or herself, things like paying the bills, getting the car fixed, cooking, cleaning, getting the kids ready for school and driving them to and from school

and sports events.

4   Those kids are probably also having a hard time coping with their parent being gone. Little kids may be more whiney because the other parent is gone, or they may even forget (for a while) what the other parent looks or sounds like. It's probably hard for a young child to understand why mom or dad's job is located so far away. Military deployments lead to other problems for teen sons or daughters. Teens don't have the other half of their support system when they are going through their hormonal changes and dealing with every day high school or even middle school drama. These are some of the most life changing, influential, and important years of their young lives and their mom or dad isn't there to help or just be with them when they need them the most. As a parent, I know that high school heartbreak is very real. A teen's loneliness for a parent she needs to talk to is real, too.

5   Military deployments are hard on families, but the family's life does not have to stop when a loved one is deployed. For instance, I found my husband's deployment easier to cope with if I did not focus so much on the end of the deployment but instead tried to live my life normally; I once again ran my errands, went to school, ate out, and had fun with my friends. Families can still live a somewhat normal life and do enjoyable things to fill the void. Parents might let small kids have a sleepover. The whole family might invite the neighbors over to play games or have a special meal. The parent and kids might decide to make a big deal out of the "I'm home! How was your day?" routine, which makes the home seem more lively. Although these things will sound trivial to some, for those missing their loved one, it really does makes things easier for all concerned. Living temporarily without a loved one isn't all bad, especially if the family works through it together.

6   Advancements in technology can also help the family stay close to the person who is deployed. Video chat and phone calls allow family members (even those in combat zones) to hear and talk to each other in near real-time. (Letters and emails are nice, but real-time talk can give everybody extra peace of mind.) A simple "Hey, how are you doing?" gets everything started. The rest of the conversation—work, school, sports, etc.—will probably come naturally. Even when families talk about the simplest, most routine things, they never want to stop talking and turn off that webcam. Of course, it may be another week or two (or more) until the family is back online together.

7   Families figure out that if they bond together, they can survive a deployment. If they unite, they realize that they can endure the six to fifteen long months without their loved one present. They'll also probably find that some of their neighbors (other military families) are going through the same thing; sometimes, in fact, the neighbor will lend a hand by changing the oil on the car or babysitting for a few hours. In this case, it's not just one family uniting but several. Deployments are definitely something that neither the military members nor their families look forward to, but they know it is necessary for the sake of their families, their country, and the nation's freedom. They also need to know that it *is* possible to endure a deployment and still be strong as a family.

Questions about Evelyn's writing:

1. Evelyn was planning to write only one essay about military life, yet she came up with seven different topics that were related to that broader topic. She also invested considerable time in freewriting and brainstorming about her potential topics. Do you agree this was a good investment of Evelyn's time? Why or why?
2. Have you ever tried to outline a draft after you've already written it, as Evelyn did? How might that technique help you? What did Evelyn gain from doing so?
3. Besides the changes mentioned in the note just above the third draft, what other changes (for instance, in terms of grammar or clarity) does Evelyn appear to have made between her second and third drafts?
4. Which of Evelyn's drafts do you think is most effective? Why?

Travis Wilson, "The Hunt"

About Travis's paper:

The following essay is by a student whose name has been changed to protect his reputation. Travis usually struggled to come up with a topic. He believed he had to have "just the right" topic in order to get started. For this paper, he was asked to write about a meaningful experience in his life. For the first time all semester, he was able to think of a topic right away and wrote a first draft close to what you'll see below in his third draft. This was his longest paper by far. You'll probably notice that it is too long. Students who have trouble coming up with length often hesitate to delete sentences or paragraphs from their papers. As you read this paper, think about what Travis could delete to make his paper stronger and more purposeful.

Draft #3

The Hunt

1   Friday, November 21, 2008 6:13 a.m. I had noticed the sun had just breaking into the foggy sky and I had looked out the window from my kitchen into the field and seen the deer that my dad and I have been after for years just standing there. I have known him for years, I knew where he grew up, I know where he lived, and he is color blind. He has been running away for years and I'm not going to let him get away with it. This time I went for my gun.

> Is this repetition effective or should it be condensed?

2   For Years he has been coming around our property and my dog hated him! He would go ballistic every time he saw him. Well opportunity struck for me to tag this beautiful monster buck. He was about 200 yards out which was perfect I didn't want him very close, if he were to see or hear me that would blow my cover. I ducked down and sneaked into my bedroom to grab my scoped rifle and threw on some camouflage.

> If you had to delete a fact or detail from paragraph 2 or paragraph 3, which one would you omit? Why?

3   Knowing the deer was colored blind was a plus so blending in with my surroundings would be for the best. The sun was just coming out, still kind of dark, but enough light to see through the scope. The darker the better, I knew I had enough time to get into position before day break.

4   I quickly turned and went out the front door of the house, I put myself in the crouched position, and ever so slowly I crept to the side of my house. I peaked around the

> It seems like something is about to happen. What creates that sense (which details or wording)?

corner to see if I could still see him and he was now lurking around over by the barn. From where I was crouched at, I had watched him take his time and go to the back of the barn, I had no shot. My self esteem had been shot down like a plane right out of the sky. I dropped my head down, and was sure that when the deer went back behind barn it was because he had seen, smelt, or heard me and bolted out of sight and back into the woods. I figured I would take a look at behind the barn, if I went inside I knew I was going to get a deer so maybe he was lurking in the pasture behind the barn.

5   I knew I was going to have to move up and over to even get a visual on my target. I threw my rifle over my shoulder and went into the prone position. The ground was freezing cold, I could see my breath coming out of my mouth and I could feel the ground just sucking the heat right out of me. I slowly started to make my way over to a bush that provided excellent cover for me, and was flush with the side of barn. I had good cover and it was here were I would lay aside the bush and wait it out for my kill.

6   This was it, I would just wait for him to come to the other side of the barn, and I would pull up on my rifle, stare through my scope, and just let him walk right into the reticule and BOOM! Well that's not how it went down, for some reason he never came out from the back of that barn. How it did go down at that bush was me waiting for the deer that never came. I got lonely, bored, and even colder than I already was. I was looking at the sky, looking through my scope to stare at the birds, I was playing with grass. I had gotten real agitated waiting for this deer. The impatience had kicked in and I was now going to go find him.

> Does this sentence make you feel cheated or let down? Explain why or why not.

7   I continued to crawl on my belly in a westerly course across the crunchy freezing cold grass. By this time I had crawled about a football field in length, I was tired, cold, wet, and I had not had my cup of coffee, and I was ready for this to be over. However I was told if I seen him I was to shoot him on the spot. This was a big deer it meant a lot of meat in the freezer and a beautiful wall mount. Anxiously I started crawling as I was ready to seal the deal and call it a good day. In the direction of West will bring me over more, and then heading south to get a sneak peak at what he is doing at the back of the barn.

8   As I crawled through tall grass I was thinking to myself that this has to be the worst part of stalking a deer, your face was getting all wet and I was getting poked in the face by grass blades that were frozen, and you end up all itchy. It felt like I was getting stuck in the face with needles. With as cold as my face was, the cold weather outside, and the frozen blades grass, It was too much, I was done, my hands were freezing, snot running down my nose, I couldn't feel my ears, the wind as so blistering that morning my eyes were watering like the Niagara Falls, the tears just kept coming. I stop to take one last quick look and low and behold he was now maybe 400 yards south of the back of the barn.

> Which details would you choose to delete from paragraph 7 or paragraph 8? Why?

9   It was such a relief to see that pretty deer standing in the middle open. It was like the movies, I could hear music playing in my head, and a gold ray shot down from the sky and shined on the deer. All of the hard work had paid off. About two crucial hours of being patient and not moving, my reward from crawling through the icy grass and getting poked in the face, and watering eyes as just moments away from being achieved.

10   Still tucked away in weeds I had crawled just to the edge of it, only enough to be able to see through my scope without having to expose myself, and blow my cover, that would not be good at all. All is set and everything was just right. No one was around to see what was about to happen I pulled the gun up to my eye and looked around, I was so nervous I was not even close to aiming at my target. Moving my gun a little to the right brought my target right into my scope. That's when I realized the time had come for me to take his life. I had never taken a life before, and was wondering what kind of person I would be and how I would feel about it if I pulled the trigger.

11   Never the less I still proceeded, taking this shot was going to be no easy task, and there are a lot of things to take into consideration when taking long distance shots. The weather, humidity, windage, bullet drop, and the Coriolis affect. The deer was approximately no more than 230 to 250 yards out. The only thing on my mind was weather, windage, and bullet drop big time.

12   I reached up to my scope to zoom in on my target a little more, and clear up the image. It was close, but a great image and crystal clear. The time had come for me to make a decision to let him live or let him die. I couldn't make up my mind, I was panicking I would look down scope, then pop out my head out and just stare at him for a minute. And then go right back into my scope. It was like a time bomb that needed defused, do I cut the red wire or the blue wire.

13   Then he stopped, turned his head and looked right at me. It was a stare down; all that panicking had vanished into the midst of the cold thin air and turned into hate and rage. I took one last look down the scope. Breathing was heavy and intense. The scope moving up and down as I took short quick breaths, my heart pounding as loud as a bass drum and beating faster than lightning strikes.

14   Taking all the air my little body could possibly hold, I took one last hearty deep breath. Everything slowed way down, as if I had taken some kind of medication. It also got quiet, No wind Just silence. Everything was in slow motion my adrenaline was at its peak, the scoped stopped moving the second I took that last breath. Quick I pinpointed where I wanted the bullet to penetrate my target, and then BOOM!

15   The world that we know, planet Earth had to have stopped spinning. The slow motion had turned into super slow motion. I had seen sparks come out of the holes of the end of the ported barrel. Following the tiny little sparks was a huge flame what had seemed to be about a foot long, come out of the end of the barrel.

16   Peaking my head over the tall disturbed grass there was nothing standing out in the open, standing up and looking through my scope and what I had saw was another story. It was without a doubt a confirmed kill. I had unloaded my firearm and set it in the barn. My hunt had come to an end and I had no longer needed my gun it was extra baggage at this point.

17   The adrenaline had really kicked in and taken affect on me. Now that I didn't have a target to focus on I noticed a lot more things. I had so many thoughts going my mind that I couldn't actually process my ideas to make sense and make them work. Instead of short

> So far, we've been focusing on eliminating text. Could or should anything be added to paragraphs 10-12? Identify what might need more explanation.

> Details: Notice the nice balance of fine details here without repetition.

fast breaths I was now taking much longer breaths, as if something had scared the life out of me. I was walking around the dead deer in circles thinking what to do next. My hands were trembling and my knees were weak. I also didn't understand the fact that it was cold enough outside to freeze water, yet I was sweating as if I was in the desert.

18   My dad had approached me with a huge smile on his face, shook my hand and let out a huge hearty laugh. He said, "Son sit down and relax, the deer is dead, and it's not going anywhere." It was all over, the patience had paid off. For shotgun season I had filled my tags. I was thinking about season after shotgun season was out and was hoping that it was going to be as difficult as this experience.

> **Conclusion:** This was Travis's conclusion in his third draft. What conclusion strategy do you think he should use here? Refer to Ch. 9 for possible conclusion strategies.

Questions about Travis's writing:

1. What do you think is the most significant part of Travis's story? Why do you think he wanted to tell this story? What should he add to the paper to make that point clearer, and where should that be added?
2. Travis wanted to build the moment up, to make it spectacular. He adds suspense, but probably builds the suspense so many times that the reader might lose interest or think the big moment is not as interesting as the build-up made it out to be. What parts of the essay could be removed in order to leave the right amount of suspense and mood?
3. Choose one paragraph with verb tense problems and correct the verbs.

Where Travis Went Wrong: A warning against plagiarism

Earlier, it was explained that *Travis Wilson* is not the real name of this student. His name was changed because he plagiarized a portion of his paper. What he did was not malicious. He wrote most of the paper himself, but in one spot, he included information from a source and did so incorrectly.

In his first draft, Travis said that he grabbed his scoped rifle and his ghillie suit. A peer reviewer asked what a ghillie suit was and suggested that Travis should add more information about that. This is the problematic portion from the second draft of the paper:

> For Years he has been coming around our property and my dog hated him! He would go ballistic every time he saw him. Well opportunity struck for me to tag this beautiful monster buck. He was about 200 yards out which was perfect, I didn't want him very close, If he were to see or hear me that would blow my cover. I ducked down and sneaked into my bedroom to grab my scoped rifle and my ghillie suit.

> This is Travis's writing.

> A ghillie suit is a type of camouflage clothing designed to resemble heavy foliage. Typically, it is a net or cloth garment covered in loose strips of cloth or twine, sometimes even made to look like leaves and twigs. Hunters wear ghillie suits to blend into their surroundings when they feel it is important for them to camouflage and hide themselves from their targets. The suit gives the wearer's outline a three-dimensional breakup, rather than a linear one. When manufactured correctly, the suit will move in the wind the same way as surrounding foliage. Knowing the deer was colored blind was a plus so blending in with my surroundings was definitely a plus. The sun was just coming out, still kind of dark, but enough light to see through the scope.

This portion is the plagiarized part.

Notice the difference in the language here. The second paragraph is more technical, and its sentences are correctly punctuated. (Travis's other sentences have frequent punctuation errors) The teacher noticed the difference too and put the paragraph into a Google search. This was the result:

A ghillie suit is a type of camouflage clothing designed to resemble heavy folia

About 703 results (1.09 seconds)

Ghillie suit - Wikipedia, the free encyclopedia
en.wikipedia.org/wiki/Ghillie_suit
A **ghillie suit**, also known as a (wookie suit, yowie suit, or **camo** tent) is a **type** of **camouflage** ... Typically, it is a **net** or **cloth** garment **covered** in **loose strips** of burlap, **cloth** or **twine**, **sometimes** made to **look like leaves** and **twigs**, and optionally ... Snipers and **hunters** may **wear** a **ghillie suit** to **blend into** their surroundings and ...

Ghillie Suit
www.bulletarchery.com/ghillie_suit.html
A **ghillie suit**, or yowie suit, is a **type** of **camouflage clothing designed to resemble heavy foliage**. **Typically**, it is a **net** or **cloth** garment **covered** in **loose strips** of **cloth** or **twine**, **sometimes even made to look like leaves** and **twigs**. **Hunters** may **wear** a **ghillie suit** to **blend into** their surroundings when they feel it is important for ...

Ghillie Suits - HARRISON TACTICAL GEAR
www.harrisongear.com/ghillie-suits.html
A **Ghillie Suit** is a **type** of **camouflage clothing designed to resemble heavy foliage**. **Typically**, it is a **net** or **cloth** garment **covered** in **loose strips** of **cloth** or **twine**, **sometimes** made to **look like leaves** and **twigs**, and optionally augmented ... Snipers and **Hunters** alike may **wear** a **ghillie suit** to **blend into** their surroundings and ...

CHEAP AIRSOFT GHILLIE SUITS : GHILLIE SUITS | CHEAP ...
cheapairsoftghilliesuitsqlog.wordpress.com/
(**Ghillie Suit**) A specialist **camouflaged** suit which lets a player **blend into** their environment. You can ... A Kids **Ghillie Suit**, or yowie suit, is a **type** of **designed** to **resemble heavy** foilage **Typically**, it is a **net** or **cloth** garment **covered** in **loose strips** of **cloth** or **twine**, **sometimes even made to look like leaves** and **twigs**. **Hunters** ...

This is plagiarism. Travis used a source for information and put it into his paper without citing where it came from. Also, he meant to paraphrase the source (in other words, put it in his own words), but instead Travis has changed a few of the words and still called it his own. This is incorrect for a few reasons:

1. Any time a source is used, it should be cited in the paper (unless it is common knowledge information).
2. Any time **exact words** from the source are used, those words need to be put into quotation marks.
3. When the information is good, but the wording is not, the writer can choose to reword it, but he needs to put it in his own words <u>and</u> structure and not keep bits and pieces the same as they were in the original material. This paraphrased information requires a citation too.

Looking for a Challenge:

Try to put Travis's plagiarized material into your own words. In class, compare your version with someone else's.

Karlos Martin, "The Helping Hand"

About Karlos' paper:

In the following student sample, the writer added length to his paper over time. He also redrafted for audience awareness. The original assignment was to write about an unexpected lesson that was learned. Karlos knew he had a great experience to write about. At one point in his life, he was cheating on his son's mother, and he knew it was wrong. His girlfriend's other boyfriend was the person who helped him to change the situation.

First draft

This draft was placed on an online discussion board for feedback:

1   The beginning of this whole situation started back in Hawaii with my little family. The only problem was getting the ticket, because once I got my check, I didn't have enough money to get them a ticket, which was a major setback. So, I let her know that she would have to wait until I got a good job in the states.

Student 2 Feedback: What do you mean by your little family?

Student 2: Where was your family and where did you want them to be? I'm confused here.

2   Later the following day after work, I decided to come home relax and watch some television, but just when I thought things were going good my ex-girlfriend Stephanie called. She was explaining to me that she still loved me, which made me fill really mushy inside.

Student 2: It seems like we just jumped in time here. I don't know what is happening.

Student 1 Feedback: Oh, no way...you KNOW that's not going to end well. LOL!

3   I thought about my son every day, but the only problem was that I was just too deep in love. Then there was one Monday I came home from school and Stephanie called me crying telling me that she might be pregnant, but she didn't want to talk about it. Two days passed by and I still hadn't received a single phone call from Stephanie. *Not one*. I'm thinking to myself: "what is going on?" I'm at home minding my business

Student 2 Feedback: It sounds like your son is really important to you. I'd like to hear more about him.

and this guy writes me on Facebook.com telling me that I'm with his girlfriend. Once I read his message, I flipped out in the worse way because his message seemed as if he was irate with me. He went on explaining to me how he left his children and their mother for *Stephanie*. I told him that we were going through the same thing and ever since then we have been friends. He tried reaching out to me in the best way in order to get me to understand the importance of taking responsibility for my son. So I told him that he was absolutely right, and from that day on my mind was clear as the Hawaiian oceans. Everything that he was telling me was what everybody else tried to telling me also. Even Alofa tried opening my eyes, but I just didn't take the time to sit down and listen. It took a man that I didn't even know just to open my eyes. I called Alofa and explained

> Student 1 Feedback: No way! That's crazy!!!

> Student 2 Feedback: Is this your wife or girlfriend back home? The paper is mostly about Stephanie. What was going on with Alofa?

her that we need to fix things up for our son and make things right. The only thing was that I was scared that I might do her wrong again. Now that I'm in control, I just have to take responsibility as a man, and do what's best for my little boy.

> Student 1 Feedback: Good ending. I like that you went back to be a dad. Good job, man!

After reading the discussion board feedback, Karlos decided that he needed to add more information about his family because he wanted the paper's message to be more about Alofa and his son than about Stephanie. He added sentences to some of the paragraphs he already had and also added more paragraphs about what was happening back home.

Second draft

This draft has feedback from his instructor:

The Helping Hand

1   The beginning of this whole situation started back in Hawaii with my little family. Alofa and I lived in Hawaii with our son. We would have our disagreements, but always prevail and make things right. We wanted to

> Instructor Feedback: Why is this essay called "The Helping Hand"? Maybe use your introduction to connect to that idea.

move back home to Southern Illinois. The only problem was getting the ticket, because once I got my check, I didn't have enough money to get them a ticket, which was a major setback. So, I let Alofa know that she would have to wait until I got a good job in the states.

2   Back in Illinois, one day after work, I decided to come home relax and watch some television, but just when I thought things were going good my ex-girlfriend Stephanie called. Stephanie was my first love, and she knows that I get soft hearted whenever I talk to her. She was explaining to me that she still loved me, which made me fill really mushy inside.

Instructor Feedback: Need pauses in between some of these words.

Instructor Feedback: wrong word.

3   Things started going downhill day after day because the kissing, hugging, and I love you expressions just slowed down and sometimes completely stopped. Seeing that I was acting the way that I was, Alofa would ask me all type of suspicious questions. It was the hardest thing to tell her, but I had no choice, but to tell her the truth. She had this look of anger, discuss, animosity, and sadness, which made me depressed from her expression. What hurt me the most was leaving my son! What I didn't realize was the trouble that I had ahead of me.

Instructor Feedback: What is the purpose of Par. 2? What do you want your reader to know or understand after reading this?

Instructor Feedback: Completely stopped with Stephanie or Alofa?

Instructor Feedback: wrong word.

4   Later that month my mother, brother, sister, and I decided to head on over to Carbondale, Illinois. Once we got there we immediately started visiting our family, and friends. Everybody wanted to know why my son wasn't with me, but I was too ashamed to tell them. What bugged me the most was the same thing that happened with my family also happened with my friends! They asked me about my son and Alofa, so I told them what I had done. Once they heard that, they lost their minds, because they know that my son needs me in his life.

Instructor Feedback: nicely focused paragraph!

5   I thought about my son every day, but the only problem was that I was just too deep in love. Then there was one Monday I came home from school and Stephanie called me crying telling me that she might be pregnant, but she didn't want to talk about it. Two days passed by and I

Instructor Feedback: Great topic sentence!

still hadn't received a single phone call from Stephanie. *Not one*. I'm thinking to myself: "what is going on?" I'm at home minding my business and this guy writes me on Facebook.com telling me that I'm with his girlfriend. Once I read his message, I flipped out in the worse way because his message seemed as if he was irate with me. He went on explaining to me how he left his children and their mother for *Stephanie*. I told him that we were going through the same thing and ever since then we have been friends. He tried reaching out to me in the best way in order to get me to understand the importance of taking responsibility for my son. So I told him that he was absolutely right, and from that day on my mind was clear as the Hawaiian oceans. Everything that he was telling me was what everybody else tried to telling me also. Even Alofa tried opening my eyes, but I just didn't take the time to sit down and listen. It took a man that I didn't even know just to open my eyes. I called Alofa and explained her that we need to fix things up for our son and make things right. The only thing was that I was scared that I might do her wrong again. Now that I'm in control, I just have to take responsibility as a man, and do what's best for my little boy.

Instructor Feedback: This is a long paragraph. Consider breaking it up at a change in topic to help the reader.

Instructor Feedback: This is a body paragraph. Maybe write a conclusion about what you learned about how to be there for your son.

From this feedback, Karlos realized he didn't have an introduction and conclusion yet. He also saw that some of the information would be unclear to someone who didn't know the full story. In short, in this revision, Karlos focused on helping the audience more.

Third and fourth draft combined

The changes made in the next two drafts have been combined here. Karlos added material for one draft and then did a subsequent draft for his proofreading.

The Helping Hand

1   I have a very special family that I love and miss very, very much. The way that I handled things with them caused a lot of animosity and sorrow. I had left them for a woman that I still had feelings for, which turned out bad. In the end, a guy named Derek really opened my eyes.

> **Introduction:** New intro added

2   The beginning of this whole situation started back in Hawaii with my little family. Alofa and I lived in Hawaii with our son. We would have our disagreements, but always prevail and make things right. We wanted to move back home to Southern Illinois. The only problem was getting the ticket, because once I got my check, I didn't have enough money to get them a ticket, which was a major setback. So, I let Alofa know that she would have to wait until I got a good job in the states.

3   Back in Illinois, one day after work, I decided to come home, relax, and watch some television. Just when I thought things were going good, my ex-girlfriend Stephanie called. Stephanie was my first love, and she knows that I get soft hearted whenever I talk to her. She was explaining to me that she still loved me, which made me feel really mushy inside. What bothered me the most was my sons face in the back of my head! So, all I could think was, "*what the heck did I just get myself into?*"

> **Transition and Purpose:** This sentence was added.

4   Things with Alofa started going downhill day after day because the kissing, hugging, and "I love you" expressions just slowed down and sometimes completely stopped. Seeing that I was acting the way that I was, Alofa would ask me all type of suspicious questions, like, "What's wrong with you, why are you acting so strange"? It was the hardest thing to tell her, but I had no choice but to tell her the truth. She had this look of anger, disgust, animosity, and sadness, which made me depressed from her expression. What hurt me the most was leaving my son! What I didn't realize was the trouble that I had ahead of me.

> This paragraph has had many changes made to it. Which do you find most helpful and why?

5   Later that month my mother, brother, sister, and I decided to head on over to Carbondale, Illinois. Once we got there, we immediately started visiting our family and friends. Everybody wanted to know why my son wasn't with me, but I was too ashamed to tell them. What bugged me the most was the same thing that happened with my family was also happening with my friends! They asked me about my son and Alofa, so I told them what I had done. Once they heard that, they lost their minds, because they know that my son needs me in his life. I knew it also. I just didn't admit it. They were blowing my ear out telling me that no man should just up and leave his child. Everything that my friends were trying to tell me was true; I just didn't see the big picture. They tried their best to warn me that being back with Stephanie was going to turn out wrong. As stubborn as I was, I still didn't do as told, so we just squashed that topic of conversation and hung out.

> **Support:** The second half of the paragraph was added.

6   I thought about my son every day, but the only problem was that I was just too deep in love. Then there was one Monday I came home from school and Stephanie called me crying telling me that she might be pregnant, but she didn't want to talk about it. Two days passed by and I still hadn't received a single phone call from Stephanie. *Not one*. I'm thinking to myself: "What is going on?" I'm at home minding my business and this guy writes me on Facebook.com telling me that I'm with his girlfriend. Once I read his message, I flipped out in the worst way because his message seemed as if he was irate with me. He went on explaining to me how he left his children and their mother for *Stephanie*. I told him that we were going through the same thing and ever since then we have been friends. He tried reaching out to me in the best way in order to get me to understand the importance of taking responsibility for my son. So I told him that he was absolutely right, and from that day on my mind was clear as the Hawaiian oceans.

> Karlos chose to divide the paragraph here. Was that a good decision? Why or why not?

7   Everything that he was telling me was what everybody else tried to telling me also. Even Alofa tried opening my eyes, but I just didn't take the time to sit down and listen. It took a man that I didn't even know just to open my eyes. I called Alofa and explained her that we need to fix things up for our son and make things right. The only thing was that I was scared of was that I might do her wrong again. Now that I'm in control, I just have to take responsibility as a man, and do what's best for my little boy.

8   I think that every father should be part of their children's lives. A lot of children in the world don't have their fathers with them. Most children without their fathers turn out either dead or in prison *especially boys* which I feel is a sad shame. Some boys turn out just right but that's not the point. All children need make role models in order to become strong minded and understand the ins and the outs of life as a male. The men are there to guide our children into success. Us guys aren't always on the up and up. Sometimes we can be dumb-founded and not even realize what's important until we bump our heads.

> **Conclusion:** Conclusion added.

Questions about Karlos' writing:

1. Usually audience awareness refers to knowing your audience's views and writing in a way that acknowledges them, respects them, and/or refutes them. How and why did Karlos need to become more aware of his audience's needs in these drafts?
2. On Karlos' first draft, he received feedback from two students. Which student's feedback would you find most useful? Why?
3. Karlos had a complicated situation to write about. Sometimes, when papers get to be too complicated, students try to write a simple version of the paper instead. How did Karlos embrace the good complication in his paper and work through the problems?
4. In the third and fourth drafts, Karlos added an introduction and a conclusion. Do they fit the paper and help the reader make sense of the message? Explain.

Rachel Beck, "Being Bullied"

About Rachel's paper:

Rachel chose to write about an experience that was meaningful to her. She was not a student to hold back. For her first draft, she just wrote everything that came to mind. When she had a question about what she should do with the paper, she included it because she knew she would have the opportunity to receive feedback.

Drafting: First Draft

When Rachel's instructor held a first draft workshop, she gladly volunteered to have her paper critiqued. Rachel's draft was projected onto a screen for the whole class to see as the teacher read it out loud. The comments that follow are from Rachel's fellow students as part of that class discussion.

Being Bullied

1   Every one has friends in kindergarten right? Why can't everyone just be nice and sweet like we were when we were five years old? Why do little kids have to get picked on for no reason at all? It's simple, they don't. When you're in elementary school you shouldn't be picked on for being too small or too tall, or the way your hair looks that day, or because of the hand me down clothes you might wear. Well that was my case, I was picked on from the time I started kindergarten till I was in eighth grade. I wasn't one of the "cool kids" or your typical little girl that loved the color pink and hung out with the girls at recess, that just wasn't me. I was the little girl who liked to play kick ball with the boys and wasn't afraid to get dirty and do what I felt I wanted to make myself happy not anyone else.

> Good sentence. The class could all relate to this.

> Change this sentence around a little. The class could get what you meant but it was a little hard to follow.

2   Yes, I had a few friends that were girls but they would always get mad at me for playing kickball with their boyfriends at recess. They'd call me names and say I was a bad friend and what not. I would get picked on for size and liking the guys my friends liked. Girls also hated me for no reason at all. I got bullied by every girl that's ever heard my name and had a friend that didn't like me, for what ever reason that may have been. I've wanted nothing but to be friends with everyone my whole life, and I've strived so hard to get it that way.

> It was suggested that "boyfriends" should go in quotation marks because they were not real boyfriends as this was still early in grade school.

3   When I was in 6th grade is when things started to turn ugly, my best friend at the time had turned her back on me and wanted nothing to do with me and tried to do everything in her power to make my life a living hell, Just because her "boyfriend" liked me. she and a couple of her friends started telling me they were going to beat me up so bad I'd need the ambulance to come get me and I'd be in

> When does the Kindergarten part end and the post-kindergarten through 6th grade vs. in sixth grade when things change again?

the hospital for weeks. She even stated that they'd meet me outside my house, which they did. Her and two other girls walked up to my house and her boyfriend, the one who liked me, was with them also. I had told my mom about it and she called the police and ran them off down the street. She wasn't about to have kids bully her daughter around for no reason at all. Then 7th grade came along and the same girls hung out together plus a few more and they did not like me either, no reason for it but I just know they didn't. one girl told me to meet her in the locker room at school during my gym hour which was her lunch hour to fight her. Yes my mom knew about this one too, and I did go to school prepared to kick the girls' ass, but yes never showed up. Another day that same school year and same hour of the day, I was running a pass down to the office and on my way back a girl started coming toward me saying she was going to beat my ass and she started walking faster, so what did I do? Walked backwards scared shitless out of my mind because this girl was a heffer, and I'm being nice by saying that much. I stood on one side of the principals door while she was still coming after me, and I said "you better stop and turn around or I'm walking right inside this door.", she stopped and did just that. Well that drama was over for the rest of the year.

> Rachel explained that the girl was taller than she was and yet she was not really afraid of being beaten up by her. Rachel added that she was shocked that they actually showed up.

> The class got a good laugh out of this comment, but Rachel felt awkward when she heard her teacher read this out loud.

4   8th grade is when things couldn't get any worse for me than they already were. The first day of school I rode the bus like normal and sat in the back, like always with girls I thought were my so called friends. But on the bus ride home that very same day, I got my hair pulled multiple times called every single name in the book. I just couldn't take it anymore, I was fed up with these girls. I stopped riding the bus after that. The few girls I went to elementary school with still hated me because of stupid reasons and just couldn't get over it. keep in mind this is when everyone used AIM on the computer. I was looking at one of the girls profiles and I seen a message that said who when and where they were going to kill me and how those girls were going to do it. the message said they were going to steal a pair of scissors from a teachers desk, drag me in to the bathroom, cut off all my hair, slit my throat my wrists the back of my ankles and knees on top my elbows, everything, they were also going to cut off my fingers and toes to torture me a little longer. Then leave me there to die, at school in the girls bathroom. Now I don't care who the hell you think you are or how badass you think you might be, but you do not post things like that on the internet for other people to read or see.<should I tell the rest? Its long.> Let's just say ending to that story was, everyone left me along after that.

> Excellent sentence. Great transition and suspense.

> Class responded with "YES"

5   When I got to highschool people knew not to mess with me because of my past and I was a new person, I was confident in who I was and did not let people get to me or try to torture me in those ways. It was a mind game to everyone and I didn't work on my any longer. If I didn't like you and you had a problem with me, you could tell me to my face or not say anything at all. Because of the way I entered highschool and changed my outlook on things is what got me away from being bullied. I couldn't let those girls talk down to me anymore and let them see it hurt me. so I just put on that face and acted as if nothing ever fased me after that. and now, people don't start shit with me or threaten to do anything. Overall

I've learned not to let people get the best of you, even if it does do not let them see it. act as if you would if you were happy and enjoyed what they were saying. When you laugh in someones face about the mean things they say about you it pisses them off because they're not getting the rise out of you they wanted.

> *After the workshop, Rachel said she had not realized how "bad her language was" until she heard the paper read out loud. We talked about how she should clean it up a little without losing too much of her voice either.*

Redrafting: Peer Editing and Draft #2

After the first draft workshop, Rachel redrafted for a peer review session. What follows is one student's feedback to Rachel. See if you agree with the feedback that was given.

Being Bullied

1   Every one has friends in kindergarten right? Why can't everyone just be nice and sweet like we were when we were five years old? Why do little kids have to get picked on for no reason at all? It's simple, they don't. When you're in elementary school you shouldn't be picked on for being too small or too tall, or the way your hair looks that day, or because of the hand me down clothes you might wear. In my case, I was picked on from the time I started kindergarten till I was in eighth grade. I wasn't one of the "cool kids" or your typical little girl that loved the color pink and hung out with the girls at recess, that just wasn't me. I was the little girl who liked to play kick ball with the boys and wasn't afraid to get dirty.

> *A star was left outside these lines to indicate that something was good. It was unclear whether the star applied to a couple of sentences or the whole paragraph.*

2   In elementary school I did have a few friends that were girls but they would always get mad at me for playing kickball with their "boyfriends" at recess. They'd call me names and say I was a bad friend and what not. I would get picked on for my size and liking the guys my friends liked. Girls also hated me for no reason at all. I got bullied by every girl that's ever heard my name and had a friend that didn't like me, for what ever reason that may have been. I've wanted nothing but to be friends with everyone my whole life, and I've strived so hard to get it that way.

> *A suggestion to add the word "all" here.*

3   When I was in 6th grade is when things started to turn ugly, my best friend at the time had turned her back on me and wanted nothing to do with me and tried to do everything in her power to make my life a living hell, Just because her "boyfriend" liked me. She and a couple of her friends started telling me " we're going to beat me up so bad you'll need the ambulance to come get you and you'll be in the hospital for weeks." She even stated "we'll meet you outside my house, right now." which they did and I was totally shocked. Her and two other girls walked up to my house and her boyfriend, the one who liked me, was with them also. I had told my mom about it and she called the police and ran them off down the street. She wasn't about to have kids bully her daughter around for no reason at all.

> *Rachel had changed this into a direct quotation. The peer rightly pointed out that she needed to change this word to "you."*

4   Then 7th grade came along and the same girls hung out together plus a few more and they did not like me either. There was no reason for it, but I just know they didn't. One girl told me to meet her in the locker room at school during my gym hour which was her lunch hour to fight her. Yes my mom knew about this one too, and I did go to school prepared to fight her and win, but she never showed up. Another day that same school year and same hour of the day, I was running a pass down to the office and on my way back a girl started coming toward me saying she was going to "beat my ass" and she started walking faster, so what did I do? I walked backwards scared out of my mind because this girl was huge in comparison to me. I stood on one side of the principals door while she was still coming after me, and I said "you better stop and turn around or I'm walking right inside this door." she stopped and did just that. At least that drama was over for the rest of the year.

> Put a period here and get rid of "and." Then start a new sentence.

5   8th grade is when things couldn't get any worse for me than they already were. The first day of school I rode the bus like normal and sat in the back, like always with girls I thought were my so called friends. But on the bus ride home that very same day, I got my hair pulled multiple times and got called every single name in the book. I just couldn't take it anymore, I was fed up with these girls. I stopped riding the bus after that. The few girls I went to elementary school with still hated me because of stupid reasons and just couldn't get over it. keep in mind this is when everyone used AIM (AOL Instant Messenger) on the computer. I was looking at one of the girls profiles and I saw a message that said who, when and where they were going to kill me and how those girls were going to do it. The message said they were going to steal a pair of scissors from a teachers desk, drag me in to the bathroom, cut off all my hair, slit my throat my wrists the back of my ankles and knees on top my elbows, everything, they were also going to cut off my fingers and toes to torture me a little longer. Then leave me there to die, at school in the girls bathroom. Now I don't care who you think you are or how "badass" you think you might be, but you do not post things like that on the internet for other people to read or see. After seeing that, my mom called the police and let them deal with it, their parents got called and after that they didn't mess with me anymore.

> Add more commas. Change the comma after everything to a period. Start a new sentence.

6   When I got to high school people knew not to mess with me because of my past and I was a new person, I was confident in who I was and did not let people get to me or try to torture me in those ways. It was a mind game to everyone and I didn't work on my any longer. Prime example, there was a girl in high school who would call me names in the hall way and she even mooned me once, trying to make me mad. But did it work? No I don't think so, I laughed in her face every time and I would even go out of my way to say "Hey what's up girl?" in the hallway. That made her more angry than I ever could have been with what she was saying to me. Because of the way I entered high school and changed my outlook on things is what got me away from being bullied. I couldn't let those girls talk down to me anymore and let them see it hurt me. I just put on that face and acted as if nothing ever fazed me after that. And now, people don't start drama with me or threaten to do anything. Overall I've learned not to let people

get the best of me. Even if it does, I do not let them see it. You should act as if you would if you were happy and enjoyed what they were saying. When you laugh in someone's face about the mean things they say about you it aggravates them because they're not getting the rise out of you they wanted. That is how I over came getting bullied throughout school.

> Good paragraph. Great ending!

Questions about feedback and revision:

1. Do you agree with the peer's comments? What type of feedback would you have given Rachel on this draft?
2. Did Rachel make good changes in between the rough draft and the peer review draft? She had said that she wanted to clean up the language. Do you think she did enough?

Redrafting: Instructor Feedback and Draft #3

Rachel made some changes based on the suggestions received in peer review. You'll probably notice that she did not change the paper as much as she could have. The following comments are from her instructor.

Being Bullied

1 Everyone has friends in kindergarten right? Why can't everyone just be nice and sweet like we were when we were five years old? Why do little kids have to get picked on for no reason at all? It's simple, they don't. When you're in elementary school you shouldn't be picked on for being too small or too tall, or the way your hair looks that day, or because of the hand me down clothes you might wear. In my case, I was picked on from the time I started kindergarten till I was in eighth grade. I wasn't one of the "cool kids" or your typical little girl that loved the color pink and hung out with the girls at recess, that just wasn't me. I was the little girl who liked to play kick ball with the boys and wasn't afraid to get dirty.

> I like this beginning.

2 In elementary school I did have a few friends that were girls but they would always get mad at me for playing kickball with their "boyfriends" at recess. They'd call me names and say I was a bad friend and what not. I would get picked on for my size and liking the guys my friends liked. Girls also hated me for no reason at all. I got bullied by every girl that's ever heard my name and had a friend that didn't like me, for what ever reason that may have been. All I've wanted was nothing but to be friends with everyone my whole life, and I've strived so hard to get it that way.

> It sounds like they took things more seriously than you were. You just wanted to play and be liked.

> Should be one word.

3 When I was in 6th grade is when things started to turn ugly, my best friend at the time had turned her back on me and wanted nothing to do with me and tried to do everything in her power to make my life a living hell. Just because her "boyfriend" liked me. She and a couple of her friends started telling me, "We're

> Fragment. Combine with previous sentence?

going to beat me up so bad you'll need the ambulance to come get you and you'll be in the hospital for weeks." She even stated, "We'll meet you outside my house, right now," which they did and I was totally shocked. Her and two other girls walked up to my house and her boyfriend, the one who liked me, was with them also. I had told my mom about it and she called the police and ran them off down the street. She wasn't about to have kids bully her daughter around for no reason at all.

> *should be She.*

4   Then 7th grade came along and the same girls hung out together plus a few more, and none of them liked me. For what reason? I'll never know. One girl told me to meet her in the locker room at school during my gym hour which was her lunch hour to fight her. Yes my mom knew about this one too, and I did go to school prepared to fight her and win, but she never showed up. Another day that same school year and same hour of the day, I was running a pass down to the office and on my way back a girl started coming toward me saying she was going to "beat my ass." She started walking faster, so what did I do? I walked backwards scared out of my mind because this girl was huge in comparison to me. I stood on one side of the principals door while she was still coming after me, and I said, "You better stop and turn around or I'm walking right inside this door." she stopped and did just that. At least that drama was over for the rest of the year.

> *You were walking backwards to face her so your back wasn't to her, right?*
>
> *Principal's*
>
> *Do you mean that she backed off after that?*

5   8th grade is when things couldn't get any worse for me than they already were. The first day of school I rode the bus like normal and sat in the back, like always with girls I thought were my so called friends. But on the bus ride home that very same day, I got my hair pulled multiple times and got called every single name in the book. I just couldn't take it anymore, I was fed up with these girls. I stopped riding the bus after that. The few girls I went to elementary school with still hated me because of stupid reasons and just couldn't get over it. keep in mind this is when everyone used AIM (AOL Instant Messenger) on the computer. I was looking at one of the girls profiles and I saw a message that said who, when and where they were going to kill me and how those girls were going to do it. The message said they were going to steal a pair of scissors from a teachers desk, drag me in to the bathroom, cut off all my hair, slit my throat, my wrists, the back of my ankles. knees, on top my elbows, and everything. They were also going to cut off my fingers and toes to torture me a little longer. Then leave me there to die, at school in the girls bathroom. Now I don't care who you think you are or how "badass" you think you might be, but you do not post things like that on the internet for other people to read or see. After seeing that, my mom called the police and let them deal with it, their parents got called and after that they didn't mess with me anymore.

> *How were you feeling? What were your thoughts?*
>
> *Missing apostrophes on possessive nouns in this section.*
>
> *All of this is just HORRIBLE! How could other people be like that???*

6   When I got to high school people knew not to mess with me because of my past and I was a new person, I was confident in who I was and did not let people get to me or try to torture me in those ways. It was a mind game to everyone and I didn't work on my any longer. Prime example, there was a girl in high school who would call me names in the hall way and she even mooned me once, trying to make me mad. But did it work? No I don't think so, I laughed in her face

> *Separate this a little; make into more than one sentence.*

228

every time and I would even go out of my way to say "Hey what's up girl?" in the hallway. That made her more angry than i ever could have been with what she was saying to me. Because of the way I entered high school and changed my outlook on things is what got me away from being bullied. I couldn't let those girls talk down to me anymore and let them see it hurt me. I just put on that face and acted as if nothing ever fazed me after that. And now, people don't start drama with me or threaten to do anything. Overall I've learned not to let people get the best of me. Even if it does, do not let them see it. You should act as you would if you were happy and enjoyed what they were saying. When you laugh in someone's face about the mean things they say about you it aggravates them because they're not getting the rise out of you they wanted. That is how I over came getting bullied throughout school.

> Tell us your mindset when you came to high school.

> Good section

> Keep revising this, but let it sit for a little while before you do that, so it will seem brand new to you again.

Questions about Rachel's writing:

1. Rachel received good feedback over her first draft during the whole class workshop. Did she take advantage of that feedback? What were some good changes that she made? What more should she have done?
2. This paper is an example of a student writing it all down in order to be able to fix it up later. How did Rachel's language choices change as she redrafted?
3. Rachel's teacher gave her many comments. Which do you think Rachel should focus on first when revising and why?
4. The last piece of advice that Rachel's teacher gave was to let the essay "sit for a while." This paper was written for a portfolio-style class, so Rachel did not have to revise it right away. How will waiting to revise it later help Rachel to revise in a new way?

Evan Brown, "An Unexpected Lesson"

About Evan's paper:

Evan knew the purpose for his paper from the beginning. He wanted it to be about how his bullying behavior stopped once he understood what it felt like to be bullied. He wasn't sure how to fill in the essay, though, and what else he wanted to say. He began his invention with some drawing to recall the event and then wrote about it in his journal. From there, he made a brief outline and then drafted his paper. With each draft, his paper evolved.

Excerpt from a journal entry about his topic:

I really strived to make people laugh, especially the people I care about. I never took time to think if I ever offended anyone. Growing up I was such a jerk with everyone outside my boys. I was probably a jerk with my crew too, but they were able to dish it back to me. Everyone else just had to take it. Looking back I can't believe I called people out like that in front of everyone.

It sure takes a lot of courage to boo someone. I was confused when I heard it. I certainly didn't like it. For someone who talked a lot about people, I didn't like to draw a lot of attention to myself.

Outline:

Pep assembly

- Talking about people while other teams got awards
- Waiting to get award
- Getting boo's from people I picked on

Learning

- I didn't talk about people I didn't really know
- I started to relate to other people better

Evan's storyboarding:

Evan drew these pictures in order to recall the moment that he would be writing about.

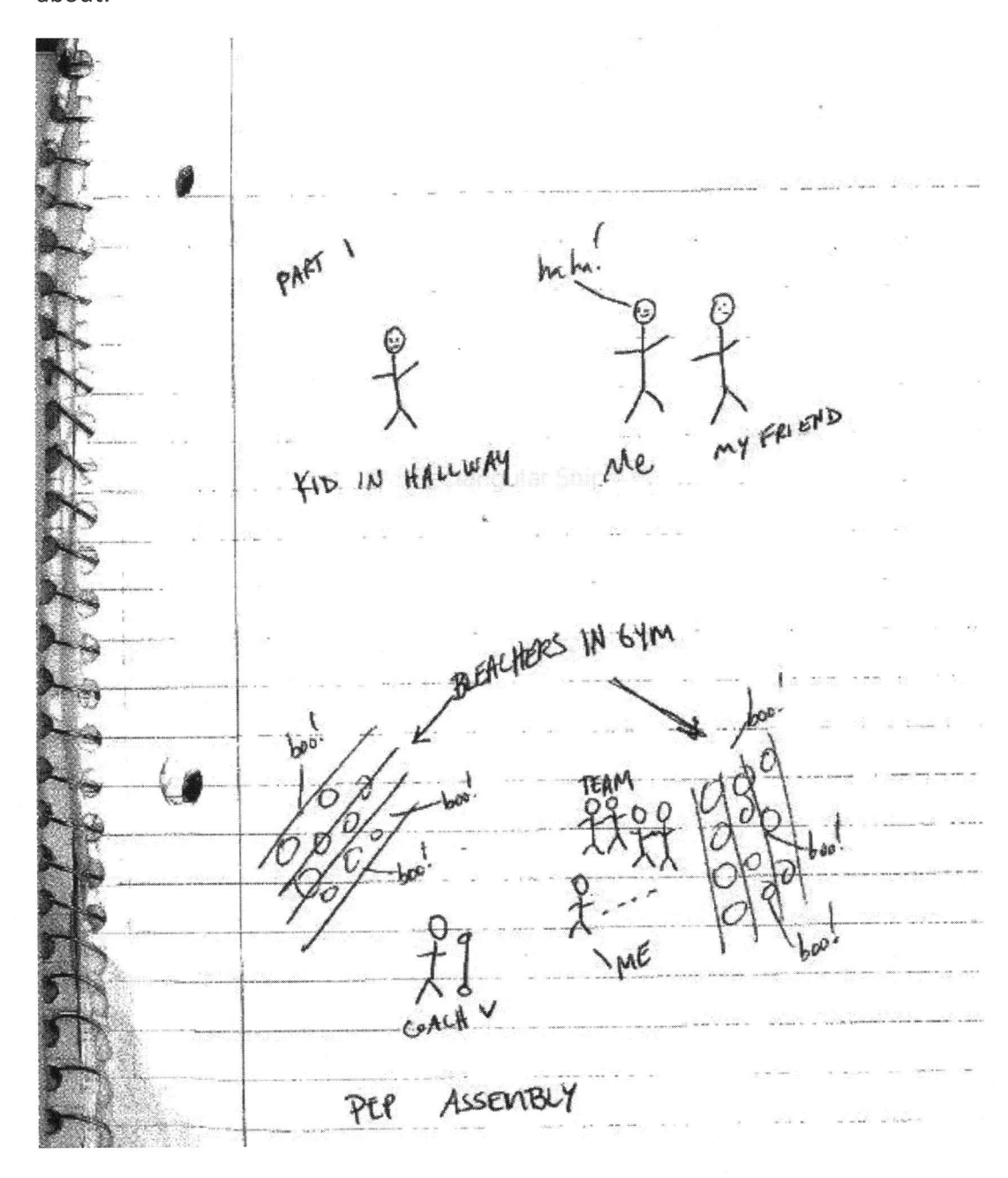

First draft:

Lesson Learned

1   "If David has one more outburst I am going to make him eat those words." The class goes for about five minutes without interruption, until David opened up his mouth to ask another aimless question. I snapped, "If you listen instead of flirting with a girl who has no interest in you Mrs. White wouldn't have to repeat herself by answering your dumb questions." David looked at me dumbfounded, so I said, "Wow you have nothing to say, or were you just not paying attention to what I said either?" I apologized to Mrs. White for interrupting the class; she seemed aggravated with both of us at this point. My job was done.

Interesting introduction. I'd like to know what happens, but I am confused about what your job was.

2   It's 10:00 a.m. and my friends and I are walking into the gym for the pep assembly at Whiteside Middle School. The students are separated by grades, and the teachers are trying to get their students to settle down. I can notice fellow athletes from across the gym. As my friends and I wait for our turn to be recognized, we kill time by making fun of people we see in the gym. We would make jokes about how people walked to get their awards. Even critique the way someone was standing while they waited.

Big jump from intro to this.

This makes it sound like your friends were all bullies too. Did they bully others as much as you did?

3   Finally, the principal called for the 7th grade basketball team to walk up! My friends and I were the best players on team, and in middle school basketball is the sport to watch. As we stand and wait for our names to be called, I stand and try my best to look cool. Our team gets a lot of praise from fellow students; some players get more than others. My friends and I always get the most applause overall on our team at past pep rallies. So I expect nothing less this time. Now it's time for our coach to announce the starters, which were us. Coach V usually gives brief descriptions about us before having us walk up to him, and gets a letter or a pin if you had already received a letter. One by one I see my teammates trying to be cool just like me as they get their pins. Before I know it the coach starts describing me, it takes me a while to know for sure if he was talking about me. As soon as I hear my name I gather myself and start my proud walk to the coach.

Why?

4   About two seconds after hearing my name my moment is ruined by loud "boos!" After the boos started spreading from other students my coach had to say something to stop them. I have never felt so embarrassed in my life. Luckily for me another one of the starters also got a few boos, but not as bad as mine. I didn't say a word through the rest of the pep assembly. Walking back to classes the same people I would make fun of now had the courage to say something and stick up for themselves. Come to find out that David got together with a few people I embarrassed along the years and started the "boo" chant. I got it the worst from my close friends because they never really had a lot of dirt to bring up on me. So now they knew how to get me, and no matter what I said back, nothing will top getting embarrassed in front of the entire school.

What did you do? How did you feel?

5   I had the reputation of hurting people's feelings, and if someone stood up to me I would just embarrass them even more. Before the pep assembly I never really had anyone in particular hurt my feelings, because I knew they didn't mean harm by jokes against me. What I didn't know is that I was hurting other people's feelings with my words. Some may think I picked on people to get attention; on the contrary, I avoided being the center of attention. Also, my family would pick those moments we're ashamed of most and make a joke out of it. I never took into consideration that other families weren't brought up like mine. Unfortunately, most people I made fun of thought I was mean and that gave me the reputation of a bully.

Maybe add an example of what kind of bullying you did.

Please explain this more.

6   Starting the next day at school I didn't make fun of people outside my close friends. And it took me a few weeks to even come back with jokes after they made fun of me for getting booed. I would never admit this back then but that pep assembly was one of the best things that happened to me in my 8 years at Whiteside.

I like that you realized this. Could you add another sentence or two to the ending?

Second draft:

Lesson Learned

1   "If David has one more outburst I am going to make him eat those words." The class goes for about five minutes without interruption, until David opened up his mouth to ask another aimless question. I snapped, "If you listen instead of flirting with a girl who has no interest in you Mrs. White wouldn't have to repeat herself by answering your dumb questions." David looked at me dumbfounded, so I said, "Wow you have nothing to say, or were you just not paying attention to what I said either?" I apologized to Mrs. White for interrupting the class; she seemed aggravated with both of us at this point. My job was done; David didn't ask a dumb question for the rest of the week. I may have won the battle, but David won the war.

Evan received specific feedback about his first draft. How did he apply that feedback in his second draft? Identify at least one significant change and evaluate Evan's success with it.

2   It's 10:00 a.m. and my friends and I are walking into the gym for the pep assembly at Whiteside Middle School. The students are separated by grades, and the teachers are trying to get their students to settle down. I can notice fellow athletes from across the gym; they have that proud look on their faces just like me. As my friends and I wait for our turn to be recognized, we kill time by making fun of people we see in the gym. I can find any reason to make fun of someone. I enjoy making my friends laugh even if I hurt someone else's feelings in the process. We would make jokes about how people walked to get their awards. Even critique the way someone was standing while they waited.

3   Finally, the principal called for the 7th grade basketball team to walk up! My friends and I were the best players on team, and in middle school basketball is the sport to watch. We have a good team too, so we all were pretty cocky walking

to the center of the gym. As we stand and wait for our names to be called, I stand and try my best to look cool. Knowing it may be 8th graders that also critique every detail about you. Our team gets a lot of praise from fellow students; some players get more than others. My friends and I always get the most applause overall on our team at past pep rallies. So I expect nothing less this time. Now it's time for our coach to announce the starters, which were us. Coach V usually gives brief descriptions about us before having us walk up to him, and gets a letter or a pin if you had already received a letter. One by one I see my teammates trying to be cool just like me as they get their pins. Before I know it the coach starts describing me, it takes me a while to know for sure if he was talking about me. I saw that because we were all so alike in how we act and played on court, those in our starting lineup have about the same skill level. But he said something about my curly hair so I knew it was me. As soon as I hear my name I gather myself and start my proud walk to the coach.

4   About two seconds after hearing my name my moment is ruined by loud "boos!" I couldn't think of anything to do beside grin at where the "boos" were coming from. After the boos started spreading from other students my coach had to say something to stop them. I have never felt so embarrassed in my life. Luckily for me another one of the starters also got a few boos, but not as bad as mine. I didn't say a word through the rest of the pep assembly. Walking back to classes the same people I would make fun of now had the courage to say something and stick up for themselves. Come to find out that David got together with a few people I embarrassed along the years and started the "boo" chant. I got it the worst from my close friends because they never really had a lot of dirt to bring up on me. So now they knew how to get me, and no matter what I said back, nothing will top getting embarrassed in front of the entire school.

5   I had the reputation of hurting people's feelings, and if someone stood up to me I would just embarrass them even more. My close friends knew I didn't mean any harm and rubbed my insults off as jokes. For example, I didn't like when students would disrupt the class by asking stupid questions. When I was younger I had problems focusing, so if something got me off topic it was hard to refocus. So since my train of thought is already lost might as well make a few people laugh. So usually I used my classmate's aimless question against them. My attitude even got me in trouble with a few teachers; I don't like people telling me I am wrong. I was so blind back then; I didn't realize they were trying to help me.

6   Before the pep assembly I never really had anyone in particular hurt my feelings, because I knew they didn't mean harm by jokes against me. What I didn't know is that I was hurting other people's feelings with my words. Some may think I picked on people to get attention; on the contrary, I avoided being the center of attention. Growing up as the only child I always felt like someone was watching me. I did it to make the people close to me laugh, and it's better to let things out than keep them in. I showed completely no respect for people I didn't know, and that made me many enemies. Also, my family would pick those moments we're ashamed of most and make a joke out of it. I never took into

consideration that other families weren't brought up like mine. Unfortunately, most people I made fun of thought I was mean and that gave me the reputation of a bully.

7   Starting the next day at school I didn't make fun of people outside my close friends. And it took me a few weeks to even come back with jokes after they made fun of me for getting booed. I would never admit this back then but that pep assembly was one of the best things that happened to me in my 8 years at Whiteside. It's no telling how many people I would have hurt and made feel like I did if I didn't learn my lesson.

Polished draft:

An Unexpected Lesson

1   "If David has one more outburst I am going to make him eat those words." The class continued for about five minutes without interruption, until David opened up his mouth to ask another aimless question. I snapped, "If you listen instead of flirting with a girl who has no interest in you Mrs. White wouldn't have to repeat herself by answering your dumb questions." David looked at me dumbfounded, so I said, "Wow you have nothing to say, or were you just not paying attention to what I said either?" I apologized to Mrs. White for interrupting the class, and she seemed aggravated with both of us at this point. My job was done; David didn't ask a dumb question for the rest of the week. I may have won the battle, but David won the war.

2   It was 10:00 a.m. when my friends and I walked into the gym for the pep assembly at Whiteside Middle School. The students were separated by grades, and the teachers tried to get their students to settle down. I could notice fellow athletes from across the gym; they had that proud look on their faces just like me. As my friends and I waited for our turn to be recognized, we killed time by making fun of people in the gym. I could find any reason to make fun of someone. I enjoyed making my friends laugh even if I hurt someone else's feelings in the process. We would make jokes about how people walked to get their awards, even critique the way someone was standing while they waited.

3   Finally, the principal called for the 7th grade basketball team to walk up! My friends and I were the best players on team, and in middle school basketball is the sport to watch. We had a good team too, so we were all pretty cocky walking to the center of the gym. As we stood and waited for our names to be called, I tried my best to look cool, knowing 8th graders would also critique every detail about you. Our team got a lot of praise from fellow students; some players got more than others. My friends and I always got the most applause overall on our team at past pep rallies, so I expected nothing less this time. It was finally time for our coach to announce the starters. Coach V usually gives brief descriptions about

---

Verb tense: Changed from "goes" to "continued" to keep the story in past tense.

Verb tense: Changed from "and my friends and I are walking." Evan made multiple verb tense changes in this paragraph.

Verb tense: Though Evan changed many of the verbs to be past tense, he did not change this one because he believes that even today, basketball is still the sport to watch in middle school.

Sentence punctuation: These sentences were combined to get rid of another sentence fragment.

us before having us walk up to him and gives us a letter or a pin. One by one I saw my teammates trying to be cool just like me as they received their pins. Before I knew it the coach starts describing me; it took me a while to know for sure if he was talking about me because we were all so alike in how we act and played on court-- those in our starting lineup have about the same skill level. But he said something about my curly hair, so I knew it was me. As soon as I heard my name, I gathered myself and started my proud walk to the coach.

4   About two seconds after hearing my name, my moment was ruined by loud "boos!" I couldn't think of anything to do beside grin at where the "boos" were coming from. Then the boos started spreading from one section of the bleachers to the other students. My coach had to say something to stop them. I have never felt so embarrassed in my life. Luckily for me, another one of the starters also got a few boos, but those were not as bad as when my named was called. I didn't say a word through the rest of the pep assembly. Walking back to classes, I thought about how the same people I would make fun of now had the courage to say something and stick up for themselves. Come to find out that David got together with a few people I embarrassed along the years and started the "boo" chant. In the days that followed, I got it the worst from my close friends because they never really had a lot of dirt to bring up on me. So now they knew how to get me, and no matter what I said back, nothing would top getting embarrassed in front of the entire school.

5   I had the reputation of hurting people's feelings, and if someone stood up to me I would just embarrass them even more. My close friends knew I didn't mean any harm and rubbed my insults off as jokes. For example, I didn't like when students would disrupt the class by asking stupid questions. When I was younger I had problems focusing, so if something got me off topic it was hard to refocus. So since my train of thought was already lost might, I thought I might as well make a few people laugh. Usually I used my classmate's aimless question against them. My attitude even got me in trouble with a few teachers. I don't like people telling me I am wrong, but I was so blind back then that I didn't realize they were trying to help me.

6   Before the pep assembly I never really had anyone in particular hurt my feelings, because I knew they didn't mean harm by jokes against me. What I didn't know is that I was hurting other people's feelings with my words. Some people may think I picked on people to get attention; on the contrary, I avoided being the center of attention. Growing up as the only child I always felt like someone was watching me. I did it to make the people close to me laugh, and it's better to let things out than keep them in. I completely disrespected people I didn't know, and that made me many enemies. Also, my family would pick those moments we're ashamed of most and make a joke out of it. I never took into consideration that other families weren't brought up like mine. Unfortunately, most people I made fun of thought I was mean, and that gave me the reputation of a bully.

Rewording: extra words were deleted here because they distracted from the main point.

Stylistic choice: The sentences were combined and re-punctuated.

Editing for style: These sentences were broken apart to make the moment last longer.

Clarification: Evan added this transition to show that time progressed.

Editing for style: Evan deleted the "So" from the beginning of this sentence to avoid repetition.

Word choice: Changed from "I showed completely no respect for people"

7   Starting the next day at school, I didn't make fun of people outside my close friends. It took me a few weeks to even come back with jokes after they made fun of me for getting booed. I would never admit this back then, but that pep assembly was one of the best things that happened to me in my 8 years at Whiteside. There's no telling how many people I would have hurt if I hadn't learned my lesson.

Questions about Evan's writing:

1. Evan tried three different invention methods before beginning to write his first draft. How do you think that helped him to have a fuller draft? Use evidence from the invention and the draft to support your answer.
2. Read the feedback given to Evan in his second draft. How would you feel if you were given this kind of feedback? Compare it to the feedback you have been receiving.
3. The editing for his polished draft focused entirely on surface issues like shifting verb tenses, punctuation, and rewording a few sentences. What issues do you think you should focus on when polishing your own drafts?
4. Compare Evan's polished draft to Terrence's on page 000-000. Terrence added and deleted material while also trying to fix surface errors. Who ends up with the more finalized paper and why?

"This Person is Very Special to Me" Essays

About "A Special Woman Known as Lucy"

During our teaching careers, we have read many different versions of what some of our colleagues call "The Dead Grandma Essay." This essay (which on occasion deals with a grandfather or some other person) has at its core a celebration of how very special the subject of the essay was. That might sound, at first glance, like a great topic for an essay. However, many writing teachers come to dread this type of essay because of the problems that often creep up in it.

We've included below an essay that we ourselves have drafted so that you'll have a better idea of the problems that this type of essay can create for the reader. (The names below are all fictitious.) Try to identify where the essay goes wrong.

A Special Woman Known as Lucy

Everyone in today's society has somebody who is special to them, and that's one of the things that makes America great, but I have someone in my life who is special in a very unique way. This person is not young any more, though she once was. This person has shared advice with me that has benefitted me greatly. More than that, however, she has always been there for me, the biggest and best qualified cheerleader in my life, a person who has shown her love for me (as well as all my brothers and sisters and cousins) in a unique and powerful way. The person I am writing about is my Grandmother.

Lucy Smith still has a reputation in my family as the most caring, generous individual any of us has ever known or likely will know. Grandma Lucy was there at the door of the hospital when my mom and dad first strapped me in my brand new Cosco car seat (or at least that is the brand my mother thinks they bought for me). She was there at my fifth birthday party (I still have the pictures, though they are those old-fashioned Polaroid things), and she was there when I graduated eighth grade and got an award for Perfect Attendance K-8. As you can tell, Grandma Lucy played an important role in my upbringing.

My Uncle Mike got a phone call from the doctor who said his ankle was not healing normally, and Grandma was there to listen to my uncle gripe all night long (which was guaranteed to happen because he started pouring himself drinks right after the doctor called), and she was the one who did her best to convince him that he was too old, at age forty-two, to begin a professional hockey career, even if his ankle was working fine. She was his shoulder to cry on, but she was also the one who reminded him that he needed to get up in the morning so he could go to work and earn a paycheck.

Grandma Lucy baked brownies for my girl scout troop. In addition, she knitted wool sweaters for the dogs at the local humane society (which they did not use, according to the director who left a message on Grandma's answering machine in a rude voice, because they didn't like the smell of wet wool on wet dogs when it rained). Grandma excelled at showing the world that it is important to be a caring person even if you are growing older.

Grandma Lucy's husband, Harold, was my grandfather. I am told he did many admirable things too but he died before I was born so Grandma Lucy took center stage in my life, proving how special a person she was time and time again.

On that Tuesday morning three years ago, Grandma Lucy was not feeling well. But, like she usually did, she trooped on, baking those brownies until my mom told her maybe she shouldn't do that if she was having symptoms of the flu like she was. So when she was admitted to the hospital five days later our family took up half the hallway in a very large corridor on the third floor west of Memorial Hospital. Our love for Grandma was very evident. (My cousin Leigh Ann could not be there because she herself was suffering through the consequences of the flu, which was not any fun for her but fun was the farthest thing from our minds too that week.)

The dietician at the hospital was getting worried over the next two days because Grandma didn't feel like eating anything, and the dietician said she would talk to a nurse because that was a very bad sign in a person so old. She didn't really have a chance to do that, however, since Grandma's heart went into cardiac arrest five minutes later. I was in an elevator at the time, headed up to see Grandma with a bunch of hand-made cards from the second grade class my Aunt Jennifer taught in Litchfield. My mom stopped me from going into the room because they were removing the crash carts (as they are called) and all the rest of the special equipment and she wanted to go in alone to look at the recently deceased face of the woman who had raised her (that is, my mom) to be a good person. We all cried hard during the next three days, which were the saddest time that anyone in Madison County ever felt, or at least it's true for all the people who lived in the northern part of the county (especially in our town) during the first week of October of that year. My Grandmother was a legend in our town, and now she was in her coffin and dead. The funeral home held so many flowers (you could see and smell how popular and loving Grandma Lucy was). The flowers were some of the prettiest you could ever see.

Lucy Smith survived the Great Depression as a young girl but never talked about it. This shows a lot of character on her part, and I hope to follow her example in my own life when I have children and then someday (years down the road) some grandchildren of my own. Until then, I will proudly be known as Lucy Smith's Devoted Granddaughter.

Questions for Discussion or Writing:

1. What traits or actions of Grandma Lucy's are mentioned to support the idea that she played an important role in her family's life? Are any of those circumstances developed in enough detail to convince you that Grandma Lucy was more special or more devoted than other grandmothers?
2. Which details seem to distract readers from the larger point the writer intended to focus on?
3. Which situations or events from Grandma Lucy's life would you like to see the writer discuss in greater detail? In other words: If the writer revised this essay, are there any areas you believe the writer should focus on more heavily? How might such a change in focus help the essay?
4. What do you think of the way the essay is organized? What suggestions would you offer the writer regarding organization?

Suggestion Box: When You Want to Write about Someone Who Matters to You

Writing about someone who matters a great deal to you can be a meaningful experience. Sometimes it leads to a good essay as well—though not always.

The trick is to find a focus that will make the essay work for your readers, all of whom have their own "special people" in their lives. If you try to concentrate on the specialness of your subject, chances are the individual will not seem very special at all. Instead, you'll end up with a generic version of the person, a cardboard character instead of a real, living human being with good qualities as well as flaws.

Here's a strategy for getting beyond the bland, generic version of someone's life: Narrow your focus. Instead of trying to discuss decades of a person's life (or even four or five years), pick one event or situation that truly sheds light on this individual's most important trait or value. Slow down and share plenty of details with your readers about this situation, particularly what the person did or did not do while dealing with this situation. In other words, do not just tell your readers about how wonderful the person is; rather, use concrete details to show how the person's true character revealed itself in this situation. (The expression "show, don't just tell" is good advice for all writers.)

"My Promise to John"

About "A Promise to John"—a successful essay about an influential person

The essay below discusses a person who was influential in the writer's life. This essay could have fallen into some of the traps inherent in the "Special Person" genre, but thankfully, "A Promise to John" manages to rise above those issues. As you read the essay, ask yourself: What traits make this piece successful?

My Promise to John

On November 14, 2001, I met John. I thought he was just another loser my mom was bringing around. I was used to that. I met him at our counseling session, when my sister and I were in foster care. I didn't expect to like him, or even love him. After a few times of meeting him, I realized he wasn't like all the other guys my mom had around. He helped my mom get her act together and be a better person. I couldn't believe how much she was changing. She was becoming the mother I've wanted her to be my entire life.

On December 6, 2001, we got to move back in with my mom. John went crazy looking for a house big enough for all of us, because his son was living with him as well. He also wanted to keep my sister and me in the same school, because he understood how difficult it was on us switching schools so much. When we got to move into the home with him, he sat us both down and explained the rules to us. As first, I thought, "This man is crazy. Did he actually think that I was going to listen to his rules? He's not my father; he's got to be insane." Then he did something I never expected. He asked my opinion on the rules. He wanted to know if I thought they were fair and reasonable. I was so shocked that I just nodded my head in agreement. I have always strived to not get close to any guys my mother brought home, because she would never keep them very long. There was something different about John though. I couldn't put my finger on it, and wouldn't be able to do so for a few more years.

I never had a cross word with John. Instead of yelling at me, he would sit down and talk to me. We would stay up real late at night watching the old black and white movies on PBS, and we would just talk and get to know each other. For some reason, we had an amazing connection to each other. I was still real cautious about it though, because I was just waiting for him to leave or end his relationship with my mom. But it wasn't happening, we got closer and closer.

I dropped out of high school four months before graduation. It was a very dumb decision, I know. My mom didn't seem to care too much; she only went to high school up until the 10th grade. But John was upset. He was real disappointed in me. I couldn't handle it, because he wouldn't talk to me. I ended up moving out of their house and in with a friend. I didn't go to my mom and John's wedding, I didn't call and talk to them. I felt like I wasn't wanted around, so I made sure that I wasn't there. I hated every minute of it. I couldn't stand not talking to him. He had become an important person in my life and I couldn't live without our connection, our bond. I felt like I was going insane with the fear of him never speaking to me again.

Then John had a heart attack. I was so freaked out. I moved home to help take care of him. Well come to find out, they were moving and there was no room for me. I ended up moving out again. I still stayed in constant contact with John. There was not a single day that went by that I didn't talk to him. I could call him and ask stupid questions that I already knew the answer to, just to have him talk to me. I was so happy to have that bond back; I wanted to soak up every minute of it.

John was there with me the day I was told I could never have children; that situation was pretty hard on me. When I found out that I was pregnant, it was a shock and a blessing all in one. John and I sat for hours just crying. He was there for me every step of the way. Right before I had my son, my mom and John bought another house. John built a room for me and my son in this house. We moved my stuff in and not long after that, I had my son.

When I had my son, Cayden, John asked me what my plan was. I wasn't sure what he meant. He asked me what I was planning on doing to make my life better for my son. I didn't know how to answer that question because I hadn't really thought about that. I should have, but I didn't. He made me promise that I would go to school and become something, do something positive with my life. I told him that I kind of wanted to be a social worker; he was so excited about that. He told me that I would be excellent at that job, because of my life hardships.

In October of 2007, John was sick a lot. We thought he had the stomach flu. He wouldn't go to the doctor though. We tried so hard to get him to go to the doctor. He started turning yellow and we were really confused. He still wouldn't go to the doctor. Finally the guys that he worked with talked him into going to the doctor. By then it was November.

The day he went into the hospital was November 17, 2007. I was on my way to my cousin's birthday party when I got a phone call from my mom. She said that I needed to come up to the hospital and get her and John's truck, because they were keeping John in the hospital. I had my cousin take me up to the hospital instead of going to the party.

When I got to the hospital, my mom was crying pretty hard. I asked her what was going on. She told me that the doctors couldn't figure out what was wrong with him, but he was urinating blood. There was so much blood in his urine that it looked like a lager beer. John was in there for about a week and they still couldn't figure out what was wrong with him.

The hospital transferred him to Barnes Jewish Hospital. He was there for four hours and they knew what was wrong with him. He had pancreatic cancer. There was a tennis ball size tumor sitting in the middle of his pancreas duct, spleen duct, and liver duct. We were crushed. The doctor explained everything to us. He said that John was already in a very bad stage, stage 4. He said there weren't a lot of options at this point, but he wanted to get the tumor out.

He wanted to do a Whipple procedure. They cut his stomach from one side to the other, basically gave him an upside down smiley face cut. His surgery took 13 hours. I sat in the waiting room the whole time, worried out of my mind. When we finally got the word that he was in the recovery room, it was like there was 50 lbs. lifted off my chest. We couldn't go see him yet and that made me mad. I wanted to be there when he woke up, but it wasn't allowed. He was in recovery for two hours. We finally got to go see him once he was back into a regular room. It was weird for me to see him like that. He was so helpless. He didn't look like John.

Through the next five months, he was in and out of the hospital a lot. He had a lot of complications from his surgery and couldn't get his pain under control. In June of 2008, they decided to start his chemotherapy. He did that for a month, then a month of radiation, then another month of chemotherapy. That was really hard to see, because he was sicker from that then before we found out what was wrong with him.

He was finally done with all of that in September of 2008. He wasn't getting any better though. When this all started he was 208 lbs.-- by the time he was done with the chemo and radiation, he weighed 130 lbs. He was in and out of the hospital a lot, still with the constant pain. By Halloween of 2008, we had a total of 486 visits to the hospital. In November of 2008, things just seemed to have gotten worse. He couldn't get up out of bed, he wasn't eating, and he didn't want to see anyone. We took him to one last doctor's appointment. It was not a good visit. The doctor said that we needed to look into Hospice care for him. He also said that if John lived past Thanksgiving, it would be a miracle.

We got hold of Hospice, they brought a hospital bed. John loved it, because he could position the bed to how he needed it to be comfortable. My mom didn't like it though, because they were no longer in the same bed. There was a nurse that came in and gave him his medicines. She would help change the diapers he was wearing at that point. She would give my mom and me a break, basically.

At this point, I was mad. I didn't understand why this had to happen to my family. Why did this have to happen to me? I was getting married and I wanted John to walk me down the aisle. Now he wasn't going to be able to do that. Then I was so mad at myself. How could I be so selfish? How could I only think of myself when John was dying? How could I only think of how this was affecting me, when I wasn't even thinking of how it was affecting John?

I sat down and had a serious talk with John. I asked him every question I could think of. He was giving me his 2002 Dodge Dakota truck, because I was the one who took him to every doctor's appointment and was there for him every step of the way. I wasn't doing all of that to get something out of it. I was doing all of that because I loved him. I made sure I told him that every day. After everything he had done for me, it was only right for me to be there for him when all this was going on.

A week before he died he got all his affairs in order. I came over to see him and he explained everything to me. He made me promise that I would let him die at home. I made the promise to him. I also got a tattoo that I made sure he saw every day before he died. I got the same tattoo on my shoulder that he had on his leg, a half crescent moon with a star in front of it, the North Star. I got my tattoo in my favorite colors, yellow and orange; he got his in his favorite colors, red and blue. In mine, though, I got his initials, JGR.

On November 21, 2008 I received a phone call from my mom at about 9pm. She was freaking out. She said that John was throwing up blood and she couldn't handle it. She said that she wanted to call for an ambulance and have him taken to the hospital. I said, "Don't do anything until I get there." My fiancée and I called his parents and asked them to watch our son. They knew what was going on and were fine with it.

I got to my parents' home at about 11pm. My mom was bawling her eyes out and sitting in the living room. I didn't even say a word to her, I went straight to John. He was trying to get the trash can to throw up in. I grabbed it and held it for him. After he was done, I wiped the blood from his mouth. He grabbed my hand and said, "Hey baby. Can you tell me something?" I told him I would tell him whatever he wanted to know. He asked me, "Am I home?" I told him that he was at home and I was going to take care of him. That was the last thing he ever said. I stayed with him all night and the next day and night. I had my mom call his kids over, because I knew what was happening. His oldest daughter and his son came over immediately. His other daughter couldn't be there; unfortunately, she lives in Chicago.

That evening on November 22, 2008 we all gathered around John's hospital bed. We all sat holding onto John and praying. At 8:22 pm John took his final breath. That was the most difficult thing in my life that I have ever done. I have never seen anyone die, and after that, it's definitely something that I don't ever want to see again. They asked me to leave the room so they could clean his body and get his body ready for the coroner. I wasn't ready to leave, but I couldn't stand to see any of that happen. I gave him one last kiss and left the room.

We had his funeral the day before Thanksgiving. He was buried at Jefferson Barracks, because of his service in Vietnam and Desert Storm. The gun salute was the hardest thing for me at the funeral. With every shot, I jumped and cried even harder. I'm not sure if it was the gunshot itself that made me cry, or what it represented. The ride back to my parents' house was so hard. When I walked into the house, everyone was there, eating and telling stories about John. Cayden was asleep in the playpen. I sat down next to it and just cried. When he woke up, I was still there. He reached out for me and I got him out. He gave me the biggest hug and a kiss on my cheek, and then he wiped the tears off my face. He said, "It's ok, Momma." Of course, I cried even more after he did that.

The next day while we were cooking Thanksgiving dinner, I couldn't help but cry while I was basting the turkey. John usually did that. When my fiancée carved the turkey, I cried again, John did that too. It was a very hard day for me. It felt like we were leaving John out of his Thanksgiving duties, like we were taking over. It's still really hard for me not to cry every time I get into my truck. When I go to his gravesite, it's not easy. My son goes up to the tombstone and kisses and hugs it and says, "That's my Papa."

It's coming up on a year that he's been gone. I am happy that I can go to his gravesite and tell him that I am going to school. I am fulfilling my promise to him. I know that he's looking down at me and he is proud of me. When I have a dream about him, I wake up smiling. I know when he comes to me in a dream that means he's letting me know that he's keeping an eye on me. He's making sure that I'm doing things the way that I should. He's helping me do the things that I need to do for me and my son.

Yes it hurts that he's not here to see it all and give me his praise, but I know that he's watching. I feel the praise every day with the warmth of the sun, the smile on my son, and the love of my son. I know he's there helping me every step of the way, just as he's always done.

I have a picture in my truck, on the sun visor, of John and me dancing at my sweet 16 birthday party. Every time I get in my truck, I look at the picture and say "Hi, John. I love and miss you." When I pull into the parking lot at school, before I get out, I look at it and say, "I'm at school again, John." For me to be able to say that to the picture every day, it helps me know that I'm living up to my word. I am keeping my promise and I will until the day that I have the job that John and I talked about. I will never stop and never give up, for John.

Questions for Discussion or Writing:

1. What details in the essay make John seem like a real person (instead of just a character someone made up)?
2. Even though this essay covers a number of years, the writer decided to depict certain scenes in detail, while summarizing other aspects of the relationship. Choose a scene that is developed in detail and analyze why the writer decided to give that section extra attention.
3. If the writer were required to reduce the essay by one-third, what would you advise the writer to leave out or condense? What material, by contrast, is absolutely essential?
4. If a friend asked you to sum up this essay's main idea in two or three sentences, what would you come up with? Could that summary truly replace the experience of reading the essay, or not? Why or why not?

Assignments and Writing Opportunities

Your own instructor can't imagine every writing situation—every rhetorical challenge—you will face. Neither can we. The journal prompts and assignments in this section are designed to get your minds working in different ways. They are designed to give your writing skills a work-out, much like the work-out your body might get if you were to go to a gym. You will learn more—and probably grow more as a writer—if you put your heart into these writing opportunities.

We think these prompts will help you prepare for new writing situations you will face in your life (within college and without) as well as in your career.

When responding to these prompts, try to write as much as possible. If you get stuck, try asking yourself, "Why?" or "How?" after the statements you have already written. That may help you to add more response.

Journal Prompts

Journal Item 1
Things Famous Writers Have Said About Writing

Choose one or two of the quotations below and write *at least* a good paragraph explaining why you chose the quotation--e.g., in what way the quote reflects your own attitude toward (or experiences with) writing.

"There's nothing to writing. All you do is sit down at a typewriter and open a vein. --Red Smith

"I wrote my first novel because I wanted to read it." --Toni Morrison

"We are a species that needs and wants to understand who we are. Sheep lice do not seem to share this longing, which is one reason why they write so little." --Anne Lamott

"We write to think--to be surprised by what appears on the page; to explore our world with language; to discover meaning that teaches us and that may be worth sharing with others." --Donald M. Murray

"I always wanted to write a book that ended with the word mayonnaise." --Richard Brautigan

"A good writer always works at the impossible." --John Steinbeck

" Writing is an exploration. You start from nothing and learn as you go." --E.L. Doctorow

"Writers are athletes of the psyche." --Lloyd Kropp

"You need a certain amount of nerve to be a writer." --Margaret Atwood

"Writing is putting one's obsessions in order." --Jean Grenier

"I like to write when I feel spiteful; it's like having a good sneeze." --D. H. Lawrence

"Getting even is one reason for writing." --William Gass

"It has been said that writing comes more easily if you have something to say." --Sholem Asch

"I publish a piece in order to kill it, so that I won't have to fool around with it any longer." --William Glass

"I talk out the lines as I write." --Tennessee Williams

"I often quote myself. It adds spice to my conversation." --George Bernard Shaw

"You write a hit play the same way you write a flop." --William Saroyan

"Literature is simply the appropriate use of language." --Cyril Connolly

"Words are, of course, the most powerful drug used by mankind." -- Rudyard Kipling

"Style is effectiveness of assertion." --George Bernard Shaw

"Great literature is simply language charged with meaning to the utmost possible degree." --Ezra Pound

"Your audience is one single reader. I have found that sometimes it helps to pick out one person--a real person you know, or an imagined person, and write to that one." --John Steinbeck

"I have no fans. You know what I got? Customers." --Mickey Spillane

"Sir, no man but a blockhead ever wrote except for money." --Samuel Johnson

"My main reason for adopting literature as a profession was that, as the author is never seen by his clients, he need not dress respectably." --George Bernard Shaw

"Poets are born, not paid." --Wilson Mizner

"Let's face it, writing is hell." --William Styron

"What is written without effort is in general read without pleasure." --Samuel Johnson

"Who casts to write a living line, must sweat." --Ben Jonson

"Easy reading is damned hard writing." --Nathaniel Hawthorne

"It is perfectly okay to write garbage--as long as you edit brilliantly." --C. J. Cherryh

"The one absolute requirement for me to write . . . is to be awake." --Isaac Asimov

"I love criticism so long as it's unqualified praise." --Noel Coward

"Asking a working writer what he thinks about critics is like asking a lamppost what it feels about dogs."   --John Osborne

"I have rewritten--often several times--every word I have ever published. My pencils outlast their erasers." --Vladmir Nabokov

"I write any sort of rubbish which will cover the main outlines of the story; then I can begin to see it." --Frank O'Connor

"Let your literary compositions be kept from the public eye for nine years at least." –Horace

"When I'm near the end of [writing] the book, I sleep in the same room with it. Somehow the book doesn't leave you when you're asleep right next to it." --Joan Didion

And last but not least:

"Writing . . . keeps me from believing everything I read." --Gloria Steinem

(The quotations above are drawn primarily from two books: *Shoptalk*, by Donald M. Murray, and *Writers on Writing*, by Jon Winokur.)

Journal Item 2
Does Writing Make You Sweat?

What anxieties, concerns, or worries do you have about writing, especially about writing for college or on the job? Be specific. Where do those concerns come from?

If you do not have many concerns or worries about your writing abilities or the writing tasks you will face in college, where does your confidence in your writing abilities come from?

Journal Item 3
Preferred Writing Conditions

Write about your usual time/place/situation for doing homework and/or writing. Then do a homework assignment in a different manner (i.e. in pencil instead of on the computer or at a desk instead of on the floor). Were there any differences in the outcome? Explore your preferences and why they seem to work for you.

Journal Item 4
Control and the Writer

Most writers do their best work when they write about something they care about. How does this idea apply to your own writing?

How do you cope with situations where you do not have total control over the topic? Can you still "survive" as a student writer when you do not have an opportunity to choose the topic? What can you do to improve your odds of success in that situation?

Journal Item 5
Asking for Help

Write about an occasion when you were hesitant (or maybe just plain afraid) to ask for help with a situation or problem that frustrated you. This might be a school-related problem or not. (Think especially about concepts or skills you were working at understanding in school, things you struggled with learning.) Why did you not want to ask for help? What was the risk? How did this situation turn out?

Journal Item 6
Share and Share Alike?

How do you feel about sharing your writing with other people? *Why* is doing that easy or difficult for you? What concerns or hopes do you have when you share your writing with other people?

Journal Item 7
Feedback

How important is it to you that you get *honest* feedback on your writing? How important is it that you get *detailed* feedback? Why are those things important to you? (Or why are they not important to you, if that's the case?) How do you feel when giving feedback to others?

Journal Item 8
Audience

Think about the first draft you wrote of your most recent paper. Who were you writing to? After you received feedback on the paper, did the audience change? Who were you writing to in the subsequent drafts? What does that audience *need to know* about the topic? What does that audience *already know* that you will not need to tell them? How does that audience *feel* about the topic? In what ways will this help you to revise for the next draft?

Journal Item 9
Revision

What did you find yourself doing the most when you revised your draft: adding, deleting, moving, rewording? What did your peers and your instructor say that your draft needed? Do you feel like you were able to change that element of your paper? What was the easiest part of improving this draft? What was the hardest part?

Journal Item 10
The Director's Commentary

If you rent or own DVDs, maybe you've listened to the DVD's audio commentary track, in which a director (or a screenwriter, actor, or film critic) discusses some of the more interesting aspects of the film. In effect, the commentator ends up reflecting on some of the choices that the creators made in the film.

You're going to do the same thing, essentially, with part of your essay. Select a <u>relatively brief passage</u> from one of your papers (maybe 150-250 words long) and <u>offer your reflections on some of the choices</u> you made as the creator of that passage. In other words, dig into your own thought process and figure out why you included that detail, or why you deleted a thought that previously was part of this passage, or why you worded this sentence the way you did. (For instance: What were you trying to accomplish with that detail or example or word choice? What concerns did you have -- or do you now have, perhaps -- about this choice or that choice which you made in the passage? How were you hoping readers would react to this question that you explored in this passage, or to this anecdote which you offered?) The more detail you go into in your reflection, the better. Writers grow when they think deeply about the choices they make in their writing.

Journal Item 11
Influence of Peer Reviews and Conferences

What influence do peer reviews and conferences have on your essays? What provides the best feedback for you? How do you sift through all the advice to know what you need to do? Or how do you manage the lack of meaningful feedback (if that has happened to you)? When is the best time to use peer review and which format works best for you, and why?

Journal Item 12
Time and Effort

How much time and effort have you been putting into this writing class? What part of this class takes the most time? What do you think an appropriate amount of time and effort would look like for the best possible success in this class? Which part of class should you spend more time on? Is there anything you are spending too much time doing?

Journal Item 13
Audience Part II

What audience do you usually write to (teacher, classmates, yourself, a thoroughly generic all-encompassing audience)? Is it always the same or does it vary sometimes? If so, when? What role do you think audience *should* play in your writing process?

Journal Item 14
Focus of Comments from Readers

What have the comments on your papers from the instructor and peer review all focused on? Is there something that you have struggled with on all of the papers or has it changed from paper to paper? What have you done to improve upon this area (or these areas)?

Journal Item 15
End of the Semester Reflection

Write about the papers you've worked on for this class. Which was the hardest and why? What kind of time and effort went into each one? Would you do anything differently now?

Journal Item 16
Personal vs. Impersonal

Do you prefer personal styles of papers or impersonal? How do you deal with the one you do not prefer? What are your strengths in the one you prefer? How will this influence what you do for the next paper assignment?

Journal Item 17
Weaknesses and Improvements

What are your major weaknesses as a writer or a student and how will you work to improve them? How does this class help? What will you do to continue building up those traits after you leave the class?

Journal Item 18
Strengths

What do you think are your writing strengths? How do you make sure to utilize your strengths? Do you think these strengths are significant enough for you to pass to the next class? Why or why not?

Assignment Bank

The following assignments are broken into two categories: open-ended prompts and focused assignments. There is overlap between these two categories, so some assignment prompts may direct you to look at another, similar assignment for more ideas.

Open-Ended Prompts

The purpose of an open-ended prompt is to give you a starting point. The goal is for you as the writer to use the ideas in the prompts when beginning your invention work. Most of the prompts will suggest freewriting, but you could just as easily use other methods of invention from Chapter 2 if you find them to be more useful to you.

1. Read through the prompt

2. Write down the question(s) or idea(s) that interest you most

3. Begin your invention work

4. Do more invention after a break. Maybe try focused freewriting or a different method of invention than what you used the first time. (See Chapter 2 for ideas)

5. Continue doing invention until you have decided what you would like the purpose/message of your paper to be. Then write the first draft.

The beauty of the open-ended prompts is that they do not ask for you to write a specific message for the paper. You get to decide what you want your message to be. Your instructor will probably just ask that the first draft of the paper relate to the prompt's overall topic or idea.

Literacy Narrative

In this paper, you'll explore your history as a reader, writer, and user of language. In particular, you can explore how various experiences (in school, at home, or elsewhere) have helped shape the attitudes that you currently have about writing, reading, and language. This assignment does not assume that you are necessarily in love with writing and reading (though maybe you are). Even if you have a more complicated relationship with those activities, you still have a literacy narrative within you. Everyone does.

Questions to explore: (choose only the most interesting or relevant to you)

- Describe how you think of yourself as a writer. Be honest.

- Do you enjoy writing? Why or why not? What (if anything) do you like about writing as an activity? What (if anything) do you dislike about writing as an activity?
- What aspect of reading (if any) do you find frustrating? When did you first start to feel that frustration?
- How did you develop the attitudes you have toward writing? Have your attitudes about writing changed over time? (How?)
- What experiences in your life would you point to in explaining why you think or feel the way you do about writing? Try to be as specific as possible.
- Who taught you what "writing" is all about? How convincing (or unconvincing) was that person's sales pitch?
- What's the best piece of advice someone has given you about writing or reading? The least helpful advice?
- How much practice have you had as a writer? What <u>type</u> of writing practice did you get in school or in your personal life? (For instance, did you have lots of practice in essay writing? Or did your practice mostly consist of completing a lot of grammar exercises? etc.)
- In what ways are your attitudes towards writing connected to your attitudes toward reading?
- What value (if any) do you see in writing?
- Discuss a time when you felt proud about something you had written.
- Discuss a concern you have about your writing or discuss a time when you realized you needed to work on some aspect of your writing. What goals do you have for yourself as a writer? In what writing-related areas do you think you might become stronger?
- Who is a writer that you admire or enjoy? Why do you enjoy that person's work?
- We'll do some freewriting in response to many of these questions. We'll examine in class how you can use that freewriting to get your first draft off the ground.

From Your Past

For this essay, you'll be writing about either a time in your life that you would like to repeat or a time that you would not want to live through again even if someone paid you a million dollars.

Some tips for this assignment:

- Brainstorm a list of possibilities before doing more invention work.

- Consider exploring how one experience was both difficult and yet also worthwhile.

- Your paper can be narrative—that is, it can tell what happened in time order (similar to Travis Wilson's "The Kill" that appears in the Draft Collection) -- or it can be organized around issues that were unique to that point in your life.

- Choose a topic you will feel comfortable writing about in detail and sharing with others--e.g., your instructor and classmates. Each of us has a right to a "private zone" in our lives. Respect your own boundaries when choosing the subject for this paper.

It's Not So Simple

Most of us sometimes reduce complex issues to clear-cut, simple observations. In other words, we opt for a bumper-sticker approach to an issue that is really complex. (Think about the average bumper sticker. They're no more than one or two sentences, and maybe just a sentence fragment of a thought.) This assignment asks you to tackle an issue or question that you believe many people (perhaps most) OVERSIMPLIFY -- something where you yourself believe it's NOT so simple.

Brainstorm a list of times or issues in your life that have been complicated.

Brainstorm a list of things that you think are really simple and easy.

Compare those lists. Is there anything in the first list that others might oversimplify? What about the second list? Is there anything on that list that maybe is much more complicated than it seems at first glance?

In class activity: Work with others in class to decide which topic(s) might be worth exploring in a first draft.

Informal Argument

Choose a topic about which you have a strong opinion. Figure out who needs to hear your opinion; this will be your audience for the essay. Consider what kinds of support you will need to provide to get that audience to see things your way.

Brainstorm a list of words, phrases, questions, situations that come to mind when you think of this topic.

For at least five days in a row (maybe even six or seven?), freewrite for ten to fifteen minutes about one or more of the things you wrote down during your brainstorming.

Now, write a first draft of your essay. The tone and the evidence are up to you. Make the choices you think are necessary in order to have a good argument. For the moment, do not worry about how argumentative you are. There's lots of room on the spectrum from subtle to "in your face." Get your first draft down; you can always change the essay later.

Portrait of Yourself Essay

Bring some pictures of yourself to class. Your pictures can be formal or casual, real or hand-drawn. The choice is yours. You will be writing about these pictures in class, and probably talking about them, too.

In class activity: Write about your own picture and why you chose it. What do you think it says about you? Would someone be able to get the "real you" from this picture? Why or why not? Share your response with the class.

Most portraits capture the subject at just one moment in time. In reality, though, each of us is a moving portrait. Who we are stays essentially the same, but our "image" shifts depending on where we are, what we're doing, or who we're around. For this essay, write about the ways that your image changes OR write about the way you choose to present yourself. You could even write about what a portrait of you would look like.

Questions to consider:

- Think of different ways that you change for different people or places. How and why do these changes happen?

- What do you do to influence how others see you? How much do others' perceptions of you matter to you?

- How would you want to be presented in a portrait? How would you be posed? Where would you be? What would you look like? What would be with you? Why?

In class activity: Look at a variety of portraits. Check out the websites for the National Portrait Gallery [http://www.npg.si.edu/] and the American Museum of Photography [http://www.photographymuseum.com/]. Discuss what differentiates these portraits from the pictures that were brought to class by students.

Essay about Learning & Education

Choose one of the topics below for your next essay topic. As part of your invention process, do a freewrite (seven to ten minutes) about at least three of the topic possibilities below. After you freewrite, go back and look through your journal entries to date. Is there anything from your journal entries that seems to match up with ideas from your freewrites?

Decide which topic below you have the greatest interest in. Your freewrites and journal entries should give you a good sense of this. Write a first draft of your essay.

- Many students say that school just isn't for them, they find it boring, they can't learn like other students. Could this be because schools often teach to just one learning style? Do you think college classes do enough to reach students of different learning styles?

- What do you think students need in order to be prepared for college? What was your experience? How did it prepare you (or not prepare you) for college classes?

- Consider what "intelligence" means to you. What should we learn while in school--and why? How should we learn in school?

- Tell about an out-of-school situation or event that taught you more than you might have learned if you had spent those same hours (or days or years) in school learning from teachers and textbooks. Explain how the situation came about, how you were involved in it, what happened, and (most important of all) what you learned from the experience (etc.).

- Jonathan Kozol, a former teacher who is often critical of the ways schools function and what they teach (or do not teach) students, believes that schools encourage too much conformity of thought and behavior. James Baldwin, a novelist and social critic, argued much the same thing in a speech he gave to teachers in 1965. Based on your own experiences or the experiences of people you know, what do you think? Are schools too focused on conformity? How so? Or is school perhaps too much a free-for-all, a place where anything goes? Explore what could be done to improve the situation (whatever the situation may be).

Essay about Work I

You are welcome to focus your essay on any of the options listed below (all of which, of course, have something to do with work or education). Whatever option you choose, your essay should include **plenty of details** and **plenty of reflection/critical thought**. Telling a story, by itself, isn't enough.

- Discuss a career field you are thinking about going into. Explore what has led you to be interested in that field. Discuss the ways in which this field is a good fit for your life: how does it relate (for instance) to your interests, aptitudes, values, and earning goals? (etc.)

- Discuss the experiences and people who have influenced the way you view the world of work, or a particular career. How would you describe your views of work? How did you develop those views? Get specific. How do those views and experiences affect your life today? How have they helped to shape the plans you have for your future?

- What's the difference between a job and a career?

- This option is the flip side of the first option above. What career would be a terrible, lousy, awful fit for you? Why? Is there anything that could happen that would make that career a good fit? Why is that career a good fit for some people, but not you? What type of personality or traits does that career require, anyway?

Essay about Families

- Choose one of the topics below. Some of these topics are more personal than others; be sure to choose one with which you will feel comfortable.

- Discuss the behavior and character traits of a television family. (As an alternative, a family from a film would probably work fine.) Describe for your readers both the behavior that this TV family typically displays in the series and what you think about the behavior or traits of the television family. (Do not just summarize what happens on the show.) Go into plenty of detail. Make your readers think.

- Describe an experience that captures a trait found in your family, a trait that is central to what your family is like or how members of your family view your family. Describe the event (using plenty of details) and show what this event reveals about your family. If at all possible, surprise your readers in some way.

- On occasion, politicians have been known to talk about the "family values" they hold dear. Does that phrase mean the same thing to everybody? Are you comfortable when politicians use that phrase or propose laws based on their own sense of family values? Why or why not?

- Discuss someone from outside your family whose actions or attitudes have influenced you as much as (if not more than) members of your immediate family. Focus on one person, not several. Go into detail about the nature of that influence (positive? negative? some other type of influence?) and how the person influenced you (what did this person do or say?)

- This last choice is almost--but not quite--a free-for-all topic about families and family life. Write an essay that evolves out of the thinking and conversation that occurs in this invention activity.

In class activity: Collaborative invention activity. Write the phrase "FAMILIES AND..." at the top of your page. Then, take the word or phrase you've been dealt by your classmate (from the list below) and discuss that topic (e.g., Families and...Anger) with the person you've paired up with. You do not have to focus specifically on your own family--you might, for instance, think about the family next door, the ways families are portrayed on TV, a family depicted in a movie you've recently seen, etc. (E.g., How does a dysfunctional TV family deal with anger compared to a so-called "functional" TV family where everybody more or less gets along and respects the other people? What sort of communication exists among George Clooney's character and his siblings in *Up in the Air*?). Take notes on what you and your partner say. (By the way: Some of these topics may seem too close to home on occasion. For that reason, respect your partner's right to "pass" on one or two of the topics you suggest.) Based on what you or your partner has said, do you see a possible topic there for an essay? Perhaps a couple good topics? List for this exercise: **Role models ... Disagreement ... Communication ... Dishonesty ... Competing needs ... Challenges ... Divorce ... Children ... Anger ... Support ... Fear .... Questions ... Perfection ... Worry ... Happiness ... Stress ... Jobs**

Focused Prompts

These prompts are traditional assignments from across the disciplines; in such assignments, instructors typically have more specific expectations for what the final paper will look like. These expectations are still, in a sense, only guidelines because an instructor may change the requirements in one or more ways. Consequently, you should always pay close attention to the specific instructions given to you by your instructor.

Analysis

To analyze is to pick something apart, examine the pieces, and put it back together again in a meaningful way.

-Attention to detail is important here. Which details did you notice? Why did you notice them? Why do you think they are important? How can they help people understand the overall meaning of the whole piece being explored?

-Examine your analysis subject multiple times. Think about what you've noticed that someone new to it might overlook. Bring these observations to the reader's attention and tell him or her why they are important.

-Think about putting together a puzzle: the pieces all have colors and images of their own, but put together, they make a bigger picture. The reader will need to be shown the details of the little pieces but also reminded of how they contribute to the bigger picture.

Campus Art

Take a walk around campus--either by yourself or with a small group of friends/classmates. Find at least one piece of art on campus that you find truly interesting. (Remember that art can take many forms: paintings, collages, sculpture, multi-media pieces, etc.)

Find a place to set up shop for ten to fifteen minutes. Jot down what the artwork looked like, what you imagine it would feel like if you were to touch it, what it resembled, how it was different from or similar to other things found in that part of campus. How did this piece of art make you feel? What was your immediate reaction? What was your reaction a few moments later? No right or wrong answers here. You're just collecting your impressions. The more impressions you write down, the better.

Go back to the artwork a couple days later. Write down any new details you notice. Take notice also of how other people seem to respond to it. Do you notice it? Do they turn their eyes away? Do they smile when they see it, or frown? (If you're brave, you might ask some of them what they think of it.)

Go home and freewrite and/or brainstorm for fifteen minutes about the piece and the reactions it draws. Speculate about where those reactions come from.

Do some more freewriting and/or brainstorming about why and how the piece was created. Speculate about what the artist was thinking as he or she worked on it. Why did the artist arrange it that way? Why did the artist choose the colors, materials, shapes that appear in the piece? (No, you can't know for sure. But speculate anyway. Offer your best guesses.)

Freewrite and brainstorm some more about how you think the artist went about composing--creating--this piece.

Write an essay discussing the most interesting ideas or reactions that came out of your invention phase above.

Song Connection Essay

Choose a song which holds some meaning for you--not just a favorite song, but a song to which you attach some significance.

Before you look up the lyrics, freewrite about why this song is important to you--what it says about you; what experience or event or theme in your life it's connected to in your mind; why this is a song that is more than just a catchy tune for you.

Find the lyrics. Try a site such as http://www.allthelyrics.com/.

Freewrite about the lyrics. Perhaps start by picking a couple lines and freewriting about those lines. Then do the same for another few lines. Then, eventually, freewrite about the song as a whole. Think about the words, yes, but at some point try freewriting about the "sound" of the song--the melody, the singer's style, the impact the instruments have in the song and on your feelings when you hear the song.

What's the "opposite" of this song? Can you think of a song or a movie or experience that this song just would not fit with very well? Freewrite about that, too.

Draw from your freewriting as you develop and shape the first draft of an essay about this song's significance in your life and why it's part of your life's soundtrack. Go beyond just telling readers why you like the song. Show your readers why the song will forever remind you of a particular moment and why the song was such a good "fit" for that moment in your life.

Website Analysis

Choose a website that is designed to be persuasive or advocacy-oriented (your instructor may provide a list or give you more guidelines). Identify the website's main goal and the audience it is trying to reach. Examine how the different elements of the website (visual and/or text and/or interactive features) make the website effective or ineffective in its mission.

- How did you know the main message?
- What additional messages or goals does the organization have?
- Where did you find the most interesting information on the page? Why do you think it is placed in this location?
- Evaluate the use of visuals (pictures, color choices, organization, etc).
- Consider looking at a different website from a similar type of organization. This will
- help you spot the ways in which your chosen website is special or unique.

Summary/Response

This assignment calls for 2 parts: a summary and your response. The summary is an explanation of the assigned reading, event, etc. The summary should be shorter than the original work and contain the main idea and the highlights (or an overview). It should also include an explanation of anything that might be relevant in your response section. The response is your opinion or evaluation of what was summarized. It often focuses in the elements that were most interesting or that were particularly well done or awful.

Tips for the summary part:

-Ask yourself what someone who is unfamiliar with the reading or event would need to know in order to "get it."

-For the first draft, it is better to include too much information than to not put enough. A reviewer can tell you which parts go into too much detail more easily than he can tell you to add something he doesn't know about.

-A natural way to organize a summary is to go in chronological (time) order.

-Keep your opinion out of this section (unless your instructor has told you otherwise)

Tips for the response part:

-Ask yourself what stood out the most to you while you read, listened, etc.

-If you took notes, read through those notes and highlight or underline the parts you think you should include in your response paper.

-Identify your reaction to different moments of the reading or event and then ask yourself why you reacted that way. For instance, if something was confusing, try to identify what was going on in that moment and why it was unclear.

-This part of the essay should be as long as (if not, longer than) the summary. This is your opportunity to share your thoughts. Explain what you thought about it and why. You should go into more specific detail in this half of the paper.

Reporting on a Presentation or Campus/Community Event

During the next month or two, look at the fliers posted on bulletin boards, the campus newspaper, blogs from student groups, etc. Find a talk, presentation, or some other special event that fits with your schedule. Attend the event.

While at the event, take notes.

As soon as the event is over, write a description of the event--what was discussed or demonstrated, who attended, what the presenter was like.

Add to that description a reflection about what you learned and/or your reaction to the event.

A few days later, reread your notes and your description and reflection. Use that material to write an essay that will help someone who was not at the event to make sense of the event.

Did you find it worthwhile? What did you learn from it? Was there anything that made you happy or angry or....? What, if anything, might have made this event better? Would you encourage people to attend a similar event in the future? Why or why not?

Essay about Work II (later in the semester)

As part of the preparation/invention phase for this essay, you will need to go online to the website for the Occupational Outlook Handbook [http://www.bls.gov/oco/], which we'll refer to as OOH for short. Look for the "Search OOH" box on the left side of the OOH site (scroll down a bit). You'll use that search box for either of the topics below.

Look up a career field you're interested in. To increase the chances you'll find an entry for this career, stay reasonably general (for instance, airplane pilot rather than American Airlines pilot). Look at the various categories of data found in a typical OOH entry: nature of the work, training/advancement, job outlook, earnings, related occupations, etc. Over the course of a few days, read as much of this material as you can. You may even want to take notes on some of it. Every so often, write down an important fact or idea from the

OOH entry and react to that idea in a brainstormed list, a quick session of freewriting, or some clustering. Then use some of that data to discuss what surprised you, what did not (and why), etc. (For instance, you could examine what skills are needed in that field and freewrite about how you will go about developing or improving your skills in that area.)

This second option also has you looking up a job in the OOH (see above), but with a different focus. Look up a career or job you've held in the past and see what the OOH has to say about it. How accurate a picture does the OOH entry paint for this job? Did the people who wrote that entry overlook something important about that job? Argue why this or that part of the career deserves more emphasis in the OOH entry.

Interview Essay

Your instructor will probably give you instructions about whom to interview. Some possibilities: someone who works in the career you plan to go into, a family member for family history, a student who has passed this class before you about how to succeed.

Preparing for the interview: Create a list of questions that you would like to know the answer to. Try to include many open-ended questions (questions that require a longer response) and list them in the order you might ask the questions. Bring a notepad and/or some other means of recording the interview with you. Ask permission to record the interview. Agree upon a time and place with the person being interviewed. Make sure you arrive on time or early.

During the interview: Take notes. Also try to make eye contact and to listen to what is being said at times. Cross off questions that have been answered. Ask follow-up questions to get even more information for your paper.

When writing the first draft of the paper, consult your notes. Try to ask yourself what someone who was not present at the interview would want to know. What is the main message that you have for the reader about the interview?

In this paper, you might want to divert from the summary/response structure. You might want to organize the paper by themes rather than a chronological retelling of the interview.

Special Writing Tasks

Preparing for an Essay Exam

You might wonder why the instructor for your history or biology class asks you to write an essay as part of a timed, in-class exam. The answer is fairly simple: Writing is an effective tool for communicating how well you understand a subject. Put another way, your instructor wants to see whether you understand important concepts in enough depth that you are able to explain them clearly in writing.

That doesn't mean, of course, that you'll always enjoy taking an essay exam. For one thing, if you're like most writers, you don't produce your best writing when time is short. However, there are steps you can take that will help you gain more control over how your essay exam turns out. Let's break those steps into two categories—things you should do *before* the test and things you should do *during* the test.

Plan Before the Test

Your job before the test is to anticipate the structure and content of the test. Doing so will help you to strategize how you can best study for the exam. Here are steps you can take.

- **Ask your instructor approximately how much of the test will be objective and how much will be essay.** Also ask approximately how long of an answer is expected for the essay questions: Is the instructor looking for a full essay (perhaps four or five paragraphs)? Or will the essay questions require shorter answers (perhaps a paragraph or two)? *An important note:* Do not complain to your instructor about the test. If you ask these questions in a polite way, your instructor is more likely to see you as a hardworking student, rather than one more student who is whining about having to take a test or as someone who is demanding to know exactly what's on the test (which is not a reasonable request).

- **Review your notes.** Look for topics your instructor has spent much time on in class--as well as things the assigned readings have emphasized.

- **Pay special attention to abstract concepts your instructor has applied to particular events, situations, or people discussed in the class.** Can you think of any *other* events/situations/etc. that you might be expected to apply that concept to during the test? (For example, let's say your economics instructor has discussed how uncertainty affected the stock market in 1929. Your instructor has also discussed the state of the stock market currently. Could she ask you a question in which you are expected to compare how uncertainty about the market today is similar to or different from the uncertainty that existed in 1929?)

- **Brainstorm likely essay questions.** Use your review of your notes (see above) as the basis for your list of likely questions. No, you won't be able to guess exactly what your instructor may ask, but you might come closer than you think. (If time allows, you might even want to form a study group for this step. Choose people who seem to be taking the class seriously. You might even ask your instructor if he or she is willing to suggest one or two members for a study group, or the instructor may be willing to let you organize such a group--for an out-of-class meeting--during the last few minutes of class time.)

- **Outline some tentative answers to the essay questions** that seem most likely to pop up on the test. Do *not* plan on using those outlines during the test (unless your instructor gives you explicit, clear permission to do so), as that would be cheating. But preparing such outlines before the test and reviewing them *before* the test is an effective study habit.

Plan During the Test

Once the day of the exam has arrived and you have the exam before you, you'll need to make more specific decisions about how to tackle the test.

- **Look over the test. Budget your time**. If the exam contains both objective questions (multiple choice, fill in the blank, true/false, matching) and essay questions, decide how much time to spend on objective questions and how much time you will need to save for the essay question(s).
  - If you are required to answer several essay questions, decide how much time you can spend on each one. Base this decision on how many points each question is worth. Questions worth more points deserve more time (since the teacher probably expects a longer, more detailed answer).
  - If you are given a choice of essay questions to respond to (e.g., "Respond to two of the four questions below"), read all the questions carefully, then choose the questions you can do the best job with during the time that is available.

- **Read the question carefully before you write.** Pay attention to what the key words in the question are asking you to do. (See the Suggestion Box.)

- **Come up with a thesis (main idea sentence) around which you can build your answer.** The details you come up with need to support or explain your main idea.

- **For each essay question, spend ten to twenty percent (10 to 20%) of the time you've budgeted for that question planning your answer.**
    - For instance, if you have twenty minutes to answer that question, give yourself two to four minutes to plan out what you will say in your essay. If you only have ten minutes to answer the question, use one to two minutes to plan your answer.
    - Be sure to *write down your plan*. Do not just *think about* how you will answer the question--get a plan on paper. Sketch out an outline of your answer. If you change your mind about the order in which you will raise different points in your answer, you can use arrows to reorganize your plan.
    - Do not spend more than twenty percent of your time for that question in planning your answer. You will still need to save plenty of time to write your essay response. (It's the essay that will get graded. Your plan will help you to write a good essay.)

- **As you write the actual essay, skip lines.** You may want to go back and add more details (examples, clarifications) in the last few minutes of the test.

- **Save a few minutes for editing**. Reread the test question and then your answer.
    - Have you have answered the question? (If not, what do you need to add?)
    - Do all your sentences make sense?
    - If time allows, fix misspelling and grammar/punctuation errors.

Suggestion Box
Use Key Words from the Question to Shape Your Answer

Teachers ordinarily formulate essay questions with great care. They have thought about what they want you to do during the exam--that is, what types of mental activities they want you to engage in. The wording of the question will reflect that. If you hope to do well on an essay exam, you will need to pay careful attention to the verb (action word) that is at the heart of the question. Here's a key to what your teacher likely wants you to do:

If the question asks you to...	...the teacher wants you to...	Example of such an essay question:
discuss (similar word: examine)	explain something (for instance, an event, a process, a problem) in detail	Discuss the challenges faced by female candidates in dealing with sexism from the media.

identify	pick out one or more things that are of special importance and help the reader understand <u>why they are important</u>	Identify the major factors that contribute to sibling rivalry in modern families.
analyze	look beneath the surface of something and discuss its deeper causes or significance	Analyze the media's role in shaping how Americans feel about the economy.
evaluate	judge the appropriateness or value of something--often in terms of a particular standard or set of rules	Evaluate the experiment your group conducted during Thursday's lab with regard to how well the experiment followed the scientific method.
argue	take a stand--one that you can support with logic (well-thought-out reasons) and details that are relevant to the class	Argue whether teachers' pay should or should not be based on how well their students perform on standardized tests. Keep the articles which we read for class in mind as you make your case.

Creating a Writing Portfolio

Many writing instructors ask their students to compile a portfolio of their work. This portfolio (which usually is due near the end of the term) is more than just a collection of the essays the student wrote. Often, students are expected to choose which pieces end up in the portfolio. In addition, most instructors ask students to include one or more reflective pieces of writing—that is, essays (sometimes journal entries) in which the writer discusses how she went about crafting her papers and why she made the choices she did in her writing.

A portfolio project might have several purposes. For one thing, it's a convenient way for the instructor to review what you've produced for the class. Yet the portfolio also allows you, as a writer, to consider the range of assignments you've taken on, as well as the various drafts you've written for each assignment. (Why were some drafts more effective than others? Did you perhaps need to write that messy first draft in order to end up with that well-organized third draft?)

You'll want to ask your instructor for details about how your portfolio should be formatted and what it should contain. Perhaps a simple two-pocket folder will do; on the other hand, maybe you are expected to turn in an electronic portfolio (an e-portfolio). Do your best to meet your instructor's requirements, as you would with any assignment. The discussion below is meant to serve as a general guide to the two most important parts of the portfolio process—selecting the right material for the portfolio and reflecting on how you make decisions about your writing as well as your writing process.

Selecting

What you include in your portfolio may be entirely up to you, but more likely, your decision will be based on the purpose the portfolio is supposed to serve.

> **The cumulative portfolio:** Your instructor may ask you to create a portfolio that is cumulative in nature, meaning that it's a collection of just about everything you wrote for the class (including all drafts of all essays, plus journal entries, posts you wrote for the course's electronic discussion board, and perhaps even notes you took during conferences with your instructor). In that case, you won't need to spend much time deciding what to include, but you will need to organize your writing with care (and perhaps even search out any drafts you've misplaced!).

> **The writing-process portfolio:** This is perhaps the most commonly assigned portfolio. In this case, your instructor might ask you to assemble a portfolio that features essays of your choosing—essays that show off different skills you developed over the course of the semester, or essays that reveal how you dealt with a special writing challenge. Maybe you'll want to showcase a range of styles you employed, or different audiences you tried to reach with your essays. Usually, this type of portfolio includes drafts from various stages in the writing process: for instance, a relevant page or two of freewriting, followed by a very rough discovery draft, and then a more focused but unpolished draft, along with a carefully revised, polished draft that truly shows what you were able to achieve. Since you are likely to include multiple versions of at least two or three different essays in this portfolio, you will (once again) want to make sure your materials are well-organized. Your reader should be able to tell what's what without difficulty.

> **The presentation portfolio:** This portfolio is not used all that often in writing classes, but it may be assigned at a later point in your academic career, particularly when you take classes in your major. The presentation portfolio includes only work that is as polished as can be. The goal here is to present yourself as a professional or near-professional to outsiders who may be judging your work for the purpose of awarding a scholarship or admitting you to a more advanced program. (This portfolio bears some similarity to the

collection of finished works which an artist might show when seeking admission to an art show.)

With any portfolio format, you should work hard at revising your work for as long as you are allowed to. Teachers want to see signs of improvement in your work. Use the revision strategies that are discussed in this book to make your portfolio essays as impressive as possible. Chapter Ten (Editing for Correctness) and Chapter Eleven (Editing for Style) will also prove helpful.

Reflecting

Reflective writing in a portfolio usually takes one of two forms: either a reflective essay or a reflective letter that introduces the reader to what's inside the portfolio. What you say might be similar in both documents, though a letter will normally be set up something like this:

November 30, 2015

Dear Ms. Berg,

Body of letter goes here.

Sincerely,
Kathy Bringer

What will you discuss in your essay or letter? Here are several questions you may wish to explore, though you don't necessarily need to discuss all of these issues. Remember, too, that even if you freewrite answers to these questions, a good reflective essay or letter is more than just a set of responses to questions. If you respond to these questions, use your answers as a jumping off point to the first draft of your essay or letter.

Questions about individual essays:

- Where did you get the idea for this essay? What did your invention process (e.g., freewriting, brainstorming, clustering) look like? How did the idea evolve?
- What audience did you have in mind when you wrote this essay? How did audience considerations influence what you included in the essay or how you organized it?
- If you were to revise this essay for a different audience, how would you change the essay?
- What types of changes did you make when you revised? Did all of your changes work? Did any of your changes lead you to experiment with other changes?
- Which change in this essay are you most pleased with? Why?
- Did any of your changes not work out as well as you had hoped? How so?
- Whom did you seek out for feedback while working on this essay? What reaction did you get?

- Why did you choose to focus on this essay for your portfolio?

Questions about your writing process:

- How do you approach a new writing assignment? Do you tackle different types of writing assignments in different ways? How so?
- What do you deal with a roadblock in your writing? How do you get restarted or get back on track?
- What does your revision process look like? How do you figure out what needs work and what's working fine?
- What were your biggest editing challenges this semester? What did you do to get a better handle on those issues?
- What you can now do (or do better) that you could not do as well at the beginning of the semester?
- Has your attitude toward writing changed at all this semester? How so?
- What do you still need to work on as a writer? What steps can you take to improve in those areas?

Sometimes writers choose to share their personal feelings about the course in the reflective essay. Keep in mind, though, that a reflective essay in a portfolio is different than a course evaluation (in which the purpose is to point out which course features worked well and what the instructor might improve in the course). A good reflective essay or letter will focus, in plenty of detail, on the writer's work—and particularly on what the writer has learned about himself or herself as a writer and a student.

Your reflective essay or letter should go through the same revision process as the rest of your work. It also needs to be edited and proofread with care.

Index

Active voice (*see also* Passive voice) 174-175

Agreement errors (subject/verb agreement) 143-147

Anecdote 106, 124-125

Apostrophes 152-153

Argumentation 60, 80, 108-110

At First...But Then... (development strategy) 112-113

Audience 24, 33, 90-93, 95, 99-100, 102, 104, 115

Audience draft (*see also* Discovery draft) 68, 87-90

Aural invention 43, 50

Baskins-Robbins problem 94

Blogs 37-38

Body paragraphs (*see also* Paragraphs) 29

Brainstorming 23, 44-45, 50, 199-201

Breaking the rules 177

Cause and effect (development strategy) 60,

Changes (types of revision changes) 8, 87-88

Clarity (being clear) 173

Closure 65

Clustering 46-47, 51

Comma splices 139-142

Commas 154-156

Comparison/contrast (development strategy) 60, 108

Complexity (*see also* Complications) 31, 65

Complications, 111-115

Conciseness 170

Conclusions 29-30, 127-128, 132

Conferences (student/teacher conference) 84-96, 206-207

Connection-making 90-93

Correctness 133-161

Critics 51-52

Debate 12

Demay, Brian 102-103

Details (*see also* Development strategies) 94-99

Development strategies (*see also* Details) 59-65, 104-116

Dialogue (in narration) 107-108

Discovery draft (*see also* Audience draft) 68

Draft—first draft 27, 53-65

Drafting 10, 12, 53

Drawing 47-48, 51

Editing 10, 12

Emotional appeals 107

Error patterns 134-136

Essay 19, 26, 27, 30

Essay assignments 254-268

Exams—essay exams 265-268

Examples (*see* Details; *see* Development Strategies)

Explaining (development strategy) 60, 105

Feedback 68, 74-86

Five-paragraph essay (*see* Formulaic writing) 31-32

Focused freewriting 42, 50

Formulaic writing (avoiding) 30-32

Fragments (sentence fragments) 137-139

Freewriting (*see also* Focused freewriting; *see also* Looping) 22, 40-43, 50, 199-201

Friends and relatives (advice from)

Global Revision 66, 87-103

Good bones 68-70

Good parts 88-89

Grammar

Grammar checker 135-136

Guido, Mike 130-131

Hansknecht, Jeanne 72-73

Humor 101-102

Hypothetical examples 106

Ideas (see also Complexity) 30-31, 40, 65

Internet (*see also* White noise) 48-49, 51, 59

Interviewing 79

Introductions 28-29, 122-127, 132

Invention 12, 39-51, 54-55, 70

Journal prompts 248-253

Learning center 86

Library 51

Localized revision 117-132

Log, writer's 16

Looping (*see also* Freewriting) 42

Main idea (*see* Thesis)

Metaphor (development strategy) 114-115

Metaphorical thinking 115

Modifier errors 149-152

Multiple development strategies (see also Development strategies) 110

Narrative (*see also* Story-telling; *see also* Anecdote) 60, 80, 106-107, 106-107

Organization 99, 111, 128

Outlining 89, 182, 230

Paradox (development strategy) 114

Paragraphs (*see also* Body paragraphs) 29, 117-119

Passive voice (*see also* Active voice)

Peer review 74-84

Peer review—approaches to 77-80

Peer review—questions for 80, 82-84

Peer review—sample 81, 216-217

Plagiarism (avoiding) 49-50, 213-215

Plexico, Van Allen 14-15

Portfolios 86, 268-271

Prewriting (*see* Invention)

Pronoun errors 147-149

Proofreading 159-161

Punctuation errors 152-156

Purpose (see also Thesis; see also "So what" question) 7, 99

Questioning 44-45, 51, 100

Questions—in introductions 125-126

Quotations—in introductions 126-127

Quotation marks 153-154

Reading (*see also* Reading actively; *see also* Reading rhetorically) 20, 33, 176

Reading actively 33-35

Reading rhetorically 36

Reader-based draft (*see also* Writer-based draft) 97

Readers (*see* Audience)

Reasons to write 17-19

Recursive writing process 11-13

Redrafting (*see also* Revision) 89

Reorganizing (*see* Organization)

Rewording 169-170

Revision (*see also* Global Revision) 8, 10, 12, 66-73

Revision agenda 69-70

Rhetoric 19-20, 25

Rhetorical moves 20-21

Rhetorical triangle 21-24

Run-on sentences 139-142

Satire 101-102

Sentence boundaries (*see also* Fragments; *see also* Comma splices; *see also* Run-on sentences) 136-143

Sentence bridge transitions 120-122

Sentence variety

Significance (*see* "So what" question; *see* Complexity)

Simile 114

Sinift, Katrina 158-159

Snapshots (thinking in snapshots) 98

"So what" question 122

Spelling 156-157

Storyboarding 48, 231

Story-telling (developmental strategy; *also see* Narrative; *see also* Anecdote) 106-107

Style 162-178

Subject/verb errors (*see* Agreement errors)

Suspense 128-129

System (writing as a system) 6

Tangled sentences 171

Tense error (verb tense) 145-147

Tension (development strategy) 113

Texting 173

Theme 26

Thesaurus 168-169

Thesis (*see also* Main idea)

They might say (strategy) 100

Title 27

TMI (too much information) 97

Tone 101, 163-167

Topic 6, 22, 26, 31, 40-41, 86, 89, 90,

Topic sentences 119

Transitions (*see also* Sentence bridge transitions; *see also* Transition phrases) 111, 119

Transition phrases 119-120

Traps (avoiding writing traps) 56-58

Tutors (*see* Writing center)

Verb errors (*see also* Tense errors; *see also* Agreement errors) 143-147

Vividness (*see also* Details; *see also* Development; *see also* Metaphor) 98

Voice 100

White noise 59

Word choice 168-170

Writer-based draft (*see also* Reader-based draft) 97

Writer's log 16

Writing assignments 254-264

Writing center 86

Writing process 5, 6-15

Writing strategies—multiple 60-65

Zooming out (in conclusions) 127

Page Numbers for Selected Features in *Use What Works*

Exercises
What Does Writing Need (Ex. 1.1), 7
Making Choices and Gaining Control (Ex. 1.2), 9
Situations Where Writing Skills Come in Handy (Ex. 2.1), 18
What Rhetorical Moves Do You Make (Ex. 2.2), 20
Examining Andrew's Invention Process (Ex. 2.3), 22
Examining the Rhetorical Triangle (Ex. 2.4), 22
Thinking about Introductions (Ex. 3.1), 29
Beyond the Five Paragraph Essay Formula (Ex. 3.2), 32
Actions and Writer/Reader (Ex. 3.3), 32
Practice in Aural Invention Technique (Ex. 4.1), 43
Pick a Trap to Avoid (Ex. 5.1), 58
Picture People Revising Their Writing (Ex. 6.1), 66
Giving Feedback on Your Classmate's Discovery Draft (Ex. 6.2), 68
Your Advice for Karlos (Ex. 7.1), 81
Workshop/Peer Review Report (Ex. 7.2), 83
Making Your Essay Longer—and More Vivid (Ex. 8.1), 98
What is the Essay's Tone? (Ex. 8.2), 101
Getting to Know Your Audience (Ex. 9.1), 104
Preparing for an Argument, Figuring Out Your Audience's Concerns (Ex. 9.2), 109
What Makes a Paragraph? (Ex. 10.1), 117
Thinking about the Goals of an Introduction (Ex. 10.2), 122
Introductions as Road Maps (Ex. 10.3), 123
Suspense Isn't Just for Horror Movies (Ex. 10.4), 128
Getting a Handle on Sentence Boundaries (Ex. 11.1), 141
Finding and Fixing Editing Errors (Ex. 11.2), 160
Starting Small—Pick a Paragraph (Ex. 11.3), 161
What's the Tone? Where's It Coming From? (Ex. 12.1), 162
Your Essay's Tone (Ex. 12.2), 165
Rewording (Ex. 12.3), 169
Add Variety—But Make It Clear (Ex. 12.4), 173
Add More Active Voice (Ex. 12.5), 175
Start Small—Try One Technique (Ex. 12.6), 176

Suggestion Boxes
Things Writers Might Improve in an Essay, 8
Debate as Inspiration, 12
Ignore the Typos for Now, 13
Give It a Try—and Then Another Try, 13
Read Plenty—Plenty of Different Things, 20
Strategies for Thinking about Audience, 24
How Do I Freewrite?, 40
Questioning for Support, 46
What Can I Do to Avoid Plagiarism?, 49
How to Use Invention Material to Assemble Your First Draft, 54

Free Noise (Potentially Helpful Noise!) from the Internet, 59
What is the Process for Creating a Revision Agenda? How Do I Get Started?, 69
Asking a Friend or Relative for Advice, 75
Making the Best of the Peer Review Situation, 77
Providing Feedback to Your Classmate(s), 78
What Questions Should Guide My Peer Review?, 80
How to Review Your Essay Before a Conference, 84
What Kinds of Large-Scale Revisions Can I Make to an Essay?, 88
What Are Some Ways to Generate More Details, 95
First, Revision...Lastly, Editing, 98
Using Dialogue in Your Narrative, 107
Using Transitions, 111
What Do Good Complications Look Like in an Essay? 112
Revising General to Specific Introductions, 124
Writing Anecdote-Based Introductions, 125
Questioning in an Introduction, 125
Questions About Questions, 126
Using Quotations in Introductions, 125
Two Strategies for Identifying Your Most Frequent Error Patterns, 134
How to Fix Fragments, 139
How to Fix Run-on Sentences and Comma Splices, 141
How to Fix Subject/Verb Agreement Errors, 143
How to Fix Verb Tense Errors, 147
How to Eliminate Spelling Errors, 157
Becoming a Better Proofreader of Your Own Work, 159
Strong Feelings That Arise in Your Writing, 165
What to Do If Your Tone is Too Informal, 166
What to Do If Your Tone is Too Formal, 167
When Repeated Words Matter and When They Don't, 169
R U txting 2 much?, 173
Essay Exams: Use Words from the Question to Shape Your Answer, 267

Looking for a Challenge
Keep a Writer's Log, 16
Find Some Rhetoric, Ask Some Questions, 25
Reading Blogs and Creating Your Own Blog, 37
Take a Topic for a Spin—Using Several Invention Strategies, 48
Wait! Don't Do It! Hold Off on Reaching Closure!, 60
Putting Invention Strategies to Work Again 70
Interview a Classmate, 79
How Humor and Satire Work, 100
Reaching Different Types of Readers, 115
Endings, 127

Beyond the Essay—Writers at Work
Van Allen Plexico (science fiction and fantasy writer), 14
Jeanne M. Hansknecht (Episcopal priest), 72
Brian Demay (on-air radio personality and program director), 102
Mike Guido (principal architect and president of firm), 130
Katrina Sinift (accounts payable at feed and grain company), 158